PROSKAUER:
HIS LIFE AND TIMES

Joseph M. Proskauer
photo by Peter Fink

PROSKAUER:

HIS LIFE AND TIMES

BY

LOUIS M. HACKER

AND

MARK D. HIRSCH

THE UNIVERSITY OF ALABAMA PRESS
UNIVERSITY, ALABAMA

Library of Congress Cataloging in Publication Data

Hacker, Louis Morton, 1899-
  Proskauer, his life and times.

  Bibliography: p.
  Includes index.
  1. Proskauer, Joseph Meyer, 1877-1971. 2. Jews in
the United States—Biography. 3. Lawyers—New York
(State)—Biography. 4. United States—Biography.
I. Hirsch, Mark David, 1910-   joint author. II. Ti-
tle.
E184.J5P943   340'.092'4 [B]   77-1697
ISBN 0-8173-9361-7

CONTENTS

IN MEMORIAM

Phillip W. Haberman, Jr.
(1905-1971)

FOREWORD

The other day Judge Charles E. Wyzanski, Jr., lamented what he called the "slump in sages" in the legal profession. In his Sulzbacher Memorial Lecture at Columbia Law School on November 12, 1975, he spoke of law and the humanities. His thesis was that no lawyer deserves to be called a leader of the bar by reason of professional skills alone; that unless he exercises them within a matrix of understanding and compassion for mankind with all its vanities and passions and weaknesses—and noble strengths— he is no more than a technician. In that regard, he declared, the profession now boasts few leaders comparable to those who graced bench and bar when he attended law school nearly half a century ago.

As a law teacher I am particularly grateful that Louis M. Hacker has taken time out from his indefatigable labors as an economic historian to remind us that Joseph M. Proskauer was one of those departed giants. To trace the rich tapestry of his career is to show what it *can* mean to be a lawyer, and modern law students desperately need to be shown. I have observed with dismay, and with considerable pity, how few of them feel the pride and eager anticipation that inspirited my law school classmates and me, children of the Great Depression though we were. It is fashionable to attribute the cynicism, the bleakness of outlook, to disillusionment at the faithlessness of lawyers in high office. The real trouble, however, is not that the profession is burdened with so many scoundrels. There is nothing new about that. The trouble is that it now offers so few true leaders whose example can encourage the beginner and provide a credible core for high aspiration.

In a narrative rich with courtroom anecdotes, Hacker pays full attention to Proskauer's skills as judge and advocate, but that is by no means all. To call the book a *biography,* as he does, belies its true scope; it is better described as an account of Proskauer's *life and times.* A vivid though impressionistic sketch of his early days in Mobile, Alabama, opens a window on life in the deep South during the trying post-Reconstruction period. The review of his years at Columbia College and Columbia Law School brings alive the process of converting a lad from the hinterland to a citizen of the world. His plunge into political life as a close friend and loyal adviser of Al Smith brings back long-forgotten personalities of Democratic party politics and the fascinating infighting that attended revitalization of government for the people in the late twenties and early thirties. Then we see Proskauer as exemplar of American pluralism—his assumption of full stature as a Jew as well as an American, first on the domestic scene and then as a major force in the creation of Israel in 1948 and in persuading Vatican Council II in 1965 to strike at the core of anti-Semitism by repudiating the centuries-old calumny of Jewish deicide. What emerges is a man who recognized the big issues of his time and grappled with them boldly. In his hands the art of the lawyer was a tool for serving not only the private client but the public weal. As I have said, it is good for neophytes to be thus shown what *they* can do with their professional training if they will but take heart.

For those who may be puzzled that Louis Hacker, not himself a lawyer, can so perceptively limn a career that was rooted and centered in the law, we should keep in mind that Hacker himself is no mere pedagogue. The ivory tower has been his habitat, but he too has stepped forward in time of critical need to grapple with public issues. In the dark days of the 1950s, when Joe McCarthyism bade fare to sterilize the academic community through neurotically exaggerated demands for political conformism, Columbia University was lucky enough to have Hacker as Dean of its School of General Studies. When university trustees threatened, more than once, to sacrifice faculty members to the crusade that had been launched against political heterodoxy in the name of supposed patriotism, Hacker took his stand for academic freedom. In case after case, working with like-minded colleagues such as Walter Gellhorn, Mark Van Doren, and I. I. Rabi, he beat back unfounded efforts to punish teachers as security risks. In 1954, for example, he threatened to resign—and publicize the reason—if the University overruled his and his faculty's decision to appoint as lecturer in Mathematics a professor whom the University of Michigan had fired under McCarthy Committee pressure. The appointment stood. It is to him as much as anyone that Columbia owes the virtually unique distinction of having yielded not an inch to the nation-wide hunt for heretics.

The full account of this struggle and victory has never been told, and I cannot tell it here. One day, however, someone will doubtless write a biography of Louis M. Hacker that will encourage educators as this book will encourage law students and lawyers.

COLUMBIA LAW SCHOOL   LOUIS LUSKY
NEW YORK, NEW YORK   PROFESSOR OF LAW
NOVEMBER 15, 1975

INTRODUCTION

It has been a matter of considerable satisfaction to me personally to see the completion and publication of this biography of Joseph M. Proskauer, the distinguished jurist and lawyer, prominent public servant, and leader in Jewish and civic causes. I have been a colleague and associate of Mark D. Hirsch at Bronx Community College (a unit of the City University of New York) for some seventeen years, and by a strange but happy coincidence my own biographical activities and scholarly interest had also centered upon another great lawyer and outstanding Jewish leader, Louis Marshall (1856-1929), a founder and president of the American Jewish Committee which Proskauer was to head in turn fourteen years later (1943-1949) through equally trying times.

As a result of this community of interest I eagerly awaited Professor Hirsch's chapters as they appeared, both from the standpoint of the professional and of the friend, for they had much to tell. I was understandably distressed when ill health forced his labors to a standstill after eleven chapters had been written, each thoroughly researched and well-documented. Fortunately, however, the distinguished economist-historian, Dr. Louis M. Hacker, who had been Dean of the School of General Studies at Columbia University and under whom Dr. Hirsch had also served for a number of years, came aboard the ship.

Dean Hacker did several things in addition to bringing the biography to completion and supplementing Dr. Hirsch's writings and research. He sought to give the book both a uniformity of style and an overall design. He underscored the many roles Proskauer had played in the different spheres of the complex world in which he had moved. These extended across law, politics, and religion, from his admission to the Bar in 1899 to his dramatic and successful appearance in Rome in 1965 at the final meetings of Vatican Council II.

It is thus the dual story of a public man's participation in a great number of civic and communal activities, always purposefully and often as leader, at the same time that he was searching for a real and satisfying sense of identity as a Jew. The combination of the talents of Hacker and Hirsch have led to a fruitful co-authorship and a book rich in detail about the man Proskauer and the times in which he lived and on which he had such a powerful impact.

*

A biographical note at this point about Mark D. Hirsch is not inappropriate. Dr. Hirsch is a native New Yorker, and a product of its public school system. His baccalaureate was conferred by the City College of New York, and his Master of Arts and Doctor of Philosophy degrees, in history, were earned at Columbia University. He taught for twenty years in the New York secondary schools, and then was for sixteen years Chairman of the History Department at Bronx Community College. He has also taught at the undergraduate and graduate levels at the City College (including its School of Education and the New York Area Studies Program), and at Columbia and Long Island Universities, and gave a seminar at Yale College. He has written a biography of William C. Whitney and numerous papers, articles, and book reviews for professional volumes and journals. In addition, he served as two-year college history consultant to the National Endowment for the Humanities in the judging of grants and awards.

Widely known as a specialist in New York City and State history, and with keen interest in urban history, he has been a frequent lecturer, the recipient of research grants, and is currently—as a "distinguished teacher" and guest scholar—a Faculty Exchange Scholar between City University and the State University of New York (SUNY). He is also a member of the Board of Editors of the New York State Historical Association. Moreover, he taught, upon invitation, the twenty-third Annual History Seminar for the Association in Cooperstown, New York in 1970 on "New York During Years of Challenge, 1914-1932."

There are other credits he has earned, but it is even more pleasant to report that Dr. Hirsch, now professor emeritus, is able, owing to improving health, to return to the library and to the writing desk, and that he is currently at work on a study of Richard Croker, with other projects in the offing. I will remember him longest and best, however, as an outstanding teacher and administrator, a sturdy pillar of our college, a champion of faculty rights, an esteemed friend to students, colleagues, and myself alike, and, above all, a scholar of integrity.

BRONX COMMUNITY COLLEGE
AUGUST 1976

MORTON ROSENSTOCK
ACTING PRESIDENT

PREFACE

A function of a Preface of a work of this kind is to acknowledge and express thanks to the many individuals, organizations, archives and libraries that rendered help to make it possible. First and foremost were Proskauer and his younger partner, constant companion, and confidant Phillip W. Haberman, Jr. They gave to both of us their time unstintingly, opened up public and private papers without cavil, read what was shown to them and if they disagreed bowed to the authors' judgments: for this book is neither "commissioned" nor "authorized" by Proskauer, his family, or his law firm. Its design, the meaning it gave to Proskauer's life in his times, and its reading of the significance of Proskauer's aspirations and successes and failures are the authors' own; and theirs the responsibility for what is here written.

It is to be deeply regretted that neither Proskauer nor Haberman lived to see a completed work. Both died in 1971—Haberman unexpectedly in his sixty-sixth year and Proskauer several months later at the age of ninety-four. This book is dedicated to the memory of Phillip W. Haberman, Jr. For not only did Haberman know Proskauer intimately—and was always ready to explain away Proskauer's impatience, bursts of temper, his quarrels with us—but he too was worldly-wise. Haberman and his wife Helen accompanied Proskauer to Rome; and Hacker, when writing the story of Proskauer's successful appearance at Vatican Council II, learned from them of Proskauer's great skills as a negotiator, advocate, and conciliator. This of a man eighty-eight years old.

Five of this book's chapters have to do with legal matters of varying complexity. For the sorting out of the data affecting them and their proper interpretation, the guidance of three members of the Proskauer firm—Haberman, George M. Shapiro, and Julius Teller—is gratefully recorded. At the request of the University of Alabama Press, Professor Wythe Holt of the University's Law School read these chapters, at points rewording and clarifying their writing, and this act of great kindness is herewith acknowledged with many thanks.

Any book, no matter how practiced its authors, needs the friendly overseeing of the publisher's editoral staff. They overwrite, introduce extraneous materials, engage in gaucheries, habits acquired over a long lifetime of putting things down on paper, which another eye and hand can detect and eliminate. The manuscript had such skilled assistance from The University of Alabama Press: from its director Morgan L. Walters and its editorial secretary Rubye H. Todd, and from Dr. W. S. Hoole, sometimes University librarian and professor of library science, who was called upon, and consented, to read critically the manuscript turned in.

It was Dr. Hoole who pruned and excised what he considered too expansive and tightened the flow of the narrative where the authors had ventured into unnecessary excursions. The authors accepted these judgments as they did much of the work of Dr. Hoole's blue pencil; an especial bow of thanks therefore for the editorial skills of the Press's staff, regular and opted.

A goodly part of the materials collected came from interviews (and in a few cases correspondence) with the many persons who had worked with, or knew personally in other ways, or had crossed the path of Proskauer and his many interests and accomplishments. Their names follow, with our thanks. First to Proskauer's three children, the late Mrs. Paul P. (Frances) Cohen, Mrs. Ruth P. Smith, and Richard Proskauer, and also a grandchild Anthony Smith. Next, to the many Proskauer partners who gave their time without hesitancy. Then to the officials of the American Jewish Committee, in particular Dr. John Slawson, Milton Himmelfarb, and Harry Alderman. Then to his lifelong personal friends Melville H. Cane and James N. Rosenberg. Many of these and those that follow appear in the text itself.

And to these others in alphabetical order: Jacob Blaustein, Philip Chasin, Judge Irving Ben Cooper, Mrs. Hans J. Curjel, Governor Thomas E. Dewey, Eliahu Elath, Max Engle, Judge Arnold L. Fein, Dr. Herbert Feis, Judge Albert Fiorillo, Judge Marvin Frankel, Joseph S. Gershman, Samuel Greason, Associate Supreme Court Justice John M. Harlan, Dr. Maurice B. Hexter, Dr. Oscar I. Janowsky, Herbert K. Kanarek, Theodore Kiendl, Milton E. Krents, Rev. Dr. Julius Mark, Father Felix A. Morlion, Jacob Nadel, Kate Pantell, Harry N. Rosenfield, President Harry S. Truman, Joseph Willen, and Charles Zunser.

Many archives were examined, these among others: the American Jewish Archives, American Jewish Historical Society, American Jewish Committee, the Jewish Theological Seminary, the Citizens Union, Columbia University's Special Collections and its Oral History Project, the Association of the Bar of the City of New York, the United States Archives. The following Libraries were utilized: those of Columbia University, the Library of Congress, and the New York State Education Department Library. Our thanks to the archivists and librarians and their staffs.

There were two primary Proskauer sources from which extracts have been made or commented upon. The first was what purported to be an autobiography and was called *A Segment of My Times,* published in 1950. The second was what we have designated here as his *Reminiscences,* made up of a series of conversations with Dr. Jerold S. Auerbach in 1961. These were taped and transcribed and added to the collection of the Columbia University Oral History Project.

A final observation. This history of Proskauer has no footnotes (but one) and many of the writings of others used are cited in the text proper. At the end of the book there has been added a Bibliographical Note of other works, arranged by categories or topics. These will indicate the wide net that has been thrown in another aspect of the preparations that went into the writing of *Proskauer: His Life and Times.*

L. M. H.
M. D. H.

PROSKAUER:
HIS LIFE AND TIMES

THE PROSKAUER FAMILY AND OTHER GERMAN JEWS

1

There are many ways of telling the story of a man. One could say that he was, in effect, the product of his lineage and recount in detail the rise of his forebears, emphasizing how they were responsible for the circumstances, environmentally and genetically, out of which he emerged. Or one could say that he was a representative man, that the times in which he lived made him, for his life consisted of action and reaction to opportunities he created or seized as he left his impress on men and events. Or, again, one could say that he was the product of his education, for all of life is a learning process and men grow and develop as their understanding takes on depth and purpose. Of these choices, the one best suited to Joseph Mayer Proskauer is the last, for his life is the story of his education.

Joseph Mayer Proskauer was born in Mobile, Alabama on August 6, 1877, the eldest child of Alfred and Rebecca (Leinkauf) Proskauer. The Leinkaufs and the Proskauers were German Jews and members of both families had come to the United States in the early 1850s. The Leinkaufs originated in Pressburg, Hungary; the Proskauers in Breslau, in Prussian Silesia. Both towns were of considerable political importance as well as commercial centers. To this extent they differed from most of the communities from which approximately fifty thousand German Jews left to come to the United States during the 1830s, 1840s, and 1850s.

The first of the Leinkaufs to arrive—an he went directly to Mobile—was Weiss, and, having settled himself, he sent for a nephew, William H. Leinkauf, who was the maternal grandfather of Joseph Proskauer. Weiss and William started humbly in the United States, as did the great majority of the German Jews, beginning as itinerant peddlers, selling their wares to the back-country farmers of Alabama. William did well. He married Caroline Bloch (whose family had hailed from the Rhineland-Pfalz), acquired a house and a store, and before the Civil War was prospering in Mobile as a wholesale and produce merchant. From the union of William and Caroline was born Rebecca, the mother of Joseph Proskauer.

William Leinkauf became one of the influential citizens of Mobile (he was the first chairman of the Mobile School Board) and he weathered the trials of the Civil War and Reconstruction so well that in 1878, in addition to his general merchandising business, he was able to establish a small private bank. He became moderately successful. In 1900 the capital of his bank was only $150,000 and its surplus $110,000—but its business was large enough modestly to support him and Joseph Proskauer's father Alfred (who was the bank's cashier), and Joseph Proskauer's brother Hugo (who was the assistant cashier).

The paternal grandfather, Julius Proskauer, also migrated from Breslau to the United States in the early 1850s, first going to Philadelphia and then to Richmond, Virginia where he remained until his death. He must have been somewhat better off than most German Jewish immigrants and somewhat older, for he was married three times and had ten children. At least one of his sons, Adolph, born in Breslau in 1838, had a *gymnasium* education. Another son, Alfred, considerably younger, was Proskauer's father. Both sons migrated with their father to the United States, and both left the paternal roof as soon as they were old enough to strike out on their own.

It was Adolph who came to Mobile, sometime just before the Civil War, and it was he who sent for Alfred after the war was over. As soon as Alabama seceded from the Union and war seemed imminent, Adolph joined up as a loyal Confederate, enlisting and being elected a corporal in the Mobile Independent Rifles, a company which was absorbed into the Twelfth Alabama Infantry Regiment and which got at once into action at Manassas Junction on July 21, 1861.

For at least fifty years Joseph Mayer Proskauer assumed (or said) he was a Southerner by associations, loyalty, and sympathies. When he went to New York, he liked to believe that some day he would return to the state of his origin. He joined a club made up of exiles like himself and he affiliated himself with the political party that controlled the public life of his native Alabama; but he soon discovered that the South was not what his sentiment, or sentimentality, had created. In fact, he learned that it was hostile to every code of decency and right with which he had associated himself. It was his friendship with Alfred E. Smith and the South's antipathy toward Smith, when he thrice sought the presidency of the United States, that deepened Proskauer's understanding. As a result, his whole life was changed.

It was by chance that the young Proskauer, at the age of fifteen, left Mobile for New York to complete his education at Columbia College and the Columbia Law School. His training at both was outstanding. As an undergraduate he had the good fortune to fall under the influence of Professor George E. Woodberry, one of the notable teachers of his time, whose passionate devotion to humanistic studies rubbed off on the young pupil and gave him a wide curiosity about persons and places and an abiding interest in pure art, particularly in poetry and music. Proskauer learned both to read and to listen with pleasure and it was this love of the arts which solaced and comforted him all his life. As a student of the law, he was one of the fortunate ones to profit from the revolutionary changes then taking place in the university's law-school curriculum. The case-method was being introduced, and under it Proskauer was schooled in those skills in advocacy that later made it possible to scramble his way by his own labors from humble beginnings to distinguished success. To his talents, Columbia added the training of his mind. In consequence, Proskauer became a versatile practitioner in the law courts—he chose the courts over the office—and was much sought after. He became a judge and he founded one of New York's great law firms.

Proskauer's maternal and paternal grandparents had left for the United States as part of that large emigration of Jews from Central Europe during the 1830s, 1840s, and 1850s. In Germany, from which most of them came, the processes of so-called emancipation—the granting of equal political, civil, and juridical rights to Jews—had been going on slowly. Jews in Germany and German Jews settling in the United States liked to believe, in consequence, that they were going to become assimilated. That is to say, they were going to be accepted at home in Germany and for the emigrants and their families in the United States, as equals socially, economically, and politically. Only their religion—as religious affiliation differentiated Roman Catholics from Protestants, and Protestants of established churches from evangelical Protestant sects—set them apart.

As a Jew, and one becoming assimilated, Proskauer nevertheless felt a sense of obligation to all Jews: to smoothe the paths for other newcomers and for the unfortunate, distressed, sick and aged. The link with his past was through philanthropic endeavor. Thus, as he climbed the ladder of his profession in New York, he accepted invitations to sit on the boards of many Jewish philanthropies. He also joined the American Jewish Committee, composed of German Jews like himself, an organization, really a pressure group, whose purpose it was to use the influence of successful Jews to overcome the disabilities or hostilities under which those less fortunate labored or suffered, whether in the United States or abroad. In time Proskauer became president of the American Jewish Committee and in this role he wrote to heads of state and legislative commissions and committees, made many public appearances, and traveled widely. This was part of the process of his becoming assimilated, and he was taking for granted that his activities would further the process for all other Jews, as well.

Then Proskauer came up against a stubborn fact: that Jews were considered different, not because they practiced another religion but because the whole Christian world, by the upbringing of its young, and the catechetical practices and liturgy of its churches, regarded them, all Jews, as the killers of Jesus Christ, the Son of God. Jews were different because they were the deicides. In short, Proskauer's assumption that he had become assimilated had turned out to be false. When he came to realize this, his Jewishness began to take on depth and, therefore, for the first time in his life, meaning. For Proskauer did something about it in two ways.

Never a Zionist, he saw that he had to accept Jewish nationalism (and run the risk of being charged with a dual allegiance) for those who sought to create a Jewish homeland and a Jewish state in Palestine. Thus, facing the bitter opposition of other German ("assimilated") Jews, and notably those who were the leaders like himself of the American Jewish Committee, he was an early advocate of Palestine partition. Only through this realistic route did he believe that the State of Israel would emerge.

And Proskauer was among those who came to understand that, if all Christians were to abandon the idea of Jewish deicide and thus strike a mortal blow at the roots of anti-Semitism, it was the Roman Catholic Church that had to take the lead. This meant not simply a declaration of disavowal, but a cleaning up from top to bottom, of its educational system, the catechetical work of its priests, and its liturgy. Proskauer was already in his late eighties, when he at last came to this understanding.

The German Jews, particularly young men and boys, who migrated to the United States in the thirty years before the Civil War, did not flee as so-called Forty-Eighters, those middle-class reformers and fighters who challenged the absolute authority of kings and princes in the Revolutions of 1848 and who lost in their attempt to have constitutional and national governments established. Indeed, it is quite doubtful that the Leinkaufs and Proskauers were personally involved. One learned scholar, Rabbi B. W. Korn, after painstaking research in all the records, could track down only twenty-eight Jewish Forty-Eighters who found asylum in the United States.

Nor should it be assumed that, as Jews, these immigrants were feeling the full weight of anti-Semitism. The Napoleonic armies, as they swept over Europe, brought with them the message of the French Revolution and of the French Enlightenment out of which it grew, of rationality and confidence in the perfectability of man, and of law, order, individual right, and fraternity, if not exactly equality.

The weakening of status and proscription also helped in the emancipation of the Jews in Central Europe. Not entirely, of course, for there continued to exist pockets of discrimination, such as special taxes, restrictions on the holding and transfer of real property, and free entrance into the universities and the professions. In Wurttemberg and Bavaria, from which many of the German Jews came, the emancipation was only partial. In the former there were occupational disabilities, limitations on the number who could enter the handicrafts; in the latter, on the number of Jewish marriages that could take place and on the ownership of land. Not until 1864 was full emancipation, equality before the law, and the right to vote, granted to Jews in most of the German states. As a result of this, the mass migration of Jews ceased.

The large movements of peoples, within Europe and out of Europe, Jews among them, from the end of the Napoleonic Wars to 1860, was a proletarian migration. Populations were on the march—in the British Isles, Scandinavia, Central Europe—from the countryside and the rural small towns and villages into the cities; and from the same sort of places overseas, crossing the Atlantic, bound for the United States, and other places, including South Africa and Australia.

Two great upheavals had taken place to account for these internal and external migrations. The first was a population explosion that almost doubled the number of inhabitants of Europe during 1800-1850, the annual rate of increase being 7.1 percent. The second was the Industrial Revolution, first begun in the British Isles, which crossed over to the western and central parts of the continent in the long years of peace after 1815. The population explosion led to a rapid growth in Europe's young people: and these were the restless and adventuresome ones who were ready to undertake the hazards of new fortunes.

The Industrial Revolution was more than the conversion of production from the cottage industries and the handicrafts into that of the mechanized and steam-powered factories. It could advance and conquer because it made possible and needed national and international markets. At home this required the building of canals, railroads, and highways, and the creation of banks and other financial institutions to collect savings, expand credit facilities, and maintain produce and stock exchanges. The modernization of cities, with their elaborate infra-structure of housing, rapid transit, municipal services of street paving and lighting, water supply, sewage disposal, educational, police, and fire-fighting facilities, could occur only when municipal financing was available. Cities, in turn, created external economies, making possible the establishment of all sorts of specialized services.

Abroad, the success of the Industrial Revolution demanded fast freight and passenger ships running on schedule and the production of those raw materials the new factories had to have to make possible continuous operation—cotton, wool, iron, tin, copper, coal, food, and other commodities. Here was an excellent example of the economic law of comparative advantage at work: it was cheaper to buy minerals and foodstuffs from the new countries across the oceans than to struggle with old mines and worn-out farm lands. Reciprocally, markets were opened up for Europe's machine-produced textiles and hardware and for its iron (and later steel) rails and shapes. The consequence signalled an enormous expansion in international trade.

The movements of Jewish peoples matched those of the general European populations and had the same general causes. Members of the lower classes, those with no education and those displaced by the new machine production, went into the factories at home or, if they were young, migrated overseas. Between the late 1830s and 1860 the Jewish population of the United States increased from about 15,000 to 150,000, of which 50,000 were immigrants largely from Germany, with smaller numbers from Austria-Hungary and Western Poland.

The German Jews came from the southern and western German lands—from Bavaria, Saxony, Wurttemberg, Hesse, and the Palatinate. A few came from Prussia. Like the rest of the European immigrants, they were humble people, usually from small towns and villages, with little money, little formal education, and relatively few skills. But many were young and for the most part boys and youths. They had courage, sturdiness, and determination to succeed in the new and (perhaps more important) not un-friendly country.

These immigrants were the second and third sons of livestock and grain dealers, petty artisans, and shopkeepers. As boys, some of them had been apprenticed in the handicrafts and the established industries. A few had climbed as high as journeymen. Large numbers had left their poverty-stricken homes to take to the road—there were too many mouths to feed and too few opportunities as small traders and craftsmen for them to re-main at home. Gathering together a few marks and somehow making their way to Hamburg, Bremen, Amsterdam, or London, they took off for the United States.

However, in the late 1830s and early 1840s the United States was not exactly the land of opportunity they had anticipated. Depression had set in following exuberant over-expansion in land speculation and public promo-tions. But even under these conditions, service industries were not as hard hit as were manufactures and construction, and young fellows who were willing to work did survive and, after 1846, even thrive. The obvious ac-tivity for such as these, requiring no capital and a little credit, where small profits could be made and stored away against better times, was that of the itinerant peddler. Of these there were literally hundreds (perhaps even thousands) who tramped the back-country roads of the United States far and wide. Bright, quick, pleasant, and always unafraid, not a few became extremely successful, ending as merchant princes, clothing manufacturers with chains of stores of their own as outlets, meat packers and, above all, investment bankers in New York.

These Jewish peddlers roamed the countryside, carrying man-killing packs on their backs. At first they peddled odds and ends—notions, bits of embroidery, trinkets, spectacles—to the womenfolk of farmers in isolated homesteads where their company was as welcome as were their colorful ribbons and laces. Shanks' mare was their first form of locomotion. Then, as one moved up the ladder of peddler-hood to the acquisition of a horse and buggy, he hawked over a wider territory, selling somewhat more pre-tentious articles, such as watches, rings and brooches, bolts of cloth and silks, and chinaware. Finally, journey's end was a small town in the midst of a thriving agricultural district, a fixed habitation and a store dealing in "general merchandise," or sometimes only dry goods, and trading on the side in the produce of the locality, whether cotton, grain, animal feeds, or packed provisions. In connection with the latter, produce men inevitably had to become small-time private bankers, discounting their customers' domestic bills of exchange and making loans with land or (in the South) slaves as security.

This was the road Proskauer's grandfather Leinkauf traveled in Mobile. It was also the route that took the Lehmans, more energetic and resourceful, out of even smaller Montgomery into New Orleans and then into New York to become rich and powerful investment bankers.

There was another pattern that led equally well to spectacular successes. Peddlers, having settled down as general merchants in growing urban communities, not infrequently took on as their specialty ready-made clothing—suits and coats for men, cloaks and suits for women. Often this led to manufacturing. Akin to these were those, the more prosperous, who moved from general stores to the founding of great urban department stores or to the creation of diversified mail-order houses where guarantee and quality, fixed price, cash returns, and quick and trustworthy service built great American mercantile establishments. Among these financial giants were Straus, Lazarus, Altman, Bloomingdale, Filene, Gimbel, Bamberger, and Hecht in merchandizing; Rosenwald and Spiegel in the mail-order business; Weber and Heilbroner, Hart Schaffner and Marx, Kuppenheimer and Sonneborn, and Levi Strauss & Co. in clothing; Morris, Nelson, Sulzberger, and Schwartzchild in meat packing; and the Seligmans, Lehmans, Abraham Kuhn and Solomon Loeb, Marcus Goldman and Joseph Sachs, Lazarus Hollgarten, and Baruch Wertheim in investment banking.

Not only had Alabama attracted the Leinkaufs and the Proskauers. The Seligmans and the Lehmans started there also. The Seligmans were Bavarians, a large family of ten children whose father was a petty and not very successful merchant. The first son to break away was Joseph. At the ripe age of seventeen he came in 1837 to Mauch Chunk, a little mining town in eastern Pennsylvania, to live with a cousin and to begin as a peddler. In six months he was able to send for brothers William and James and in four years for Jesse. By this time all four were located in Lancaster, Pennsylvania where they had a store and were "general merchants." James, well off enough to own a horse and wagon, was the first to go to Alabama. What he found there impressed the other three, for in 1841, having amassed a capital of $5,000, they too went to Mobile out of which they ranged far and wide, establishing their headquarters in the up-country cotton town of Selma and renting buildings and opening general merchandise stores in the villages of Greensboro, Eutaw, and Clinton. In a year they sent for the five more Seligman children, two sisters and three brothers, and in the next year for the father and the last of the sons.

The other four brothers were Henry, Leopold, Abraham, and Isaac, and the sisters were Rosalie and Sarah. The sisters chose to stay in New York (where they quickly found husbands) and the restless Seligmans divided their forces, leaving the four smaller boys with them. Never missing an opportunity, they opened a store in 1846 at 5 William Street in lower New York, which carried the sign "J. Seligman and Brothers, Merchants."

One brother-in-law, however, was sent to St. Louis and the other to Water-town, New York where he opened his business of "Dry Goods and Importers."

By 1850 the Seligmans had left the South. The California gold rush had begun and larger opportunities beckoned. Joseph moved to New York to make it the family headquarters and Jesse and Leopold were dispatched to San Francisco to sell general merchandise to the miners but, more impor-tant, to buy their gold and dispatch it east. By 1852 Joseph was one of New York's important gold traders and the first German Jew to become a private banker.

The Seligmans thrived during the Civil War. Earlier, in Watertown, they had met and become friendly with a young army lieutenant named Ulysses Simpson Grant, whose regiment was stationed nearby, and this friendship plus the astuteness of the Seligmans as merchants later made them important suppliers of the Northern armies. As soon as the war was over, the firm of J. & W. Seligman & Co., Bankers, appeared. New York was its center, and there were branches in Frankfort (to which Henry and Abraham went) and London (where Leopold and Isaac were in charge) and offices in San Francisco and New Orleans. Raising foreign funds for the building of America's new railroads was their forte, and they did very well, indeed.

The Seligmans, then, did not remain Alabamians and Southerners. The Lehmans did, first as peddlers, then as general merchants, owning slaves and undoubtedly dealing in them and, when the Civil War broke out, they were Southern patriots. There were three Lehman brothers and they left their parents behind in a small Bavaria town. The first to go was Henry, aged twenty-two in 1844, and he made directly for Alabama, peddling north along the Alabama River, selling his wares to the cotton-growers and the general farmers in Alabama's Black Belt country. A year later he es-tablished a general store in Montgomery, the state's capital, dealing in dry goods, hardware, bagging, and seed. He did so well that within two years he was able to send for brother Emanuel, who was then twenty, and in another four years for brother Mayer, who was a year older. The store now bore the sign "Lehman Brothers, Grocers," but they were also brokers, for they bought and sold cotton and gray cotton goods.

Henry, the eldest, who had started the family off, died of yellow fever in 1855, when he was thirty-three. During the 1850s Emanuel had been the firm's agent in New York. He made frequent trips there, getting ac-quainted with the city's money dealers and their ways, for New York was the apex of the cotton triangle, handling and financing the ginned cotton as it came from the Southern ports and then forwarding it to Liverpool, Eng-land, Britain's cotton center.

An agent like Emanuel obtained his funds and maintained his liquidity, so that he could expand his operations in either or both of two ways: he could sell (and discount) the domestic bills of exchange he received for the dry goods and hardware he sold to Alabama cotton farmers, or he could sell (and discount) the sterling bills he received from London, after the ginned cotton he had bought was landed in Liverpool. In 1858 Emanuel, still the Southerner in his loyalties to King Cotton and the slave system, established himself permanently in New York. There he began to function also as a bills dealer—the beginnings, in other words, of a private banking business. At the same time Mayer was carrying on in Montgomery.

The outbreak of the Civil War was a trying time for the two brothers. The Northern naval ships threw a tight cordon around Confederate sea-ports and blockade-running was a risky and often unsuccessful business. Mayer, hoping for an early end of the war and the resumption of the cotton trade, with a partner bought cotton and warehoused it. Emanuel made oc-casional trips to Europe to try to sell Confederate bonds and, very likely, also to get some cotton past the patrolling Northern frigates.

After the war Mayer stayed in the South for three years, just long enough to set up the firm of Lehman, Durr & Co. in Montgomery and that of Lehman, Newgass & Co. (Newgass was a brother-in-law) in New Orleans. Both called themselves cotton dealers.

In New York Emanuel had been branching out, first as a produce broker handling not only cotton but also petroleum, coffee, and sugar, and ex-panding his dealing in bills. In 1868 Mayer joined Emanuel and the office of Lehman Brothers, Bankers and Brokers, formally made its appearance. Up to the turn of the century Lehman Brothers continued as produce brokers and private bankers (rather than public underwriters), financing all sorts of novel American company promotions. This was a true example of the role the money man could play as innovator or entrepreneur.

It was Philip Lehman, Emanuel's son, who embarked the Lehman firm on its later sensational career as investment bankers. With him were ac-tively associated at the start three of the sons of Mayer, Sigmund, Arthur, and Herbert H., as well as numerous cousins and the men the women of the family married. There was money for all, so that Mayer's sons could pursue other interests more seriously than they did their banking. Arthur, by carefully cultivating his good taste and with judicious advice, became one of America's great art collectors. (He willed a superb body of the work he had gathered, together with money for a building to house it, to New York's Metropolitan Museum of Art.) Irving (another son) studied law, was quickly named a member of the New York State Supreme Court, and later became chief judge of the Court of Appeals, where he was a very good jurist, if not a great one. Herbert H. was elected governor of New York, when Franklin D. Roosevelt ran for the presidency, and after a number of terms served in the United States Senate. In both offices he was hard-working, conscientious and, of course, scrupulously honest, if never brilliant. He left hosts of admirers and a tradition: men with large fortunes could be elected to public office where they could, and would be, good public servants.

These were outstanding examples of great successes of Jews in the Old South, the pre-Civil War South. There were others who did more modestly (Proskauer's maternal grandfather Leinkauf was a case in point). Yet, when they entered into the civic life of their communities, they were elected to public office, two even to the United States Senate (Judah P. Benjamin of Louisiana and David Yulee of Florida).

Here, then, was proof of the stoutly held belief of Jews that assimilation was possible without absorption and loss of identity. Such prejudice as there was against them, was directed against them as aliens, not as Jews. There are many recollections of the friendliness with which hard-working young men, trudging along dusty roads with their peddlers packs, were received in the back-country of the rural South. Once settled in, however, as shopkeepers, traders, brokers, all members of the middle class, many doors were open to them. They had, as Rabbi B. W. Korn once wrote, on a footing of equality, full "social, political, economic, and intellectual status and recognition."

And this, of course, was the heart's desire of every Jewish emigrant, to be a member of a minority in the midst of a dominant culture, whose prevailing mores he accepted, unquestioningly. And the German Jews of the Old South were anxious to do so: to vote as the majority did, to hold and swear by its prejudices, to raise the same alarms at threatened dangers, and rush to its defense, even if it meant supporting a Civil War. Then they belonged, and their peculiarities, their Judaism, their German speech they used at home and taught their children, were acceptable as eccentricities or peccadilloes.

But there was another difference. The Old South was the slave South. It could defend itself and survive only if, built into its entire institutionalism, was the assumption that the slave, the black, was the white man's inferior in every way. One "belonged," then, if one bought and sold slaves, used them, and treated the blacks with familiarity, patronizingly, and, at times, with the harshness that a lower order of being was accustomed to or, it was assumed, required.

The rub was that one "belonged" only because one was a white. But once the stability, sanctions, or mores of such a society disappeared—once the blacks were freed by an act of war and, in the face of that, once they were legally disfranchised as a result of the seizure of political power by the white masses, the lower middle class, in the New South (all this happening when Proskauer was a young man)—then ancient hostilities and prejudices were revived. For the New South was on the defensive and suspicious of all outsiders. Therefore, Roman Catholics were aliens because they unquestioningly accepted the guidance of a foreign power, the Vatican. Blacks were inferior and thus, it was believed, would always remain so.

And Jews were the despised and feared people who were responsible for the death of the Son of God as well as being members of an "international conspiracy."

To this extent, when the young (and even the older) Proskauer stoutly maintained that he was a Southerner and proud of it, he was sentimentalizing a world of which he had heard from his elders and in which they had found a false acceptance and security. This make-believe world had been built upon a set of false values. The New South into which Proskauer was born and which he left never to return, was an uneasy, turbulent, even a violent South. Its ways and habits of life rejected every rule of conduct he, as a German Jew, had learned to respect and accept. It took him a long time to find this out: in fact, he did not find out until 1924-1932, when his friend Alfred E. Smith was three times defeated for the presidency—in each case the deciding force being the hostility of the New South.

There was something else Proskauer discovered and it took him a lifetime to do it: that complete assimilation, for him, a Jew, could not work. Indeed, he believed, it would never work until the individual was treated— liked or disliked, consorted with or avoided—as a single, solitary person, and not as a faceless member of a race, religion, or people, ever under suspicion because tagged with a something that was repugnant to the dominant culture. Toward that time, strangers, aliens, members of minorities had to band together for their protection. And for what end? To prove (in this case) that Jews could create a state of their own, where they could order their own lives as do peoples of other states, with all their follies and triumphs. Even more important: once and for all to make the Christian churches see the great wrong, perpetrated and perpetuated over two milleniums, that their doctrine of the Jews, all Jews, as deicides, had wrought, and to disavow it and remove it from the education of their young and the liturgy of their churches.

GROWING UP IN
MOBILE, ALABAMA

2

Proskauer's father, Alfred, arrived in Mobile in the late 1860s or early 1870s, having been sent for by his oldest brother, Adolph, who had set himself up in business after his return from the war. Adolph must have done fairly well as a cotton commission merchant, certainly up to the depression of 1873, for the South had to grow and sell cotton to survive. Alfred was also doing well. In the mid-1870s he married Rebecca, daughter of William Leinkauf. They had three children, Joseph, born in 1877; Hugo, in 1879; and Adelaide, in 1881.

But the family circle included more than those, for Jews are known for and fond of their clannishness and like to maintain close ties even with distant relatives. In the friendly circle were Grandfather and Grandmother Leinkauf; the Blochs (whose daughter Leinkauf had married); the other sons and daughters of the Leinkaufs and their children; the Kochs, one of whose daughters Adolph had married; the other Koch children and their offspring; and Adolph's three children. Joseph Proskauer once wrote that he had "hundreds of cousins."

The head of the tribe was Grandfather Leinkauf. He owned a large house and kept a barouche with a spanking team of horses. Indeed, he was a man of importance in Mobile, prominent in civic affairs and a leading merchant. When times were out of joint, particularly after the depression of 1873, he was able to keep his head above water. Like all Jews, he had a strong sense of family obligation and was able and willing to help those who faltered (as he did Proskauer's father and younger brother).

Joseph Proskauer sensed these difficulties as he grew older. Nevertheless, for a young boy Mobile must have been a pleasant, exciting place to live in during the 1880s. In his *A Segment of My Times* (1950) he related this incident:

> . . . there was the afternoon drive down the shell road along the Bay, through groves of giant magnolias and live oaks festooned with Spanish moss. Fanned by a breeze redolent of salt-tanged bay and magnolias, regaled on special occasions with food and drink when we came to Fredericks at the end of the drive, I would come home fully convinced that I lived in a wonderful world where I could love and be loved and all was 'right as right could be.'

As much as the boy loved Grandma and Grandpa Leinkauf, he apparently adored Uncle Adolph, his Confederate hero who, as a soldier in the Mobile Independent Rifles, had fought at Manassas Junction, in the bloody Peninsular Campaign, at Chancellorsville (where he was wounded), at Gettysburg and at Spottsylvania, where he was again wounded, this time severely. He was transferred to Mobile to recuperate, and in January, 1865, as the war neared its end, he obtained permission to leave for Germany in order to restore his health.

Meantime, during his four years of service to the Confederacy, he was promoted from corporal to sergeant to captain, and, finally, to colonel of his regiment. According to Joseph Proskauer's *Reminiscences,* Adolph was first denied his promotion to colonel "because he was a Jew," but the official history of his regiment, the Twelfth Alabama (of which the Mobile Independent Rifles was a unit), states that the military board which examined Adolph discovered that he knew "more about tactics than any of the examining board. . . . He was gallant officer."

Adolph was the idol of Proskauer's childhood. There were so many tales to tell and Adolph undoubtedly told them to admiring companies of boys, in the manner of all returned soldiers. Indeed, Adolph was a prepossessing man: a passport to Europe (where he went in 1865 and again in 1871, 1877, and 1879) described him as being five feet, ten and one-half inches tall, with a low forehead, dark eyes, small nose and mouth, dimpled chin, dark hair, flowing side whiskers, fair complexion, and a full face. Apparently, Adolph was a bon vivant who dressed in the height of fashion, smoked cigars, was a connoisseur of wine, and liked his rum neat. He must have cut a figure in every society in the Jewish community as well as in the civic life of Mobile. He was elected twice to the Alabama legislature, in 1869 and 1870. He became a member of the esteemed Société Francaise de Bienfaisance of Mobile in 1870, president of Mobile's Jewish Congregation Shaarai Shamayim in 1873, and a Master Mason in 1875. When Carl Schurz visited Mobile in August, 1865, Adolph chaired the meeting and was toastmaster at the banquet tendered Schurz by the German-Americans of the city.

It is not surprising that the younger brother, Alfred, Joseph Proskauer's father, lived in the shadow of the older. In any event, Alfred was very much the junior partner of A. Proskauer and Co., commission merchants, who represented the Lehman Brothers, and undoubtedly it was he who minded the store while Adolph was occupied with his various civic responsibilities and his frequent trips to Europe.

The modest business did not do well during the depression of the 1870s, for when Adolph returned from his last European journey in 1880, he found A. Proskauer and Co. in bankruptcy. However, there was a refuge for Alfred in his father-in-law's private bank (which had been established in 1878). Adolph remained in Mobile until 1887, at which time he and his family moved to St. Louis. There he enjoyed varying success, was prominent in its associational life, and died in 1900.

Inevitably, Alfred was the eclipsed, subdued, and perhaps defeated one. Proskauer, the son, recalled this of his father:

> He was an isolated sort of very junior partner in Grandfather's little bank. He never wanted to take a vacation. He always wanted to be on the job all the time. He was well-liked. I don't think he had the gift of friendship. He was tremendously self-sacrificing and always helped others. I got a feeling of responsibility and sense of obligation to duty from him.

This comment sounds very much like the dutiful son paying his respects to a long-dead father. On the other hand, it was in the image of the outgoing, energetic, forceful uncle, with his zest and appetite for life and good living, with his hankering after going to far places, that Joseph Proskauer was to cast himself.

A boy's upbringing, in addition to his being sheltered, protected, and loved by his family, includes his schooling, religious training, and companionships—to say nothing of the countless frustrations of "growing up." Among these many activities, the youthful Proskauer learned also to be passionately fond of music and particularly of the piano, although not to play it. His mother and his grandmother's brother, Joseph Bloch, were musicians—the latter a self-styled "professor" who taught music appreciation at Spring Hill College, a Jesuit academy in Mobile. Young Proskauer was also an indefatigable reader. With his several cousins he was enrolled in a private elementary school run by his grandaunt. There he remained until he was nine. Then, for the first time, he ventured out into a wider world inhabited by both Jews and Gentiles: he entered Barton Academy, a public school which had been founded in 1835. There, in that old institution, he was taught the three Rs, grammar, history, civics, and studied English literature, Latin, and Greek, and he was introduced to physics, chemistry, and mathematics. All this was in line with the new secondary school curriculum that the U. S. Commissioner of Education, a distinguished philosopher and educator, was then expounding. So well did he learn that, when he was graduated from Barton in 1892 at the age of fifteen, Columbia College of New York City readily admitted him, albeit with some minor conditions.

For young Joseph in Mobile there were, of course, both boyhood friends and foes. Among the former he had one with whom he was particularly close, the son of the rector of an Episcopal church, in whose home he spent many happy hours. Among the latter there was at least one who constantly harassed him, and Proskauer never forgot him. While in Barton Academy he was waylaid and his nose bloodied by a band of youthful toughs known as the "Goubil Gang," because, as they said, he was a "Christ Killer." Although banged up again and again, he fought back on his own behalf and later to protect his younger brother Hugo from the same tormentors. In his seventies he recorded these events at Barton in *A Segment of My Times:*

> I entered the junior grade and there, for the first time, encountered the

mystery of anti-Semitism. I was, so I believed, a good boy. I was a patriotic American, and my uncle had surely earned for my family a deserved reputation for loyalty to Alabama. My father had close Christian friends. I treasure still the silver cup which had been given to me as the first-born of a member of the Order of the Mystics, one of the societies responsible for the Mardi Gras pageants which gave Mobile the proud title of 'Mother of Mystics.' Membership in that order gave a sense of 'belonging' in a common fellowship.

It was the earliest in a long series of bloodied noses, physical and metaphorical, that have marked the life of myself and every other American Jew. And as I still puzzle today over the why and wherefore of this amazing phenomenon in free America, I experience the same sense of bewilderment that came over me when I backed up against the fence on Conti Street and tried to trade blow for blow with Rene Goubil and his followers.

Years later, in his eighties, Proskauer was to learn the "why and wherefore" of anti-Semitism, particularly why what he had been doing with all his power "to destroy this ugly excrescence on the American way of life" had been unavailing. He had been reared in a Jewish family which "was not piously Orthodox, but it was observant"; that is to say, it adhered to the tenets of Reform Judaism, as did virtually all German Jews in America. There had been a small Jewish community in Mobile as far back as the 1830s. The new immigrants swelled it, so that in 1841 a formal congregation, Shaarai Shamayim (Gates of Heaven), was organized. Five years later a synagogue was established. In 1876 there were about six hundred Jews residing in Mobile. At the synagogue there was a succession of rabbis and transfers of the institution to larger quarters. Because this was the inclination of the congregants, the ritual of the synagogue increasingly followed the more relaxed practices of Reform Judaism. The Minhag American prayer book was adopted; the services and responses, first in German, were later in English, and not Hebrew and an organ was acquired and a choir trained.

The Sabbath began on Friday night and was celebrated in the Proskauer home. The whole family attended services in the synagogue on Saturday. The important holy days—the Passover, Rosh ha-Shanah, Yom Kippur—were properly observed. Schools were established for religious instruction and young Proskauer attended one regularly, the one taught by a new young rabbi, Oscar J. Cohen, who came to lead the congregation in 1888. Proskauer, now in his teens, was swept off his feet by the slightly older man, well-educated (at Columbia College), well-trained, and devoted to his congregation, particularly the young members. A passage in A Segment . . ., reciting the spell the young rabbi had cast over him, is all but idyllic in its quality:

> After I have passed my three score and ten, I still thrill as I remember the glee with which I celebrated, under his tutelage, the Maccabean Victories, the delight I had when Haman was caught in his own toils, the sense of glory I felt

in Miriam's Song of Triumph. But much more than to the glory of these merely historical phases of our Jewish life and tradition, I warm to the recollection of my response as I sat there, in our little synagogue, with the windows open and the sunlight streaming in when I heard the choir intone *Lift up your heads, oh ye gates,* I felt that the gates of the Ark were really lifting themselves up, as Rabbi Cohen took one of the scrolls of the Law from which to read the morning lesson. He gave me a sense of immanence of a divine spirit, firing me with a glow that made me Jew through and through, loving my religion and its traditions. He greatly influenced my secular education, but his priceless gift was to my soul.

As Rabbi Cohen and young Proskauer became closer friends, they discussed many things other than religion, among them the vast world beyond Mobile. As his day of graduation from Barton Academy neared, the topic was often college. "Tell me about Columbia College, Rabbi Cohen; tell me about New York."

Cohen responded enthusiastically. For he, himself, when a boy, had heard about the Lost Cause and the New South that had emerged after the Civil War and Reconstruction; and had seen them coldly in the harsh light of reality. (It took Proskauer years to come around to that viewpoint: the New South would have cabined, cribbed, and confined him, breaking his spirit; or it would have chewed him up and spit him out.)

Mobile was a small city when Proskauer was growing up. With a population of about thirty thousand, it had stopped progressing. But it was an old American city and it had been fought over and won and lost by the soldiers of different countries almost a half dozen times. Residents of Mobile took pride in the fact that it had been ruled for varying periods under five flags—those of Spain, France, England, the Confederate States, at last, the United States. Each had left its traces in the names of streets and avenues and in the architectural styles of their houses. The main thoroughfares were lined with magnificent shade trees, live oaks, magnolia, banana, and Japanese plum. Most of all, the city, like New Orleans, seemed French and Roman Catholic, and, like New Orleans, celebrated many old church festivals and carnivals. It was little wonder, then, when Proskauer as a much older man living in New York, that he was closer to Catholics than to Protestants, a fact which partially explains his ease in working with the former in their struggle against the latter. He believed that it was up to the Roman Catholics to be the first to tackle the root case of anti-Semitism; that is, the idea of the Jews as the deicide people.

Mobile lay at the mouth of the Mobile River, an ideal place for a town, a stockade, and a depot for traders and proselytizing priests who seized the opportunity to work their way north and east up the rivers into the Indian country. Both the English and French did this. Before the town stretched the Bay of Mobile with its sandy shores lined with lofty pines and inlets and beaches. At the entrance to the bay were islands which had once been fortified by the English, for they were merchants who used their foothold in Mobile Bay to expand their commerce into the whole Gulf of Mexico region.

A young fellow, like Joseph Proskauer, learned a lot about all these things in school. The area's terrain and climate encouraged other interests and these were to remain with Proskauer all his life. Mobile's climate was subtropical, its winters mild, its summers hot and humid, its rainfall heavy. As early as February or March flowers began to bloom profusely throughout the region—pink and red azaleas, purple wisteria, the small white flowers of the many privet hedges, and many more. All this was conducive to an out-of-doors life. Young Proskauer sailed and fished in the coastal waters, tramped the woods and beaches, and climbed the hills and bluffs around the bay. The wooded areas about the city were filled with wild game birds and animals. All of this made lasting impressions on the boy, impressions that were to serve him well during his long lifetime. After he moved to New York, he bought a country place at Lake Placid in the Adirondacks, which he kept as nature had created it. There he found the same kind of endless rural pleasures as he had had as a boy in Mobile. And when he traveled, as he did so much later in life, he visited cities, to be sure, but he was constantly returning to the simpler joys of his country life.

Spain did not give up West Florida, of which Mobile was a part, until 1813, and then by force. Meanwhile, settlers had been streaming into the Mississippi Territory, for "cotton was king," and the rich Black Belt, stretching across the central half of Alabama, beckoned planters with their slaves. In 1819 Alabama became a state. There followed, notably in the 1850s, the golden age of Mobile. It was the port into which the cotton poured and out of which went the supplies for the planters and villages of the back-country. In 1849 Alabama led all the states in cotton production and in 1859 it was second only to Mississippi. Slaves made up nearly half of Alabama's population by 1860; in fact, in the Black Belt their proportion was 66.4 percent.

First, cotton came down the Alabama and Tombigbee rivers to Mobile by keelboat and later by steamers. In the late 1850s, when the Mobile and Ohio Railroad was running the western length of the state, Mobile's docks, warehouses, cotton presses, railroad terminals, and boats multiplied. From the port ships sailed directly to New York and later by iron packet boats to Liverpool. By the time of the Civil War, Mobile was the second largest port of the South and its leading railroad center.

The City of Mobile was of sufficient importance in the 1830s to have a branch of the Bank of the United States. Water and gas pipes were laid down. The Barton Academy, perhaps the pre-war Deep South's best public school, was established. In the 1850s Mobile housed other banks, many flourishing mercantile establishments (cotton factors and commission men, mostly, merchants buying supplies for and selling to upcountry planters), lumber mills, a few small iron foundries, and it boasted of newspapers and theaters. By 1860 its population had grown to 30,000—Alabama's largest city.

Mobile was a loyal Confederate city during the Civil War and its young men (Uncle Adolph among them) went off to fight. United States ships kept up a continuing blockade patrol of the waters off Mobile Bay, but some cotton kept on moving out and some supplies coming in. Even the famous C.S.S. *Florida* (built like the *Alabama* in Liverpool) was able to slip through the Union cordon to be refitted and remanned and sail out again. After the fall of New Orleans only Mobile and Galveston remained. Admiral David G. Farragut, who had ascended the Mississippi and reduced New Orleans in 1862, moved on Mobile, August 5, 1864, with a large fleet of wooden frigates and iron monitors, ran through the mine fields and pounded his way past Forts Gaines and Morgan, guarding the entrance to Mobile Bay. The forts surrendered August 23, and the Confederate flotilla defending the city was defeated. However, it was not until April, 1865 that Union soldiers entered Mobile itself. By that time its commerce had been dead for almost a year and so was the city's affluence.

Mobile did not revive or recapture its former preeminence—not during Proskauer's boyhood and, in fact, not until the 1930s, when the New Deal began to pour large sums into the South. The city lost population from 1870 to 1880 and its inhabitants in 1890 numbered no more than they had in 1860. The South began growing cotton again as soon as the war was over; but the chief producing area shifted to Texas, so that cotton receipts in Mobile were only 200,000 bales in 1890 as compared with 800,000 in 1860. And as railroads began to criss-cross Alabama during 1870-1890, interior towns were freed of their dependence upon Mobile as their supply and banking center.

Efforts were made to maintain the city as a port, and federal funds were appropriated for digging and widening a channel. By 1896 it had reached a depth of twenty-three feet, enough to accommodate the larger freighters. But by that time the cotton factoring and cotton commission businesses were dying industries and the little firm of A. Proskauer and Co., along with many others, went into bankruptcy. Some capital was diverted to the expansion of the region's lumber cutting industry; however, real growth did not begin taking place until a full decade after Joseph Proskauer had left for New York. There were some public improvements in Mobile during his boyhood: the city streets were paved, the water-supply system became a municipal utility, an electric railway was begun, and the fire department became a unit of city government. Yet Mobile's population rose slowly— to only 38,000 in 1900 and 50,000 in 1910.

Despite his profession of loyalty to Mobile and the South and an occasional statement that he wanted to live in Alabama after he was graduated from college, he never returned, except to visit relatives. By the time he had earned his degree in law from Columbia, he was a confirmed New Yorker.

PROSKAUER AT COLUMBIA UNIVERSITY

3

In June, 1892 Joseph Proskauer journeyed to New York to stand the examinations for admission to the freshman class of Columbia College's School of Arts. He had made the proper preparation; in fact, he had been put on notice that the tests were going to be difficult, for Columbia was the equal, if not the superior, of any other American college. The institution was known to be particularly interested in the further education of youths who had already traveled far along the road toward the country's upper middle class. The written tests covered a wide variety of subjects, including Latin and Greek, English grammar, composition, and literature, mathematics, and French or German.

Proskauer did very well indeed, receiving chiefly As, a few Bs, and a couple of Cs (which he later worked off and converted to As). Thus, on October 3, 1892 he was admitted and enrolled as a freshman. All together, his class numbered only sixty-four students.

In a single block in New York's already well-settled East Side, from 49th to 50th Streets and from Park to Madison Avenues, was crowded the inadequate physical plant of Columbia College, a highly complex educational institution. The site had been chosen in 1879, presumably as a temporary way-station in the hoped-for march northward into greener and wider space. But as time went on and funds for a move did not materialize, in the small area were erected buildings to accommodate more than two thousand students and some four hundred instructors. The largest structure was Hamilton Hall, the home of the School of Arts, with faculty offices, classrooms, lecture halls, and a large reading room for students. Also on the same site were the library (which also housed the School of Law), a small chapel, the School of Mines, the Electrical School (which was also the boiler house), and the administrative offices. There was one spillover to the corner of Park Avenue and East 51st Street, where a gymnasium had been erected, and another to the south side of East 49th Street which contained two annexes. The College of Physicians and Surgeons extended from West 58th to West 60th Streets between 9th and 10th Avenues, adjacent to Roosevelt Hospital, Vanderbilt Clinic, and the Sloane Maternity Hospital, all affiliated with Columbia and furnishing teaching facilities, medical and surgical services, wards, and necessary out-patient departments. Oddly, there were no dormitory facilities, largely because the majority of the students were local residents. Thus, out-of-towners like Joseph Proskauer had to fend for themselves. During his seven years at Columbia he lived with relatives—for the first two years with cousins of his mother at 48 West 97th Street and for the remainder of his stay with a

paternal uncle, Joseph Proskauer, at 116 West 136th Street. He was fortunate to be able to do so, for his resources were slender and he was forced
to pick up all sorts of odd jobs—tutoring, taking boys on trips, and acting as
a "stringer" or campus correspondent, working on space for the New York
Commercial Advertiser.

There is no doubt that young Proskauer was at first very much alone, a
stranger in a strange land, for most of his fellow students were New Yorkers. He was confronted by an exacting regimen and he worked constantly
at it. Later in life, in his autobiographical fragment, *A Segment . . .*, he admitted he worked too hard. He was lonely and he considered himself
"something of a novelty" to his classmates. But he had the urge to succeed, an urge which, as he put it, "brought in its train a certain impulsive
assertiveness. I soon recognized this as a kind of gaucherie in myself."
Perhaps, Proskauer was too severe on himself. Had he behaved more the
Jew, as Saul Bellow, Philip Roth, Bernard Malamud, and others have
pointed out, he would have known that this anxiety, doubt, self-torture,
and compelling necessity to excel were his natural traits.

Proskauer's Columbia College program for the first two years was set; all
the courses were required and there were no electives. As a freshman he
had fifteen hours of classes, distributed among Latin, Greek, rhetoric,
mathematics, history, and German. As a sophomore, he had sixteen, distributed among Latin, Greek, history, mathematics, German, literature,
and chemistry. In his junior year he enrolled in history, political economy,
logic, and psychology, and eleven elective hours. In his senior year he
chose a minimum of fifteen hours of electives, including any courses he
desired from the institution's varied offerings, for by that time Columbia
College had formally become "Columbia University in the City of New
York." Following the current fashion of using the German universities as
a model, it nevertheless maintained a strong "college." There were separate faculties for all major divisions, each headed by a dean, and all under
the direction of the president and a Board of Trustees. Along with this
came the long-heralded announcement that the University had acquired a
large property on what was to be known as Morningside Heights, from
West 116th Street to West 120th Street, between Amsterdam Avenue and
Broadway (then named "The Boulevard"). The move was to be accompanied by two independent, but affiliated corporations, Barnard College
(for women), to be located on the west side of "The Boulevard," and
Teachers College, to be located on the north side of West 120th Street.

These were the accomplishments of Seth Low, a graduate of Columbia
College and a wealthy citizen of Brooklyn, who had been that city's mayor
from 1882 to 1886, and had consented to become Columbia's president in
1889. John W. Burgess, an older man, and Nicholas Murray Butler, a
younger one, both holding the Doctor of Philosophy degree from German
universities, had been the leaders in pressing for the upgrading of the

college. Of course, Low was sympathetic to the change. Indeed, he was the one who had led in getting the pledges together to make possible the acquisition of the new site, himself furnishing the funds for the erection of the first building, the handsome Low Memorial Library which was completed in 1897. The Law School, in which Proskauer was a student, was housed in that new structure.

In 1892 the Board of Trustees approved the purchase of part of the Bloomingdale Asylum on Cathedral Heights. Years before, or so the story goes, the trustees had refused to purchase all of this property, an excellent and large piece of still undeveloped land running from West 110th to 120th Streets and from what is now Morningside Drive to Riverside Drive, believing it much too spacious for their needs. As a result, part was bought for the Cathedral of St. John the Divine and part for St. Luke's Hospital.

When the University and the Cathedral of St. John made their moves, the old Bloomingdale Asylum buildings were still standing. In fact, two of them remain today and are being used by Columbia and the Cathedral. One, the charming little red brick edifice known as East Hall (the first home of the School of General Studies), faces the Low Library on the upper campus. The other, a wooden structure, is the Cathedral's exhibition hall and is located where some day, it is hoped, the south transcept of the Cathedral will be built.

The Board of Trustees contracted to pay $2 million for the Bloomingdale Asylum land and took possession of it in 1894. An impressive architectural plan, linking all the projected buildings together—lying within their own gates, protected by their own lawns, an enclave as part of, yet aloof from, the city that was beginning to grow around it—was agreed on. The firm of McKim, Mead, and White, which had designed the Low Memorial Library (a charming example of the so-called Renaissance Revival style of classical architecture), laid out the general plan and supervised the construction of the various halls as funds were raised. In time all of the projected buildings were erected, although more than a decade passed before the University's College and the Law School were able to move into buildings of their own, Hamilton and Kent Halls, respectively.

In his first two and one-half years in the University, Joseph Proskauer earned chiefly As and Bs and signed up for honors in mathematics for his first two years and in English for his third. In his junior and senior years, under the elective system, he took courses in calculus, history of philosophy (the lecturing professor was Nicholas Murray Butler), political and constitutional history of the United States (under the distinguished John W. Burgess), and in the political and constitutional history of England (under Herbert L. Osgood). One of his favorite instructors was a young man named James Harvey Robinson who taught the history of modern Europe, always relating it to the growth of man's mind and the progress of society. Proskauer registered for at least one course and one seminar with Robinson and audited several others. In his later years he always glowed when he talked of Robinson, for Robinson has opened for him many doors —"The intellectual and moral links between the past and the future,"— links which Proskauer never forgot. And Robinson must have liked his eager young student, for he personally invited him to enroll in his seminar on the Procedural Methods of the Inquisition, but, alas, Proskauer had already chosen to enter the Law School and thus had to decline.

Proskauer, after his early lonely start, developed many friendships, some of which he retained for a long time. Despite the facts that he was always capable of independent judgments and led much more often than he followed, he possessed a passion for comradeship. In his boyhood he had found one such friend in his Uncle Adolph. In his mature life he was to find another in Alfred E. Smith. In his teens and early manhood it was George Edward Woodberry, professor of literature at Columbia University, who lifted his spirit and made his pulse beat faster. As late as 1944, when Proskauer wrote an essay about Woodberry for *The Saturday Review of Literature,* he excitedly expressed the same enthusiasm for his old teacher as he had felt when he was sixteen.

Woodberry was indeed a remarkable man and teacher. His courses in comparative literature, criticism, drama, and poetry were among the most popular in the University. Students considered him their friend. His office door was always open. They came early to his classes and waited outside the lecture room before the bell so they could crowd up front to catch every word. As Lionel Trilling has written, his students' "personal loyalty lasted through his life and [their] devotion to his memory lasted through their own lives." Besides Joseph Proskauer, James N. Rosenberg, Melville Cane, Henry Harkness Flagler, Frederick P. Keppel, Harold Kellogg, John Erskine, and Joel E. Spingarn were among the many distinguished graduates who sang Woodberry's praises. Proskauer, himself, declared that Woodberry was "The greatest teacher I ever knew."

> to men who, like myself [he added], lacked the divine spark he gave a kind of sixth sense by which we could feel the glory and beauty of literature. . . . If the reader senses in this 'merely personal' outpouring a note of passionate devotion for an exalted teacher, he may be sure I have tried to put it there and that it is shared with me by many other men.

Woodberry was responsible for the formation of King's Crown, an undergraduate literary and social club the members of which pursued serious literary interests. The *Columbia Literary Monthly,* with Proskauer as one of the editors, was revived under his sponsorship and Proskauer and James N. Rosenberg edited an *Anthology of Columbia Verse, 1892-1897* which included poetry written by Woodberry's students, particularly Proskauer, Rosenberg, Keppel, and Cane.

The Woodberry cult survived far beyond college days. To celebrate his first decade at Columbia, he was given a testimonial dinner in 1900. Present were more than a hundred of his former students. Joseph Proskauer, newly graduated from the Law School served as master of ceremonies and President Seth Low and Dean of the College J. Howard Van Amringe were among the speakers.

The creation of the Columbia University Club (Woodberry was a prime mover) was one of the consequences of the dinner. And then came a rude shock for Proskauer and Rosenberg and their friends. Proskauer and Rosenberg had been invited to become charter members of the new club, but the matter of their being Jews raised its ugly head—and both young men withdrew their names. Later, upon the urging of their friends, they permitted their names to be proposed again through the customary channels, after the club had been organized. But this time they suffered the ignominy of being blackballed. Many years later, after both Proskauer and Rosenberg had become distinguished lawyers in New York, they were approached again. Rosenberg was stiff-necked about it, laying down as a condition that the club's directors expunge the earlier humiliation of the blackball. When they refused, Rosenberg declined to join. But Proskauer was elected and became a member. Possibly, his decision was a part of the process of the assimilation he believed in: proving, in a genteel company, that there was no essential difference between himself and his associates.

The Woodberry magic continued to hold, however. In 1909 old students formed a Woodberry society, with Proskauer as one of the initiators. They visited and corresponded with their mentor, sent him presents, and held dinners in his honor. More importantly, they helped finance the publication of two of the three biographies he wrote after he left Columbia University and they collected among themselves a large enough sum to assure Woodberry ("as poverty and oblivion closed in on him," wrote his biographer, Joseph Doyle) a pension of over $2,000 a year.

Woodberry died in 1930 at the age of seventy-five. Columbia University waited eighteen years to make some amends for the wretched way it had treated this gentle and inspiring man. A collection of Woodberriana was displayed, including eight hundred of his letters to his friends, Proskauer among them. A University Convocation was held in his memory, presided over by Acting President Frank D. Fackenthal; and among the several speakers were Woodberry's old students, Cane, Erskine, and Doyle.

After Proskauer had settled in at Columbia and had overcome his compulsion to excel, his life began to take on the normal characteristics of young collegiates of his time and class. He joined societies, usually of a literary bent, often ending by being an officer. He became a member of a chess club and of the Columbia Debating Union; he appeared in theatricals; he entered oratorical, essay-writing, and debating competitions, in each of which he excelled. He had dates, went to dances, wrote verses to girls, and was the recipient of theirs—but he evidenced no serious emotional involvement until he met Alice Naumburg when he was a Law School student.

Most of his social life was in the company of a small group of college companions with whom he drank in beer taverns, frequented the theater in New York, and went for jaunts out into the country. Closest were three who, with Proskauer, formed a tight inner circle of their own. They were all Jews: Alfred L. Kroeber, who became an internationally recognized anthropologist and a professor at the University of California; Carl L. Alsberg, later chief of the Bureau of Chemistry of the United States Department of Agriculture and from there dean of the Graduate School of Leland Stanford University; and James N. Rosenberg, distinguished specialist in the law of bankruptcy, who at 70 quit the law cold to become a first-class graphic artist and almost as good a painter. Proskauer was also close to Irving Lehman, of the banking Lehmans, who was a fellow law student (and later chief judge of the New York State Court of Appeals), and Melville H. Cane, an outstanding lawyer and equally good poet. Together, these five friends hunted and fished in Canada and in the Adirondack Mountains. Proskauer and Kroeber formed what they called the "Adirondack University," a cover for taking boys from New York's settlement houses along with them to Big Moose Lake for nature walks and simple instruction in woodcraft.

At Columbia University it was in intercollegiate debating that Proskauer found his greatest triumph and which eventually directed him toward the study of law. In time he was recognized as one of the University's outstanding student speakers. In March, 1897, when Proskauer was a first-year Law School student, teams from Columbia University and Harvard University met in Carnegie Lyceum to debate the popular election of United States senators. Columbia opposed the selection of senators by the state legislatures and Proskauer, as the anchor man, spoke last for his team. He openly attacked the domination of New York State's Republican Party by "Boss" Thomas C. Platt (who had just had himself chosen senator for a second time), making these pointed remarks:

> State legislatures owing their position to the boss are tools of the boss, and their consciences are in his pocket. He can therefore choose his own Senators. Under the system proposed by us, however, he would have to be pretty careful with his nominations, as the large number of shifting votes which have such patent influence in deciding all elections, must needs be taken into account.

Columbia University won the contest and went on to debate the team from Chicago University on March 25, 1898 in Madison Square Garden. The subject was: *"Resolved,* that the policy of increasing the United States Navy is wise and should be continued." Columbia took the negative.

Proskauer was again the anchor man, speaking last and making the summary in rebuttal. Columbia again won. Stated the New York *Tribune,* which fully reported the meeting, Columbia had "won a decisive and well-earned, if somewhat unexpected victory." And as for Proskauer, he was hailed as "a college orator of the first class." (Even after he had been graduated from Law School, he coached Columbia's debating teams for a number of years.)

It was inevitable that Proskauer, even as a student, should be drawn into New York City politics, at least on its fringes. The city had for three decades been dominated by Tammany Hall which controlled the local Democratic Party, with the usual consequences: plundering of the public till, massive profits from contracts, and corruption in the Police Department. In 1894 a Committee of Seventy, made up of leading citizens, appeared to challenge Tammany Hall. And it was as a watcher at the polls for this so-called "Good Government Party" that Joseph Proskauer took his post in the Sixth Assembly District. He was seventeen years old.

Tammany Hall lost the election and a Republican was chosen mayor. Out of the Committee of Seventy emerged the "Citizens Union," a body which Proskauer at once joined and with which he was long identified. In 1897 Seth Low, president of Columbia University, ran for mayor of the recently consolidated New York City on the Republican-Reform ticket, and Proskauer spoke for him at rallies, usually under the auspices of the Citizens Union. Low was defeated. However, in 1901 he ran again, was elected, and promptly resigned from the University. Meanwhile, Proskauer, having been recently admitted to the bar, ventured into somewhat deeper political waters. In 1900 he joined a district Republican Club, made speeches, and placed his name on a primary ballot for election to the state's congressional convention. He lost and soon entered the Elkus firm as a law clerk. By now he had become weary of politics.

There was a second element of New York's complex life into which Proskauer moved as a young student—"philanthropic endeavor," he called it. Even then he was expressing his limited, nay, optimistic idea of what he considered his Jewishness; that is, the obligation of the presumed assimilated Jew to smooth the journey for other Jews, alien Jews, along the same road he had traveled. In other words, he wished to make easier their absorption into the American way of life.

> In the decade from 1890 to 1900 there had been a large influx of eastern European Jews into America, many of them fleeing from the persecutions of Czarist Russia [Proskauer wrote in *A Segment...*]. The Lower East side of New York City was densely populated with these immigrants, and it became a matter of great concern for American Jews to see to it that they, and especially their young people, were trained in the traditions and ideals of our country.

This mission into a strange country peopled by fellow Jews he had never met before took Proskauer to the Educational Alliance on East Broadway, the heart of the Lower East Side in 1898. There he became both a leader of young boys, meeting them one evening a week, and a Big Brother, visiting their homes and talking with their parents. The organization, known as the Peter Cooper Club, was conducted in "accordance with parliamentary law"; and under this procedure he discussed with his young charges "current political and social topics" and, by recitations and talks, sought to instill a familiarity with English literature. "By such devices," he explained, "we brought home to these youths some substantial degree of knowledge of our country, its history and its ideals, and the literature of England and America." On Sundays and holidays the club members were encouraged to develop their athletic skills. The boys were taken on hikes and excursions into Bronx Park and, farther afield, into the wooded sections of Westchester and the neighboring counties. As a Big Brother he sought during his home visitations to explain his aims to bewildered parents. As he wrote,

> One of the most serious problems was to maintain those family relationships which appeared to be threatened by the Americanization process. On the part of the parents there was an uneasy feeling that their boys were growing away from them; on the part of the boys there was the correlative feeling that the old folks were too much behind the times.

All together, Proskauer found his labors, including his explorations into the life of the East Side, "an arduous, but interesting undertaking." He maintained his association with the Educational Alliance for five years, until 1903, at which time he withdrew to devote his entire time toward earning a living, for he had meantime become engaged to Alice Naumburg and needed to establish himself in his profession as quickly as possible.

There can be no doubt that Joseph Proskauer was fortunate in the time he was able to study law. In 1896, when he entered Columbia Law School, he found himself in one of the two leading schools in the country. (Harvard was the other.) Its repute was attested by the size of its classes and the fact that its students came from all sections of the nation. In his entering class there were 100 men in a student body of 351. These came from 57 different colleges and universities, the greatest concentrations being from Columbia, 32; Yale, 32; College of the City of New York, 26; and Harvard, 25.

One element of the so-called "revolution of 1891," of which Proskauer and his fellow-students were beneficiaries, was the decision to choose entering classes on the basis of individual merit and future promise and not on family prominence or religion. Prior to 1891 the basis of instruction in Columbia Law School had been the lecture-textbook method. A handful of professors addressed large captive audiences in a prescribed curriculum which had not changed for years. They expounded the nature of the law, public and private, *ex cathedra,* presumably based on ancient principles, that seemed to be fixed and immutable. These discourses were supplemented by close study of established textbooks. Student participation in classes was in the form of recitations learned by rote, rather than in the give and take of frank discussions. Professor Theodore W. Dwight, who was the "Warden" of the Law School, defended what he called "the old New England and the old Columbia method" in these words:

> The method adopted in the Law School seeks to inculcate great principles of law, leaving to the student to apply them by his own reasoning to special cases as they arise. It is thus truly educational by drawing out the powers of the student and giving him comprehensive views. It is in sharp and as we think most favorable contrast with instruction by concrete cases, which leaves the student without a guiding principle to connect them. Law is nothing without logic, and true logical methods should be pursued, and the student trained not merely to think on the spot, instead of acquiring his knowledge simply by absorption.

In 1891, after years of debate amid growing dissatisfaction and with President Low pressing for thoroughgoing change in the curriculum, selection of students, and classroom procedures, the philosophy of the school was entirely recast. "Warden" Dwight accepted retirement and two of his colleagues, who thought as he did, resigned.

A good deal of the instruction in the new program was based on the case system, inaugurated at Harvard University. A three-year program, which required regular and full attendance, was set up. There was an increase in the number of hours of weekly attendance—a minimum of fourteen a week which were made obligatory. Beyond the first year, which was set for all students, the elective system operated for the rest of the program, within a vastly expanded choice of courses. A full curriculum in public law, the first in the country, was offered in conjunction with courses in private law.

The "revolution" was made possible and successful because President Low was able to win William Albert Keener away from Harvard. In 1891, at the age of thirty-five, Keener was named professor and the school's first dean. Keener was versatile in many fields, brilliant and exciting in the classroom, and thoroughly committed to the case system of instruction. In 1888-1889 he had published in two volumes his *A Selection of Cases in the Law of Quasi-Contracts.* Four years later this was followed by his *A Treatise of the Law of Quasi-Contracts.* Both works established him as a pioneer in his approach to the study of law. As he himself explained,

> While [the case method] of teaching does not at all proceed on the idea that the common law is wanting in jurists, its advocates regard the adjudged cases as the original sources of our law, and think it is better for the student under proper advice and guidance, to extract from the cases a principle, than to accept the statement of any jurist, however eminent he may be, that a certain

principle is established by certain cases. . . . [In class] the student is required
to analyze each case, discriminate between the relevant and [the] irrelevant,
between the actual and [the] possible grounds of decision. And have thus discussed a case, he is prepared and required to deal with it in its relation to
other cases. . . . By this method the student's reasoning powers are constantly
developed, and while he is gaining the power of legal analysis and synthesis,
he is also gaining the other object of legal education, namely, a knowledge of
what the law actually is.

With Keener came three other new professors: Francis M. Burdick,
George W. Kirchwey, and George M. Cumming. They joined George F.
Canfield and Henry W. Hardon, already members of the faculty. The new
public law program was given by these four men, all of whom, leaders in
their fields, also were on the Faculty of Political Science: John W. Burgess, professor of political science and constitutional law; Munroe Smith,
professor of Roman law and comparative jurisprudence; Frank J. Goodnow, professor of administrative law; and John B. Moore, professor of international law and diplomacy.

In his first year in the school, 1896-1897, Proskauer was enrolled in
classes in elements of jurisprudence (Keener); equity (Keener); contracts
(Cumming); real and personal property (Kirchwey); torts (Burdick); criminal law and procedure (Moore); and common law pleading and practice
(Hardon). The case method was used in equity, contracts, pleadings,
torts, and real and personal property, each course being preceded or accompanied by a standard treatise, as a sort of concession to the inflexible
among the alumni.

In his second year Proskauer was able to choose from among twelve
courses (each usually meeting twice weekly), of which two, comparative
constitutional law (Burgess), and administrative law (Goodnow), were in
public law. In his third year he had fifteen courses to choose from, including the whole gamut of private law, as well as, in public law, insurance, municipal corporations, taxation, and comparative jurisprudence.
Proskauer took advantage of the open system and the generous opportunities the program offered for becoming acquainted with so many aspects of
the law, its procedures, and its practice. He took sixty-four hours of instruction, embracing twenty-one different subjects, and was graduated
high in the top quartile of his class. There can be no doubt that he was a
good student.

A history of the Columbia Law School, published in 1955, characterized
the new program and the great weight it gave to electives as a "smorgas-
bord of legal tidbits," but it went on to say that despite "the atomization of
the curriculum the system did manage to educate lawyers which was to a
large extent due to the personalities of the men who were doing the teaching." Proskauer, reminiscing about the faculty in his *A Segment . . .*,
agreed:

William A. Keener [he wrote], the Dean, was a coursing hunter who ran us relentlessly to earth if we faltered or quibbled or failed to grasp the nettle; John Bassett Moore, the greatest international lawyer of our time; Francis Marion Burdick, mild in manner but stern in demand that we get to know all that he knew (which was all there was to know) of his subjects; George W. Kirchwey, who could make the hairsplitting of the early doctrinaires of the law of real estate seem alive; all these great teachers set the pace which their colleagues followed.

It was not until 1910, thirteen years after its arrival on Morningside Heights, that Columbia University School of Law had its own home in Kent Hall. Beginning in 1901 the students began publishing *The Columbia Law Review* which quickly became an outstanding journal with an international reputation.

In June, 1899 Proskauer received his LL.B., took the New York State bar examination, and in the fall of 1899 set out to look for a job. Inasmuch as he had gone back for summer vacations in Mobile in 1896, 1898, and 1899, he talked of his deep attachment for the South and hinted of his return to it. But it was in New York that he was destined to make his home and seek out his life's career.

MARRIAGE AND
BEGINNING LAW PRACTICE

4

When Joseph Proskauer was a student in the Columbia Law School in 1898, he met Alice Naumburg, the oldest daughter of Max and Theresa Naumburg, middle-class but not affluent German Jews. Alice was four years Proskauer's junior and at that time completing her freshman year at Bryn Mawr College. Five years later, after a typical courtship of their time and class, Joseph and Alice were married. The Naumburgs became, therefore, a part of Joseph's life, particularly the family of Elkan and Bertha Wehle Naumburg, because they were the wealthy ones and the arbiters of family taste and social deportment and much of what the Max Naumburgs did undoubtedly was guided by "what their cousins Elkan and Bertha would say."

The Naumburgs, natives of a small village in Bavaria, had migrated to the United States in 1850. The head of the family was a Reform rabbi and with him had come at least three sons and several grandchildren. They settled in Baltimore and there the sons established a characteristically Jewish mercantile enterprise, dealing in drygoods and notions and specializing in men's ready-to-wear. Two of the grandsons successfully operated a typical lower-middle class Jewish business and then struck out on their own. The first was Elkan, born in 1834, and the second, his cousin Max. Elkan was the pathbreaker. He left Baltimore in the 1880s for New York, first setting up as a "merchant" and later specializing in the manufacture of men's clothing. As the business grew, it came to be known as Naumburg, Kraus, Lauer & Co. In it there were jobs for several other Naumburgs, among them young Max.

Apparently, Elkan was made for success. Like other German Jews, such as the Seligmans and the Lehmans, he saw that the next step upward was from merchandising and manufacturing to banking; in short, to become a note-broker discounting commercial paper. In 1894 the firm Naumburg, Lauer & Co., "Bankers and Note Brokers," made its appearance. Meantime, Elkan's two sons, George and Walter Wehle, had gone to Harvard College and both had returned to enter the family banking business. Elkan had taken one of his original partners (Lauer) with him into banking; the other remained in men's clothing and this one, along with cousin Max, formed the firm Naumburg, Kraus & Co.

Cousin Max's life crossed the life of Cousin Elkan at many points. The latter, a wealthy man, became a patron of the arts. His fondness for music inevitably became an interest of Cousin Max's growing family (he had three daughters and a son). Here, at any rate, was the basis for their many formal visits to the Elkan Naumburg home. There was always chamber music (en famille); and, on more pretentious occasions, when the musical great of New York assembled, talk of the plans of the creation of the Oratorio Society (of which Leopold Damroach and Elkan were the leading spirits) and of the activities of Theodore Thomas, a conductor and close friend of Elkan Naumburg. Out of this, in 1905, Thomas was instrumental in persuading Elkan to finance the first free concerts in New York City's parks, building a magnificent outdoor bandstand for them in Central Park.

Elkan died in 1924 and in 1931 his two sons sold out E. Naumburg & Co. to Shields & Co. By then it was one of the largest dealers in commercial paper in the United States. Until their deaths the sons, like their father, continued to support various sorts of musical activities in New York and at Harvard and Princeton Universities.

Max Naumburg, on his part, continued as a clothing manufacturer and did passably well. He educated his children, lived in solid comfort on New York's West Side, sent his wife and daughters to boarding houses, or "hotels," in New Jersey or the Catskill Mountains for summer vacations. However, he was in no position to encourage Alice's marriage to Joseph Proskauer who had not yet proved he could support a bride in comfort. As he put it to the young couple, he and his wife would not consider a formal understanding, let alone a wedding, until Joseph was able to demonstrate his ability to earn $5,000 yearly.

There is no question that Proskauer was very much in love with Alice. His letters to her became more and more ardent as the years stretched out. Alice, for her part, had been thoroughly schooled by her mother in a middle-class ritualistic dance: she was to be maidenly, proper, and avoid compromising situations, such as appearing openly and obviously in "love." Above all, she was to avoid "talk." Dutiful daughter that she was, she played the game by these rules: there was nothing ardent about *her* letters to Joseph. In fact, she cautioned the impetuous young man that he was writing her too often! Proskauer, humiliating though it must have been, kept a tight check rein on his romantic spirit. Perhaps it was Woodberry's training that held him back. As he saw it, his task was to attend to his business and accomplish what he had set out to do in the practice of law. (Interestingly, Proskauer's close friends, Rosenberg and Cane, did follow their inclinations. Both regarded the practice of law as something by which they earned their livings. Their real vocations were the life of the creative spirit, Rosenberg as a skilled craftsman in the graphic arts, and Cane as an accomplished writer of poetry.)

To Proskauer, on the other hand, law was his vocation and his abiding and sustaining love, with the quest for the humanistic life secondary (but always in his consciousness). This is why Proskauer worked so hard to be a success—that is to say, as an outstanding practitioner at the New York bar —but it is also why he did not become very wealthy as a lawyer. So, in these early years, Proskauer applied himself with great assiduity to all those qualities that make for real accomplishment at the law. He accepted the conditions in the law firm in which he worked without complaint. Even in his college days he had decided that his real interest was in advocacy. He therefore cultivated the skills of public speaking and of argument at the bar. These required a ready tongue, a good memory, and the capacity to win friends, both among judges and juries. He was to guard against antagonizing. He must always keep full command of the facts and legal precedents involving a case. He must remember that at the American bar success in advocacy requires more than forensic skill, however. It demands skill in preparation and in writing of briefs, for in controversial or important suits there would always be long chains of appeals from the lowest to the highest courts. Here again, as Proskauer well knew, complete command of legal precedent was involved, precedent as laid down in English and American courts: the full sweep, in short, of the Anglo-American common law in both its historical development and its changing patterns of adjustments. Thus, a capacity for concentrated study, a cultivated and quickly-to-be-tapped memory, a wide education, and writing skills were the basic tools with which he had to work.

In short, as Senator Charles Summer is said to have written, "A lawyer must know everything. He must know law, history, philosophy, human nature, and, if he covets the fame of an advocate, he must drink of all the springs of literature, giving ease and elegance to the mind and illustration to whatever subject he touches." With this as his credo, Proskauer worked at becoming a *court* lawyer and not an *office* lawyer. In fact, after he left the bench to set up a law firm of his own, much of his business initially came from the office lawyers who had sought him out for *their* trial or appellate cases.

In addition to all this, Proskauer wanted of course to win the hand of Alice Naumburg and thus to show all the Naumburgs that he could play the game under the conditions they had set, and make money. He wanted money enough to indulge himself and his wife in their modest desires— long vacations in the New York north woods, foreign travel, buying and reading books, and listening to music—and to become an advocate, a public one, for Jewish causes.

Upon graduation from Columbia Law School in 1899, Proskauer made the rounds of the law offices, seeking work. This hunt narrowed itself automatically, for he received no help from the Columbia Law School faculty and only a few law offices in the city were open to Jewish clerks. Moreover, secretaries to judges were party plums dispensed by district political bosses, so there was no help or leads in any of these quarters. After a good deal of knocking on doors, in September Proskauer obtained a clerkship with the small Jewish firm, Bullowa and Bullowa, at a salary of $8.00 a week. Unhappy about the limited opportunities offering themselves to him, he and his friend, Rosenberg, who had experienced similar difficulties, went into partnership and hung out their shingle as Rosenberg and Proskauer on January 1, 1900. They did this and that for two years and then quit. Their most important cases had to do with litigation involving their own fathers, in which they cut their eyeteeth on some of the intricacies of law and procedure as well as with appellate practice. They won both cases, but the financial returns were small.

At the end of the second year of practice Joseph wrote to Alice who had meanwhile transferred from Bryn Mawr to Barnard College:

> My best recollection is that I've taken you to only one dance this winter; and on each of the two occasions that we went to the theatre, dear girl, we resolved not to go without *expressly* having your mother's approval—which she gave. At the sociable, I danced with every old girl there, excepting one; and I did my duty pretty well at your Aunt's. I know we've tried to meet your father's wishes about being discretely sensitive and I think we're not blameworthy. ... And it seems to me that the best thing to do is to tell the truth to these relatives who have a right to expect it ... that we're fond of each other but that our engagement awaits my practice.

Proskauer and Rosenberg got jobs in March, 1902 as clerks with the law firm of James, Schall and Elkus at $20.00 a week. Although the firm had been established in 1897, it now revolved around the youngest partner, Abram I. Elkus, who was destined to play a prominent role in Proskauer's early education.

Abram I. Elkus was a new, rising star, but of the second or third magnitude, in the life of New York. His father, born in Posen, Poland, had migrated to the United States in 1833, long before the great East European Jewish movement began, and settled in Mobile. Later, after the Civil War, he had moved to New York City, where his son Abram was born. Abram was educated in the city's public schools, including City College, and had studied at the Columbia Law School. At the age of thirty he was a partner of James and Schall and at thirty-five, two years after Proskauer and Rosenberg began working for him, the head of the firm. Meanwhile, the senior members of the firm had died.

There were two *causes célèbres* of the day in which the young Joseph Proskauer played a minor, behind-the-scenes role. One concerned Captain John D. Herlihy who was in command of the Eldridge Street police station in the heart of the Lower East Side between September, 1899 and November, 1900. He had been brought to trial for failing to shut down prostitution houses in his precinct. He had been found guilty in the Court of General Sessions; but there had been a reversal in the Appellate Division of the Supreme Court which had been sustained in the Court of Appeals. In 1902 Herlihy was being tried again, this time with Elkus in charge of the defense forces. The trial resulted in a hung jury and the district attorney announced that Herlihy was to be brought before a jury once more. At the same time the Police Department filed charges for derelictions of duty against Herlihy and his superior, Inspector Adam A. Cross. Herlihy was suspended and later dismissed, but the departmental trial of Cross was pressed and begun before a deputy police commissioner in March, 1903.

It was at this point that Proskauer had his day in court. He conducted Cross's defense in the best tradition of advocates, filling the record with objections and exceptions, while from time to time Elkus stepped in to cross-examine the prosecution's witnesses. This went on for two months, with the trial commisioner reserving decision and asking for briefs. On May 6, 1903 Cross was adjudged guilty and dismissed from the force.

The stage was now set for an appeal—another point at which the advocate had his innings, as the suit for Cross's reinstatement came before the Appellate Division of the Supreme Court. The case became front-page news, when it was announced that Elihu Root, now returned to private practice after having served as Secretary of War under Presidents McKinley and Theodore Roosevelt, had, as a friend of Cross, joined with the Elkus firm to argue Cross's appeal. Proskauer was assigned the role of liaison and to prepare his brief for Root. Because there was no exchange of briefs required, the attorneys for the appellant had to display all the skills of advocacy they possessed, conceding what was indefensible and bearing down where the law allowed a reasonable doubt. The Proskauer brief was a skillful one of this genre. There was no point in trying to argue that no disorderly houses were in Cross's district, for there were hundreds of them and they flourished openly. But had Cross neglected his duty, or were not the failures at enforcement the fault of others? The brief went to Root in due course and Proskauer waited. Just before the case was to be argued Root summoned him. To his unconcealed delight, as Proskauer much later recalled his triumph, Root approved the strategy of his brief and "launched into an argument of the entire case to me right there in his office and then asked me whether he knew his lesson properly." It was Proskauer who had had the lesson, both in his careful preparation and in the use of a highly trained memory. And when Root made his argument for Cross in June, 1904, the decision was a unanimous one for Cross. He was reinstated as inspector, the proceedings were annulled, and Cross—to further sweeten the victory—was awarded $50.00 in costs.

Proskauer's second case was a civil one, started in 1902, against the United States Steel Corporation and its fiscal agent, J. P. Morgan & Co. The Elkus firm represented a stockholder, J. Aspinwall Hodge, who was seeking to restrain the House of Morgan from converting $200 million of United States Steel stock into a similar amount of bonds (with a commission of $10 million for itself, while making the bonds a prior lien and thus weakening the claims of the equity holders). Proskauer was put to work preparing the initial arguments and the accompanying opening brief, all this in a highly complex matter whose opening guns were set off in the New

Jersey Court of Chancery. More than a restraining order was involved in this suit. It was for high stakes. If Morgan could be stopped, then the carefully devised plans he had worked out for banker-control of the great new mergers his firm was organizing were in serious jeopardy. The counsel that thronged into New Jersey, as a result, was a dazzling company. United States Steel was represented by Gutherie, Cravath and Henderson, with additional counsel. Morgan was represented by Francis Lynde Stetson, the original begetter of the idea of the holding company, or merger. Joining Elkus and his junior Proskauer were three leaders of the New York bar, Frank Bergh, Alan H. Strong, and Edward B. Whitney. The first round went to Hodge, the plaintiff, as the New Jersey vice-chancellor ruled that his claim was a legal one on the ground that the Morgan partners, as members of the board of the corporation, had a personal interest in the conversion.

An appeal was taken to the New Jersey Court of Errors and Appeals, where the case was presented by brief, without oral argument. The lawyers for United States Steel and Morgan emphasized that the conversion of stock had, at least in form, been properly authorized and that the House of Morgan had in addition been given the power to obtain an option on everything above $100 millions of the transfer with additional commissions. In February, 1903 the vice-chancellor was unanimously reversed, essentially because the New Jersey corporation statutes were drawn so loosely as to allow all the hanky-panky that had taken place. The court found no "conflict of interest" (our modern term) on account of the contract between Steel and Morgan by men who were directors of the one and partners of the other, because the statute merely required notice of such transactions to the stockholders and did not explicitly condemn such insider manipulation. Other aspects of New Jersey's code had also been technically complied with.

Thus, Proskauer lost his case—but David had stood up to Goliath. He had gained in two ways: first, he had learned that the state corporation law of his time was not sophisticated enough to cope with banker-manipulation of the giant corporate mergers of the day; and, second, he had gained the approbation of his senior, Abram I. Elkus, who rewarded him with an increase in salary sufficient to appease Alice Naumburg's parents. At last, young Proskauer seemed to have a bright future, even though he was not yet earning $5,000 annually. The Naumburgs permitted the engagement to be announced on January 10, 1903 and on October 14 Joseph and Alice were married in the Naumburg home, the ceremony being officiated over by Dr. Felix Adler, founder of the Ethical Culture Society which the Naumburgs had joined.

The young couple set up housekeeping in an apartment at 823 West End Avenue, near enough to the Naumburgs for the regular round of family visiting. A year later Rosenberg was married and he and his wife moved into the same building. Within seven years the Proskauers had three children, Frances, who was born February 5, 1905; Ruth, born August 4, 1907; and Richard, February 24, 1912.

Proskauer was now able to assume these mounting obligations. There was no doubt that his usefulness to Elkus was increasing and, at the same time, his own education was broadening into new areas. Soon, the firm's name included the junior partner, to wit, Elkus, Gleason, and Proskauer. Working with Gleason, whose business had much to do with industrial accidents involving jury trials, gave Proskauer added experience. But it was Elkus who developed greener pastures and, as a by-product, Proskauer took still new steps in his education.

Elkus, an East European Jew and a native-born New Yorker, was watching other East European Jews making their way out of the Lower East Side, pulling themselves up by their own bootstraps, prospering, and slowly becoming politically important. Elkus joined Tammany Hall in the 1890s. Upon the death of his senior partner, James, he took over in the creation of his own relations and contacts with the New York Democracy. He became an active worker in the East Side Seymour Club, of which a Tammany-appointed minor court functionary named Alfred E. Smith, was a member. He did all the bread-and-butter work that a loyal membership constantly was calling for and getting and received his rewards also in the customary fashion—in trusteeships, receiverships, estates management, and the like which were always dropping as crumbs from the tables of Tammany judges. But Elkus' new business clients were also becoming forces to be reckoned with and this, too, aided him in his Tammany connections. And as he was aided, so was his junior partner, Joseph Proskauer.

Their clients, East European Jews almost entirely, as they moved out of the petty buying and selling of the Lower East Side, were seizing the opportunities for specialization a great city afforded. They were setting themselves up as merchants or middlemen dealing in furs, or woolens and worsteds, or linings and canvases, or embroideries, all having to do with the requirements of the needle trades. These called for skillful assistance and guidance, and the servicing of such needs. Elkus set about formalizing. He did this through the establishment of trade associations: to help in the regularization of their business practices, their relations with their workers, the financial arrangements they made with creditors and debtors, their protection in bankruptcy proceedings. (Political connection—which was exactly what Elkus was developing—helped, naturally.) Proskauer became intimately acquainted with this kind of work and the East European Jews who came with it, so that he learned of the many ways these East European businessmen, hanging on with their fingernails, could obtain a modicum of security—and thus survive and sometimes even climb higher.

In 1911, Proskauer had a first-hand opportunity to see how other East

Europeans, this time as workers, earned their meager livelihoods and the precarious conditions under which they labored. On March 26, 1911 a flash fire swept through the Triangle Waist Factory, located in the upper stories of a loft building near Washington Square. There, more than eight hundred men and women, most of them young girls and almost all of them East European, found themselves trapped behind locked doors. Within minutes, 146 were dead from burns or smoke inhalation or being dashed on sidewalks after plunging from windows. Many of those who escaped were permanently maimed and scarred.

Following this tragedy there was such a hue and cry that the New York State legislature was compelled to take cognizance of the unsafe and unsanitary factory conditions in which so many of New York's workers toiled. The legislature was controlled by the Democrats with two New Yorkers, both good Tammany stalwarts, directing its work. One was Robert F. Wagner, the presiding officer of the Senate; the other was Alfred E. Smith who was the majority leader in the Assembly. The result of the efforts of these two men was the establishment of a State Factory Investigating Commission in June, 1911. As its counsel another loyal Tammany man was named—Abram I. Elkus.

The commission began to hold hearings at once and continued to function actively until 1915. It looked into fire hazards in existing factories and other occupational risks, and authorized the drawing up of remedial legislation affecting workmen's compensation, hours of work of women and children, and the creation of decent factory conditions. Public hearings were held in New York, Troy, Schenectady, Syracuse, Utica, Rochester, and Buffalo.

The Elkus offices, as a matter of course, heard much of what went on in the commission and all of this contributed further to Proskauer's education and to his widening familarity with the life and labors of the people of the city and of his East European co-religionists. It also gave him his golden opportunity: Elkus' involvement permitted Proskauer to do increasingly the court work of the firm and it was in these years that he sharpened his great skills in advocacy and developed the beginnings of his reputation as one of the outstanding trial lawyers of the New York bar. When Elkus was named by President Woodrow Wilson ambassador to Turkey in 1917 and when, in 1919 and 1920, he was picked by Alfred E. Smith, now serving his initial term as governor of New York, first as chairman of a commission to provide a plan for the reconstruction of the government of the state and then to fill a vacancy on New York's Court of Appeals, it was Proskauer who was left to mind the store. It was in these years, too, when Elkus was engaged in his public duties, that Proskauer became a friend and more and more the trusted adviser of Governor Smith. From these many experiences he profited long and fruitfully.

It is possible to throw a good deal of light on Proskauer, the lawyer at work, because of the recollections of two members of the increasingly important law firm with which he was associated. One was Albert L. Fiorillo who served a clerkship under Proskauer during 1920-1923. The other was Jacob Goldberg who, in 1914-1929, after starting as the office errand boy, moved up to be managing clerk and then managing attorney. According to these two associates, Joseph Proskauer appeared early every day at the office to read his mail. From 9:15 to 9:30 he was closeted with Goldberg, his office manager, who had already read the daily Law Journal and marked it for Proskauer's perusal. The office's forthcoming calendar and the progress of cases it was handling next came up for discussion. Clients were routed by Goldberg to firm specialists (by this time its business had been departmentalized) or to trial lawyers, with both Proskauer and Elkus standing by to take over, provided the importance of the suit or the client required specialized attention. Both Fiorillo and Goldberg emphasized the scrupulous care with which Proskauer prepared himself for court appearances. Because the opposing counsels and judges knew this, there was an elan about the proceedings and matters moved with a dispatch from which all, notably Proskauer, handsomely benefited.

Proskauer constantly advised Goldberg and his colleagues that every case was to be prepared as though it were destined for the Appellate Division of New York's Supreme Court, in whose lowest division jury trials involving important cases and criminal suits initially took place. In this fashion it would be tightly drawn and if won, would serve to repel a possible appeal from the other side. If lost, it would be the foundation for a more effective appeal by their side. Proskauer insisted that every attorney going to trial should have both a brief and a written set of charges to the jury, ready for the judge for his instructing the jury on the law.

Proskauer was the good leader. He worked harder than anyone else in the office. He learned quickly how to single out competent juniors, helped in their development, and gave them their heads, consulting frequently with them and respecting their advice. Two of these young men, who grew with him and who later became prominent members of the New York bar, were Samuel C. Worthen and J. Alvin Van Bergh. This plan left Proskauer free for the exercise of his own talents in the courts, for increasing participation in communal and civic affairs, and for the pursuit of his own enjoyments, his long summer holidays at Lake Placid, his friendships, reading, and attendance at musical concerts.

Meanwhile, Proskauer early had learned that showmanship was more than half the battle in court work. He prepared for every appearance with meticulous care and used his highly cultivated memory to give him ease and confuse his adversaries. With but a few notes, more particularly concerned with what his opponents were likely to say, he was ready to argue a case or an appeal. He would sometimes go to court without even taking his briefcase. The juniors would then ask J. Alvin Van Bergh, "How about his notes? How about his briefcase?" The reply was usually, "He hasn't asked me to bring anything."

Proskauer's younger associates fell in readily with his methods and learned how to assist him. Once, he was retained on short notice to argue an appeal, and the trial record was especially voluminous. He laid it all out on a table, divided it into segments and units according to theme and point, and then parceled each unit out to a different member of the staff for study, analysis, and a digest. He was thus well prepared and in time. Van Bergh was an especially valuable aide to Proskauer. In these earlier years he began to do most of the reading of the law. Proskauer once entered the room where Van Bergh was looking up a problem for him, and the younger man began to tell him about the cases he had found, but which apparently were contrary to the point Proskauer was interested in making. "Now please," Proskauer stated, "I know about those cases. I know that those cases are against me. Will you please find a case that I can win on?" A day or two later Van Bergh found a very good case and, when he told Proskauer about it, the latter said, "Van, now, that's what I want!"

Proskauer possessed another quality, a politeness almost verging on courtliness, which he invariably employed in his relations with his associates and in his deportment toward judges and juries. Goldberg recalled one such incident, involving Judge Irving Lehman, then on the Supreme Court. Proskauer was late in arriving for a case and it remained for Goldberg to tell Judge Lehman that Proskauer was on his way. Lehman warned Goldberg that he would wait only five or ten minutes more and Goldberg fled to the corridor to avoid the judge's further annoyance. In a few minutes Proskauer arrived, with only time enough to be apprised of the situation inside and of Lehman's anger. Although Proskauer and Lehman had been classmates at the Columbia Law School, Proskauer was wise enough not to trade on familiarity. With gravity he apologized to the bench and then, turning to the jury, repeated his regrets with the same courtesy. Judge Lehman replied that he did not mind and the jury nodded understandingly.

Proskauer's court performances, notably in appeals cases, had a finesse about them that left other lawyers filled with admiration. He knew all the arts of argument. He knew that repetition, skillfully used or disguised as that, was notably effective in holding the attention of the judge before him. Whitman Knapp, one of New York's very good lawyers, once described a performance he witnessed which displayed all the virtuosities Proskauer possessed. The place was the same New York Appellate Division whose bench Proskauer later graced. In making his oral argument, Knapp said that Proskauer told the court at the outset that he "had three points."

> He stated [Knapp continued] the first point and then said, 'that was my first point, your honor.' Then he recapitulated and went on to his second point. Then he said, 'Those were my first and second points,' and reviewed

the two together. Then he stated the third point, and 'by way of summary,' reviewed the three of them. Each point was identical to every other point. But you didn't get that impression as you were listening to him. You got the impression that each time you were hearing something new, and it wasn't until you were all through and you were wondering how the court below could have been so stupid, that you recognized the artistic performance you had witnessed.

It was in the cross-examination of witnesses that Proskauer shone, for it was here that all the skills of advocacy he had worked so hard to perfect really received their tests of fire. So highly thought of was he by his fellow practictioners that he was called upon frequently to tell them about what he was pleased to call the "art of cross-examination." One such occasion was in 1940 before the Bar of the City of New York, under the auspices of its Committee in Post-Admission Education. (The lecture was reprinted in the *New York Law Review,* July, 1940, under the title "You May Cross-Examine.") Proskauer started by pointing out that the handling of an adverse witness had its dangers and he counseled discretion. What was the purpose of cross-examination? It was either to prove or to discredit a vital point. "I rarely cross-examine just to show that a witness is a liar or an exaggerator or generally to create an atmosphere," he said. Proskauer stressed the necessity for concentration and pointed out that sometimes, if the vital point had been singled out, the examiner had to lay the preparation for his case early in the direct. He gave this example from one of his experiences:

I was trying a case once where the plaintiff had brought an action against the inventor of an oil-cracking process and the Texas Company. The claim was a very simple one. It was that the patent owner had assigned a 40 per cent interest in the patent to the plaintiff by written assignment and that with knowledge of that assignment the Texas Company had paid some large sum, I think three or four million dollars, to the patentee. The assignee had gotten no part of it, so he wanted an accounting for some million dollars or so. His story was that he had a written assignment; that when the patentee began to negotiate with the Texas Company he came to the assignee and said, 'I want to borrow your assignment. The Texas Company wants to see the original,' and that he lent it to this patentee, and that the patentee had never returned it to him.

That is a very simple story and if badly told a very difficult story about which to cross-examine. But, fortunately for the defense, the plaintiff had a very assiduous lawyer, and he produced on a sheet of yellow paper what purported to be a carbon-copy of a letter from the assignee to the patentee saying, 'You remember I lent you the assignment on a certain date and you promised to return it. You haven't returned it yet. Please send it to me at once.' Some of my colleagues were vociferous in the desire to have me urge the trial justice to exclude that paper as a self-serving declaration. I finally prevailed in my contention that there was no jury to be affected and that something might come out of that paper, and it was marked in evidence. It was pretty close to adjournment time when I took the carbon copy and just asked the substance of these questions:

Q. Did you write this letter yourself?

A. Yes.

Q. What kind of typewriter did you write it on?

A. On an old Smith Premier, and I've got it up at my hotel. I brought it from my home in Pennsylvania in case any questions were asked.

I said, 'Show me the letterhead on which you wrote the original,' and he produced a letterhead, and I superimposed this copy on the letterhead, and said, 'You notice that if I superimpose this copy squarely there are four lines of typewriting in the letterhead.' But he said, 'Perhaps I didn't put them in quite flush.' And I said, 'That's all for tonight.'

We were to have an expert next morning, but he failed to appear and I telephoned to a printer after adjournment (after first having raised the yellow sheet to the light and having read a watermark, 'Patten copy') and asked the printer when it was made. He said his catalogue showed it was first made in 1935, nearly ten years after the date of the letter—This is the kind of thing lawyers dream about, but it never quite happens—I telephoned to the Patten Paper Company at Appleton, Wisconsin. They confirmed that report and I arranged for an officer of the paper company to fly to New York at once.

Next morning a tall young Swedish-American named Lindbergh came in and testified that he recognized this sheet of paper, that it was undoubtedly of the manufacture of his company, of which he was secretary, that that watermark was adopted years after the date of the letter and the paper couldn't have been before that. He had the minutes of the board of directors in which they resolved to abolish the old watermark and use the new one. This was an efficient fellow, and I thought it was enough; but he also produced the bill from the die-maker for making the new watermark. If my memory serves me right, the plaintiff took the witness stand and testified that he was mistaken, that this was a copy of a copy, and without great difficulty I got a decision from the presiding justice.

The moral, if the story has one, is that all during the direct examination you try to pick the things that are going to give you material for your cross-examination and to use for the body blow.

But there was another method in cross-examination, too. In Proskauer's words: "It requires infinite patience, infinite tact, and a memory for carrying innumerable details in your mind until you weave them all into the final fabric." To illustrate the necessity of the examiner's being constantly on the alert, he often told the following story:

I was representing a real estate broker in that case and he was suing a man who had a very attractive French wife. She was on the witness stand. There were no women on the jury in those days, but there were twelve men all looking intently and rapturously at this lady. She testified through a French interpreter to a conversation between her husband and the broker in which her husband said that all negotiations were off. It was as simple as that. When

my adversary said, 'You may cross-examine,' I hadn't the remotest idea of
what to ask her. As I rose I got a flash and inquired in what language the conversation took place, she said in English. I said, 'Now you will answer the
rest of my questions in English.' To the rest of my questions she answered,
in effect, 'Je ne sais pas, monsieur.' I think it was the shortest and perhaps
one of the most efficient performances in which I have ever been able to
indulge. . . .

   After all, cross-examination is a noble part of the noble art of advocacy. It
is one fundamental process for applying the acid test to fallible human testimony. It is the furnace through which we have to pass the evidence of weak
human beings in order to smelt out from it the residuum of real truth. And it
is because cross-examination makes so much and so deeply for the ascertain-
ment of truth and the registry of a just and true verdict, that all of us lawyers,
engaged eternally in the quest for truth, regard it as a magnificent part of the
tradition of the great profession which we serve.

Judges respected Proskauer. James A. Foley, one of New York's outstanding surrogates, once said to Fiorillo: "Young man, you could not
possibly be with a finer firm." Another judge said of Proskauer: "You
know, it's really a pleasure for a judge to try a case when a capable attorney is practising before you." And said another, before a group: "I
never argue with Joe Proskauer because he always knows what he's talking
about."
   Proskauer was not unaware of his skills. One morning, when he was in a
great hurry, he took time to tell several people who were in his outer office,
"Well, gentlemen, I will see you tomorrow morning. I have an appointment this afternoon, and I'm going up to charm the Appellate Division."
Goldberg described an unusual scene before the same court. Proskauer, in
arguing his appeal, referred to a page in his brief and asked that the
justices do likewise. Every justice turned to it. Then again, he requested
that they turn another page for a point that he was making. Again all the
justices complied. It was almost as though he were instructing a class!
Fiorillo remembers that there was a famous case in those earlier years,
conducted by a glittering array of counsel on both sides, some of the New
York bar's outstanding lawyers, among them Nathan Miller, Max D.
Steuer, and John W. Davis. Judge Nathan Bijur was presiding. One of
the spectators remarked, "Now here are all the great lawyers of New York
City!" But a man next to Fiorillo replied, "Yes, but Joe Proskauer isn't
here." Fiorillo, only a clerk in the firm, glowed with pride.
   The word "duty" was writ large in Proskauer's lexicon—the necessity
for working in other vineyards. Proskauer had become increasingly active
in civic and communal affairs and, everywhere, instead of simply putting
his name on a letterhead, he assumed posts of responsibility. He became
president of the Young Men's Hebrew Association and sat on the Board of
Trustees of the Federation of Jewish Philanthropies. He was a member of

the City Club, an association concerned with good government. The Citizens Union was an old love and he served on its Executive Committee, its City Committee, and its Committee on Legislation. In the last connection he gained a reputation for his knowledge and advocacy of social reform and amelioration, and for his efforts to safeguard free speech and assembly. He was a member and a committee worker on all the bar associations, being particularly active in the affairs of the Association of the Bar of the City of New York and the New York County Lawyers Association.

During these years he was drawing closer and closer to Alfred E. Smith, as adviser and friend. In 1918, when Smith had been elected to his first gubernatorial term, the vote had been challenged in a number of districts by his defeated opponent, Governor Charles S. Whitman. Proskauer successfully defended Smith in the courts to his claim to a fair election. Four years later, in 1922, Proskauer was Smith's manager in his campaign for reelection. Such a public record and such private devotion merited reward and in June, 1923, when a vacancy occurred in the New York Supreme Court, Smith asked Proskauer if he was interested. The unexpired term was to run for the balance of the year, after which he would have to stand for election on his own, virtually without party backing, for Proskauer's attachment had been to Smith personally, and not to the New York Democracy. Proskauer hesitated. He consulted his associates and his friends. From both he received encouragement. He accepted and the appointment was well received by the press. In October he decided to run for the full term of fourteen years as an "independent Democrat." This meant he was not bending the knee to Tammany Hall or paying "contributions" to its campaign fund. Social workers and friends of municipal reform flocked to his standard. Stated the *Voters Directory of the Citizens Union,*

> [Proskauer's] integrity, high character and ability, both as a citizen and a judge, mark him unmistakably as the possessor of rare qualifications, for the judicial office which he now holds by appointment, and for which the Citizens Union is glad to endorse him.

Proskauer won, bade farewell to his private practice, and took his seat on the Supreme Court bench, from which, on January 1, 1917, he was elevated by Governor Smith to the court's Appellate Division. He could have ended an honorable judicial career on New York's Court of Appeals, perhaps the federal bench; but two things stood in the way. He had thrown in his fortunes with Al Smith (and in so doing had made an enemy of New York's newly elected Governor Franklin D. Roosevelt) and judicial calm and decorum were not hot enough for his blood. On April 1, 1930 he resigned to start the building of another law firm in which he was destined to be the unquestioned and unchallenged senior for more than forty years.

TAMMANY HALL AND
ALFRED E. SMITH

Within the twenty years of Proskauer's early manhood, that is, up to the outbreak of World War I, New York City was transformed into the mercantile, commercial, shipping, and banking center of the United States and one of the world's great metropolises. The creativity of its citizens in all walks of life was unequalled anywhere. The city contained the country's most important docks and warehouses. The New York port was receiving a bewildering variety of goods from almost every country in the world and, in turn, was sending out America's great supplies of wheat, cotton, meat, and other commodities, including its own manufactured products.

A good part of this development was the result of the great burgeoning of New York City's banking and credit facilities. In the twenty years between 1890 and 1910 its banking resources increased 250 percent, as contrasted with only 26 percent for the nation. This concentration of money and credit was hastened by the location of America's largest investment banking houses in the city, among them the firms of J. P. Morgan & Co., Kuhn, Loeb & Co., Lehman Brothers, and the Seligman Brothers. They were helping in the financing of the corporate merger movement then taking place in the country, in heavy manufacturing, mining and smelting, in the railroad industry and in life insurance companies. In total, their "interlocking directorates" and the establishment of "communities of interest" virtually directed the economic growth and development of the United States.

By 1910 New York City was a significant manufacturing center. By 1914, 10 percent of the country's manufacturing establishments were within its borders, a concentration exceeded only by Pennsylvania and New York State. There were important metals refining and processing plants located around the rim of the city's harbor, but light manufacturing (which required the existence of managerial skills and an adequate and quickly trained labor supply) predominated. Among the leading products were women's clothing, the fabrication of white goods, furs and leather, metals, jewelry, diamonds and other precious stones. Following closely behind were the distributive trades which also required specialized skills and particularized forms of credit. New York was filled with the offices and warehouses of wholesalers and jobbers, all dealing in and distributing throughout the country a miscellaneous array of goods and commodities, including piece goods, china and tableware, embroideries, leather goods, tobacco products, drugs, pharmaceuticals, toiletries, and many, many others.

All this was facilitated by another factor than the purely economic—the demographic. Between 1870 and 1915 New York's population had grown from slightly more than one to more than five million people. This increase had come about in part by the political consolidation of the city and in part because of immigration, particularly during the decades 1890 to 1910. The newcomers had brought with them many skills, urgently needed in the mounting metropolis. And, fortunately, the City of Greater New York was able to provide them with adequate social and public services, such as electricity, hospitals, housing, schools, rapid transit, water supply and sewage disposal, port expansion, railroads, and recreational facilities.

The creation of "Greater" New York as an enlarged political entity with a full measure of home rule speeded up these diverse processes and provided the setting and opportunities for spectacular enterprise and growth. It was a large stage where great talents could perform and, inevitably, attract national attention. It is no wonder that men of different backgrounds and tastes, like Joseph M. Proskauer and Alfred E. Smith, joined hands to work together in a common cause.

The City of Greater New York, which formally emerged on January 1, 1898, had grown by bits and pieces. During 1874-1895 the state legislature had permitted Bronx township to be annexed to the original city; in 1895, it approved the addition of an area which pushed its northern boundary up to Yonkers; and in 1897 it had sanctioned the absorption of Brooklyn, Queens, and Richmond. (The charter of New York, amended in 1901, set up a frame of government which, in its larger particulars, is still operative.) There was a mayor, elected at large, a comptroller, and a president of the Board of Aldermen. There were five boroughs, Manhattan, Bronx, Brooklyn, Queens, and Richmond, and each empowered to elect its own president. General authority over the city and broad questions of public policy, the most important of which was the city's financing, were vested in a Board of Estimate and Apportionment made up of these eight elective officials.

The legislative branch consisted of seventy-three aldermen, elected by districts, with clearly defined powers: the adoption of a building code; the issue of special revenue bonds for specified purposes; the making, amending, or repealing of all police, fire, park, and building ordinances and regulations; the authorization of the purchases of the city without public letting of contracts; and the control of public markets. The mayor had the right of veto of city ordinances (which could be overridden) and the creation of departments, including their heads, for the city's complex functioning, such as parks, education, docks, police, fire, and health.

Coterminous with the five boroughs were the five counties of New York, Bronx, Brooklyn, Queens, and Richmond. These were state units of government. They had their bodies of elective officials: the higher criminal and civil courts (from which appeals could be taken to the New York State Court of Appeals), the surrogate's courts, and the sheriffs' and registers' offices. From the counties were also elected representatives to the two houses of the state's legislature.

Consolidation and a unified financial system made possible the establishment of an elaborate municipal infra-structure, composed of public-works and improvements to facilitate settlement, movement, the flow of goods and services, police and fire protection, and the amenities of daily living. In consequence, real estate values rose, making possible an increase in tax receipts and, more important, an expansion of the city's borrowing capacity to finance long-term capital works. However, the legislature held a check rein on these obligations. The city's tax levies were limited to 2 percent of average realty valuation over a five-year period and its borrowing capacity (through the issue of bonds) to 10 percent. Otherwise it was on its own.

During 1898-1914 New York City was able to borrow almost one billion dollars to finance this infra-structure of public works, including water supply, transit systems, schools, bridges, docks, ferries, streets and other necessities. During 1898 alone borrowings, or bonds issued, totaled $21.1 million, and the annual average for the period came to $852.6 million.

For the greater part of the years following consolidation, the politics of New York was dominated by the Democratic Party, that is, Tammany Hall. The party in New York County and its leader, or "boss," by understandings with the leaders of the Democracy in the other counties, virtually controlled every aspect of the city's functioning and life. The party nominated or appointed judges, high and low, and dominated public improvements. It also controlled all matters that had to do with the business of public and private improvements and construction, including the letting of contracts and the bonding and insurance of their recipients; as well, the land that was to be acquired for them had to be purchased or condemned by court action. For the latter, exceptions or variances to building and zoning codes were often sought and either granted or denied.

Presumably, public officials had the power of life and death over these matters, but Tammany Hall was actually the authority. In consequence, the party had its own highly controlled organization and a hierarchy of power and function. At its top was the "boss," not so much by the consent of the members of the committee as with the approval of the "leaders" of the wards or assembly-district clubs. They were to be consulted on political matters having to do with their own bailiwicks; they ruled supreme as regards the protection of establishments in their own districts associated with "organized vice"—that is, gambling clubs, houses of prostitution with their street walkers, runners and pimps, and saloons that kept illegal hours and served women and children. At the local level "protection" meant the connivance of the police and their corruption and the sharing of the "take." It was the business of the ward or district leaders to get the vote out and to assure the loyalty and "regularity" of the voters. In certain measure, although this role has been exaggerated, they also were to run their clubs as social and eleemosynary centers. The local leaders held city jobs which were really sinecures. They were commissioners, court clerks, registers, deputy sheriffs, and their subordinates. The captains of smaller electoral districts held lesser political posts. All these worked together, hard and faithfully, as dispensers of jobs. Unskilled workers obtained job referrals from the district clubs in construction, particularly those having to do with public letting. The less able got licenses as street vendors. Clubs were given free legal advice and legal aid. There were occasional picnics, and, for the needy, baskets of food on the Thanksgiving and Christmas holidays and throughout the winter sacks of coal. But the clubs, by no stretch of the imagination, took the place or even supplemented the charity organization societies of the city, all of which were private philanthropies.

The funds that flowed into Tammany Hall and into the pockets of its leaders, so that they did not have to hold regular employment in the ordinary sense, political or private, came from a variety of sources. And Tammany was, of course, the vehicle in the creation of opportunities for corruption. It flourished as long as corruptors could appear, operate, and thrive. The buying and selling of public offices, judgeships notably (the price tag ran anywhere from $10,000 to $50,000), and the forced contributions from office holders at election time were only the lesser sources of revenues. So was the pocketing of campaign-fund surpluses after expenses of elections had been met. The "shakedowns" of the purveyors of and dealers in "organized vice" (the funds usually flowed to the district leaders and others) was also a minor part. Almost all of it came from the business, more particularly the capital improvements, public and private, in which the rapidly expanding city was engaged. Private properties were condemned or acquired for the erection of public buildings or the laying out of approaches to bridges and tunnels. Politicians with prior knowledge and for a price obtained first choice at acquiring properties in the rights-of-way or the abutting ones. Companies seeking franchises or contracts for public improvements were willing and did pay for them, either by fraudulent campaign contributions or by agreeing to buy services, such as trucking, hauling, excavating, insurance, and the posting of bonds for performance, from firms in which the bosses were silent partners. Exceptions to zoning and building codes could be bought for a price, as could reductions of tax assessments.

The consequence of all this was that the Tammany leaders and their subordinates were wealthy men and, as a result, remained in power for long periods of time. When "reform" movements appeared sporadically, they were short-lived for two reasons: first, they concerned themselves only with the obvious and lesser evils—the existence of "organized vice" and the involvement of the police in its protection; and, secondly, they were incapable of obtaining control of the political (and therefore, economic) mechanisms which ruled the city. Mainly, this was because they could not organize at the grassroot level. As a result, mayors of the city came and went. Some were elected on "reform" or "fusion" tickets, some started out as Tammany designees and broke with the party, but most of them were obedient political stalwarts. Nevertheless, Tammany continued to keep control because its ways and influences were built so deeply into the habits and operations of the city and its business. This power was maintained as late as the 1930s.

The parade of the city's mayoral administrations during the years when Proskauer was growing to maturity in New York demonstrates the validity of these observations. Judge Robert Van Wyck, member of an old Dutch family and a good Tammany organization man, held office as mayor for two terms, 1898-1901. New York, after a brief interval of "reform," became again a wide-open city and "organized vice," with the usual police involvement, flourished. The "Fusion" forces, led by the reforming, good-government Citizen's Union, which had appeared in 1894, nominated Seth Low, a Republican, one-time mayor of Brooklyn, and president of Columbia University, and he won a three-cornered contest. But he held the post for only one term, 1902-1903. In the next election Tammany closed ranks and won easily. Low was followed by George B. McClellan, son of the Civil War general, a Princeton graduate and a man of taste and scholarly interests. He bowed to Tammany for his first term, 1904-1905, and the stalwarts and the Tammany Tiger were at the controls again. In his second term, 1906-1909, however, the office having been extended to four years, he broke with the bosses, but he did not know how to break with the system and build up his own organization.

Tammany picked the next mayor, Judge William J. Gaynor, an independent Democrat, who was intelligent and honest, but indifferent to or incapable of taking over leadership. The Fusionists once more were successful and their candidate, John Purroy Mitchel, an independent Democrat, held the mayoralty during 1914-1917. There then followed a long Tammany rule. John F. Hylan was mayor during 1918-1925, and James J. Walker, 1925-1933. When Walker resigned as a result of the personal scandals in which he had become involved, John P. O'Brien completed the unexpired term. In the following election the Fusionists with a Republican candidate, Fiorello H. LaGuardia, won. He remained in office from 1934 to 1945, and the thoroughgoing changes he effected in the conduct of the city's affairs and its business relations virtually ended boss rule in New York City. The Tammany Tiger was not dead, but its teeth had been drawn because its larger sources of revenue were once and for all cut off.

Because Tammany Hall was run largely by Irish Catholics, most of its plums, judgeships, nominations to the Board of Aldermen and the state legislature, commissionerships, and other positions of power went to them. This is understandable enough. The Irish-Catholics, a minority group which as immigrants had arrived in New York with little education and less capital, were despised by New York's middle and upper-middle classes. They in turn came to understand that recognition and even affluence lay in controlling the city politically and its affairs economically. Tammany Hall, which they succeeded in taking over fully in the last quarter of the nineteenth century, was the vehicle to achieve these: but Tammany's strength, as has been pointed out, was in its ability to organize the voters and maintain their "regularity."

When other minority groups, notably the workers among them, demonstrated their willingness to accept this pattern of loyalty and "regularity," Tammany Hall was prepared to take them in as junior partners. Slowly, therefore, there began to appear, first, German, then Jewish, and later Italian names among the nominations—a few judgeships here and there, a few scattered seats on the Board of Aldermen and in the state assembly. As long as middle-class Jews (like Joseph Proskauer) considered themselves "independent" Democrats, however, and their interest in "reform" made them uncertain quantities in New York City politics, Tammany could disregard them. Proskauer played a public role only because Alfred E. Smith himself began to deviate from the pattern.

The Tammany bosses who ran the city over this long period were only four in number. The one who ruled longest was Richard Croker, an overbearing, rapacious man, overt in his greediness. He became a boss in 1885, but resigned following Tammany's defeat in 1894 and moved to England to live on a large country estate. In 1897 he returned to New York and re-established himself as boss until 1902, when he retired permanently to a home in Dublin, Ireland. When he died in 1922, he left an estate valued at more than five million dollars.

Croker's successor was Charles F. Murphy, who was boss from 1902 until his death in 1924. His only public office was that of commissioner of docks in the Van Wyck administration. But he too accumulated a large fortune. He established what came to be called "New Tammany Hall." His hand within the iron glove was more skilled than Croker's and he was more subtle in his handling of men and affairs—until he was crossed, as in the case of McClellan, and then he could strike swiftly and unerringly. Thus, Murphy encouraged clever young men to rise in Tammany Hall and through it to great heights in the government of the State of New York, the outstanding among them being Alfred E. Smith, a good Roman Catholic, and Robert F. Wagner, a good Protestant. Murphy kept his subordinates in line and trafficked in public offices like all his predecessors; but he was alert to the opportunities for private gain from the great expansion of the city's relations with businessmen and companies. He was the silent partner in a contracting and trucking company, a catchall which he used to permit him to participate, at his own price, in many of the city's public contracts. He made money as a supplier to the people who had leased the city's docks under his commissionership, and he got the contract, through his brother, for the excavations for the Pennsylvania Railroad station. When he died, his estate was worth more than two million dollars.

During 1924-1929 the boss was George W. Olvany, another product of the "New Tammany." Olvany was a lawyer and he was satisfied to get his share of the city's business through his own firm. His law office was estimated to have made at least one million dollars annually, not only from the largess of the courts in trusteeships and receiverships, but also from the companies which had dealings with the city. His successor was John F. Curry who fell on hard times almost at once. He was Mayor Walker's man, instead of the customary reverse relationship. When Walker's irregularities in office became public knowledge, Judge Samuel Seabury finally unhorsed him and Curry's leadership came into question.

There was a more compelling reason for Tammany's decline. The onset of the Great Depression of the 1930s, with its accompanying mass unemployment and the drying up of private investment, necessitated public intervention, through spending, on a gigantic scale. The State of New York sought to create relief and make-work agencies as early as 1930, but only the federal government, following Franklin D. Roosevelt's election in 1932, could mobilize the great fiscal resources necessary for the inauguration of new public works and the creation of jobs. All the various projects associated with the New Deal—CCC, WPA, PWA, a series of housing administrations—emanated from Washington and were supervised by federal authorities. Jobs and contracts were created by an officialdom which never thought of the need for seeking the approval or using the channels of Tammany Hall. Among them, Fiorello La Guardia, Harry Hopkins, and Harold Ickes had made the Hall and its sachems even less than an ornamental institution.

Alfred E. Smith, a third-generation New Yorker, whose family had always lived on the Lower East Side, was born in 1873. He was of Irish-Catholic descent, although there were strains of Italian, German, and English in his heritage. His father was a small businessman who owned carts and teams of horses which he rented out. Young Alfred was destined for an education and higher things, perhaps the priesthood. He attended a neighborhood parochial school, but when his father died penniless in 1886, young Alfred, now thirteen years old, dropped out of the eighth grade of his school. This was the end of his formal education. His mother supported the family by opening a small grocery store; it was not more successful than the father's business had been and Alfred became the chief breadwinner. He drifted through a succession of jobs at low wages. Once he even dreamed of becoming an actor. Meanwhile, he kept up with his parish church and played a prominent part in its amateur theatrical society. But as his earnings improved he abandoned this youthful ambition and, at eighteen, accepted a job in the Fulton Fish Market. Two years later he was hired as a workman in a Brooklyn pump works.

As a youth, following in the footsteps of his father, Smith joined the

Seymour Club, a Tammany Hall district club in the Fourth Ward (among its members as we have seen was Abram Elkus), where he performed characteristic chores and became friendly with the faithful. He was a hard worker and early showed intelligence and maturity of judgment. In addition to being friendly and quick and skillful with his tongue, he was needed as a youthful recruiter. Soon, the district leader found a public job for him and at once his fortunes began to mend. For $800 a year, at the age of twenty-two in 1895, Smith became a minor judicial functionary, first as a process server, then as an investigator attached to the office of the Commissioner of Jurors. With his mother and the younger children now provided for, and as his status improved, he was able to get married in 1900 at the age of twenty-seven.

In 1903 Smith took a big leap forward by announcing that he was willing to run for the Assembly. He got the nod from his district leader, obtained the nomination from his district convention, and was elected handily. Now his education really began. He was a loyal member of the organization and listened to what the bosses of Tammany told him. As an earlier history of New York State said, Smith had "liberalism, industry, fair-mindedness, sense of humor, and ability as a speaker," and he soon attracted attention on both sides of the Assembly and among the advocates of reform. Members of the Citizens Union (in which Proskauer was a power) called him "intelligent and active, somewhat above average of machine men." Two years later, in 1908, he was described as "Increasingly active and aggressive, very much above average in intelligence, force and usefulness, though still inclined to follow machine in support of two bad measures." He "disappointed the expectations of those who believed he would make proper use of his increased influence" and he was inexperienced. Despite these criticisms, he was not overlooked.

In 1910, and for the next four years, the Democrats controlled the state and, with majorities in both houses of the legislature, Smith had a chance to demonstrate, now as lawmaker, how far he had advanced in his education. He was picked his party's leader of the Assembly and he and Robert Wagner, in a similar position in the Senate, steered through the legislature a significant body of social legislation. Following up the findings of the 1911-1915 Elkus State Factory Investigating Commission (which Smith chaired in a number of cities), the New York legislature passed laws regulating factory sanitary conditions, sought to eliminate fire hazards, set up a six-day working week and a workmen's compensation system, and was responsible for one of the country's early widowed-mothers' pension acts. And to delight the Citizens Union and particularly Proskauer, enacted laws calling for ballot reform, direct primaries, and ratification of an amendment to the Constitution of the United States, providing for the direct election of senators.

It was at the New York State Constitutional Convention of 1915, summoned to modernize the ancient and creaky structure of government, that

Smith received universal praise. The convention was controlled by the Republicans with Elihu Root in the chair, but it was Smith who dominated the proceedings and led the discussions. His familiarity with the processes, duties, and functions of government compelled admiration. Moreover, he was fluent in speech, possessing a rough tongue and a wry and salty wit, and unbeatable in debate. Matthew and Hannah Josephson, two of his biographers, wrote:

> The number of subjects he discussed was fantastic: the salaries of the members of the Legislature, the role of emergency measures in procuring undesirable legislation, home rule for cities, the budget and appropriation bills, apportionment of seats according to population, the role of special privilege, impeachment of methods, bond issues and taxation. Also the short ballot, reorganization of the state departments, the minimum wage, education, waterpower and conservation projects, civil service, and many others.

The Citizens Union praised him, as did the Republican greats who were there to make use of his knowledge and skills.

When the new amendments to the constitution were submitted en bloc in a referendum to the electorate, it failed of approval. But Smith had his own opportunities, when he was elected governor in 1918, and again in 1922, 1924, and 1926, to carry out the reforms he had proposed in 1915. Said the state history, previously quoted, of Smith's accomplishments:

> Although there was no area of state activity that was not influenced by his policies, his major accomplishments were the establishment of a system of centralized and responsible government (with an executive budget), the adoption of a body of welfare legislation that surpassed that of any other state, and the revitalization of the democratic spirit when democratic thought and practices appeared to have lost their effectiveness.

Smith failed to stand again for the Assembly in 1915, but, instead, he was rewarded by his election to the office of sheriff of New York County during the two years, 1916 and 1917. The position had no important duties, but the ancient office carried along with its salary many fees and perequisites, all totaling $60,000 annually. Now, for the first time in his life, he was able to put something by so that he could pursue his political career. The next local (and last) public office to which he was elected was that of president of the Board of Aldermen in 1917. He served only one year. In 1918 he was nominated by the Democratic Party for the governorship of the State of New York to run against the Republican incumbent, Charles S. Whitman, who was standing for reelection to a third term. It was at this point that the fortunes of Joseph M. Proskauer and Alfred E. Smith were drawn together, to be joined closely for almost twenty years.

PROSKAUER
MEETS SMITH

6

Proskauer had been brought into the 1918 gubernatorial campaign by his older partner, Abram I. Elkus, who headed the "Independent Citizens Committee for Alfred E. Smith." It was at this time, too, that Smith involved in his fortunes Mrs. Belle Moskowitz and Robert Moses and they plus Proskauer added a flavor to a campaign that interested (and possibly annoyed) the regulars of Tammany Hall. Smith made no effort to disguise his awareness of the great role Tammany played: it was to roll up the large downstate Democratic plurality which was needed to overcome the traditional strength of the upstate Republicans. But the amateurs with their fresh skills, the clever publicity they introduced (Mrs. Moskowitz's contribution), the witty speeches (Proskauer's), and the intelligent research (Moses'), were directed to the growing numbers of uncommited independent voters, those who were more likely to be attracted by an appeal to intelligence than to party loyalty. Smith's campaign struck all the right notes. He was elected governor of New York State, but with the Republicans controlling both houses of the legislature.

Smith, the clever politician who was determined to stay alive, realized he could continue in public life only be assuming the role of the intelligent opposition. For this he needed Proskauer, Mrs. Moskowitz, and Moses more, and Tammany Hall less—Mrs. Moskowitz and Moses to go to Albany with him as his "kitchen cabinet" (an early "Brain Trust"), and Proskauer to remain in New York to write key speeches and state papers and give counsel.

Tammany Hall sensed its inferior role: its loyal son had quickly grown to be certain of himself and to be his own man. He honestly meant his increasing devotion to public programs of social reform. And those closest to him, as Matthew and Hannah Josephson put it, were "descendants of kings of Israel, rather than of kings of Erin." Somewhat wryly, this ditty was sung at private Tammany gatherings: "And now the brains of Tammany Hall/Are Moskie and Proskie and Mo-o-o-ses."

In 1927 Henry F. Pringle, in an unfriendly biography of Smith, declared Smith was being characterized by his friends as having a "Jewish mind":

> Certainly [he wrote], to an increasing degree, his closest advisers have been of that race. One of the first was Mr. Elkus, who managed his 1918 campaign. A later one was Joseph M. Proskauer, now a justice of the Supreme Court and one of the ablest legal minds in the country. Among his present close associates, in addition to Mrs. Moskowitz, are Clarence M. Lewis, another lawyer, and Robert Moses, his Secretary of State. But Mrs. Moskowitz, whose talent it is that she can dream the dreams of an idealist and labor for

their realization as a pragmatist, is the most important of them all.

To be in opposition and always to keep fences in repair, a politician must take the offensive. Governor Smith did this at once and on two occasions. The first was the idea of Mrs. Moskowitz, the second the handiwork of Proskauer. The former proposed that Smith create a nonpartisan "Reconstruction Commission" to plan for the complete reorganization and simplification of the state government. If the legislature balked, then Smith could ask a group of distinguished citizens to sit on such a commission and to finance it themselves.

On January 20, 1919, with acceptances immediately in hand, the Reconstruction Commission was announced from the Governor's office with fanfare. Elkus was appointed chairman. Among others on the commission, each willing and ready to serve, were Charles P. Steinmetz, George Foster Peabody, Alfred E. Marling, V. Everit Macy, Bernard M. Baruch, Mortimer H. Schiff, and Michael Friedsam. To make certain that Governor Smith was always to be involved, Mrs. Moskowitz was chosen as executive secretary and Moses as research director. Elkus quickly declared that the commission would pay its own bills.

Before the year was over the master plan had been revealed. Approximately two hundred offices, boards, agencies, and commissions were to be combined into sixteen proposed new departments. The secretary of each was to be responsible directly and personally to the governor who, along with the lieutenant-governor and the comptroller, were to be elected for four-year terms. And the governor (working with his cabinet) was to prepare an executive budget made up of revenues and expenditures for each fiscal year. The over-riding purpose was, of course, the creation of a responsible central authority, thus cutting out unnecessary personnel and saving the state's money.

It took a decade for this program to be carried out. Governor Smith was reelected in 1922, 1924, and 1926, and Mrs. Moskowitz, Moses, and Proskauer continued to serve with him. By the end of his terms Smith had achieved more than reorganization, conservation, and an executive budget. He had increased state aid to education, revised the workmen's compensation law, prepared a plan of protection of women and children in industry, developed a public works program, including the building of hospitals, prisons, bridges and a state park system, made possible ownership of the state's waterpower facilities, and reorganized the state's state tax program. These activities, pursued with diligence and intelligence, inevitably made Alfred E. Smith a national figure and a presidential possibility. Here was also a man, it quickly came to be noted, who was willing to risk his growing reputation by defying the forces of obscurantism let loose by the "Red Scare," the work of President Woodrow Wilson's attorney general, E. Mitchell Palmer.

The New York legislature had responded to this general call for witch-hunting by opening its 1920 session with the expulsion of five newly elected Socialist assemblymen from New York City districts, charging them with "plotting to overthrow our system of government by force." The year before, the legislature had established a joint legislative committee, under the chairmanship of Senator Clayton R. Lusk, to devise ways and means for the state's doing its share to overcome the so-called "Red Menace." The Lusk Committee far and wide announced its discovery that it was through the school teachers and the schools that this dirty work was being done. Accordingly, in March, 1920, Lusk introduced in the Senate a series of bills amending the State Education Law. They were passed by large majorities. The first bill, in effect, imposed a loyalty oath on all school teachers. They had to prove "good moral character" in order to be certified, and their certification could be withdrawn "for any act or utterance" that allegedly threatened the "welfare of the country or that is not in hearty accord and sympathy" with the government and institutions of the State of New York and the nation. A second bill provided for the licensing by the Board of Regents (through the State Commissioner of Education) of private schools, the test being that their courses of instruction did not discriminate against the public interest. Licenses were also required of school authorities and teachers having to do with the instruction of both adults and minors over sixteen. Another measure (the so-called Lusk-Fearon Bill) might have had the effect of outlawing the Socialist Party, for it gave the Appellate Division of the State Supreme Court authority to act as a special tribunal to determine the fitness of a political organization desiring to nominate candidates for public office.

Governor Smith held public hearings on a miscellaneous collection of Lusk bills, including all those referred to, on May 14, 1920. Five days later he vetoed all of them. He had planned to do so from the very beginning, but required a little time for Proskauer to write the appropriate veto messages. The request from Smith to Proskauer went as follows, as Proskauer reported it in his autobiography thirty years later:

> [Smith] called me on the telephone. He wanted, he said, to accompany his signature of each repealer with a message. Would I submit drafts to him and include 'some highbrow college stuff?' I did. In one of the drafts, I quoted Thomas Jefferson; in another, Benjamin Franklin, and in the third I quoted a passage from De Tocqueville's *Democracy in America*.
>
> A day or two later his messages appeared, substantially in the form I had submitted, but with the addition of that personal touch which gave peculiar tang to his every utterance. I noticed especially one change he had made: he had eliminated the quotation from De Tocqueville.
>
> That night . . . Belle Moskowitz called to say . . . she was instructed by the Governor to give me this message in his own words: 'Tell Joe I'm supposed to know Thomas Jefferson. But if I had ever used that quotation from that

French————, everyone would know that Al Smith never wrote that message.'

Smith's thinking and Proskauer's language are worth recording. Thus, on the Lusk-Fearon Bill, in which a state court was given the power of outlawing parties of whose principles it disapproved:

> No matter to what extent we may disagree with our neighbor, he is entitled to his own opinion, and, until the time arrives when he seeks by violation of law to urge his opinion upon his neighbor, he must be left free not only to have it but to express it. In a state, just as in a legislative body, the majority needs no protection, for they can protect themselves.
>
> Law, in a democracy, means the protection of the rights and liberties of the minority. Their rights, when properly exercised, and their liberties, when not abused, should be safeguarded. It is a confession of the weakness of our faith in the righteousness of our cause when we attempt to suppress by law those who do not agree with us. I cannot approve a bill which confers upon three judges, learned though they be, but nevertheless human, the power to disfranchise any body of our citizens.

And this on a measure which sought to disqualify from the legislature any member-elect of a party whose methods might tend to overthrow the government, by empowering that body to examine members' qualifications before seating them:

> The Constitution provides that the Legislature shall be the judge of the qualifications of its members. This great power has always involved a great responsibility, and the precedents in all legislative assemblies show that it has been exercised with the greatest caution and upon the rarest occasions.
>
> To permit this bill to become law would be to give apparent legislative sanction to making an exception to the rule, and such a law might undoubtedly be invoked as a justification for the arbitrary exclusion of a minority. The mere statement of the provisions of this bill seems to me sufficient to condemn it.

And this on the Lusk education bill with its varied devices of loyalty oaths for teachers and licensing for private schools:

> In effect, it strikes at the very foundation of one of the most cardinal institutions of our nation—the fundamental right of the people to enjoy full liberty in the domain of idea and speech.
>
> It deprives teachers of their right to freedom of thought; it limits the teaching staff of the public schools to those only who lack the courage or the mind to exercise their legal right to just criticism of existing institutions. The bill confers upon the Commissioner of Education a power of interference with freedom of opinion which strikes at the foundations of democratic education.

Meanwhile, the trial of the five expelled assemblymen continued. The Bar Association of the City of New York had from the start strongly voiced its disapproval by appointing a committee, headed by Charles Evans

Hughes, to assist in their defense. Of this important committee Joseph Proskauer was a member. The Assembly persisted, however, and after a long trial voted the conviction and expulsion of the "Five." The next day, September 16, 1920, Smith issued a proclamation calling for a special election in their districts. It was unconscionable that a quarter of a million people should remain unrepresented, he said, issuing this statement:

> Although I am unalterably opposed to the fundamental principles of the Socialist party, it is inconceivable that a minority party duly constituted and legally organized, should be deprived of its right to expression so long as it has, honestly by lawful methods of education and propaganda, suceeded in securing representation, unless the chosen representatives are unfit as individuals.
>
> It is true that the Assembly has arbitrary power to determine the qualifications of its members, but where arbitrary power exists, it should be exercised with care and discretion, because from it there is no appeal....
>
> Our faith in American democracy is confirmed not only by its results but by its methods and safeguards against revolution. To discard the method of representative government leads to the misdeeds of the very extremists we denounce and serves to increase the number of enemies of orderly, free government.

On these notes of defiance and commitment, Smith's first gubernatorial term ended. The next two years he was out of politics, for the Republican currents in the 1920 elections were running too strong. At the June Democratic National Convention, held in San Francisco, Smith was placed in nomination for the presidency as a favorite son and received great applause. (The nomination went to James M. Cox of Ohio with Franklin D. Roosevelt as his running mate.) In September, Smith was renominated, unopposed, for governor in the Democratic primaries. Now, again, he called upon Proskauer to direct his campaign. Proskauer pleaded his lack of experience in political management and the fact that he was not a member of Tammany Hall. No matter, said Smith: Tammany would take care of the politics and it would be Proskauer's task to get out the independent vote. Proskauer thus formally became chairman of the "Citizens Committee for Alfred E. Smith," as Elkus had been two years previously. Against Smith the Republicans nominated Nathan L. Miller, a distinguished lawyer and former judge of the New York State Court of Appeals.

Smith and Proskauer tried valiantly, but the hostilities President Wilson had created in his fight with the Senate over the League of Nations, among them his alienation of important ethnic groups, were too much for Cox's shoulders. Harding's election by a landslide was anticipated. He carried New York and Smith lost, although he ran almost half a million votes ahead of Cox. He also did very well upstate in strong Republican districts, but was defeated by a plurality of only 74,000 votes.

Smith spent the next two years as a private citizen, holding the post of

chairman of the board of directors of the United States Trucking Corporation. In 1922 there was little likelihood he was ready for retirement. Thus,
he was easily persuaded to agree to accept once more the gubernatorial
nomination, but he announced he would not countenance the names of the
wealthy newspaper publisher William Randolph Hearst (who was threatening to enter the lists through his self-financed "Independence League")
or Mayor John F. Hylan on the ticket with him in any capacity. Hylan's
blustering that he would withdraw municipal patronage from Tammany
Hall budged neither Smith nor Charles Francis Murphy, its boss. Hearst
and Hylan reluctantly withdrew and Smith was nominated unanimously at
the party convention and, under pressure from Murphy, the Democracy
closed ranks and named Dr. Royal S. Copeland, health commissioner of
New York City and a Hearst newspaper columnist, for the United States
Senate.

Once more was Proskauer called into service to manage a Smith campaign, this time in the capacity of chairman of the "Citizens Committee" of
independents. It became more than that, for Tammany Hall was pushed
into the background. Copeland took separate headquarters, and the Democratic State Committee was charged with taking care only of the lesser
nominees on the party ticket. It was Proskauer's strategy that the campaign was to be run entirely on the issue and responsibilities of state
government, a decision in which Smith gladly concurred, for he was eager
to take the offensive. His familiarity with every aspect of government and
its problems and his amazing memory served him well. Smith attacked
Governor Nathan L. Miller and his record on all fronts—for his hostility
toward labor; for stifling home rule; for his indifference to traction problems and public power development; for his extravagance in office; for his
opposition to the creation of a scientific budget system and direct primaries; and—this from a man presumably under the thumb of Tammany
Hall—for Miller's subservience to the Republican machine and its local
bosses.

Miller kept on retreating in the face of a steady barrage of charges and
proved ineptitudes. On one occasion, after Miller had maintained that he
had saved the state $25 million, Smith replied, "If Governor Miller says he
saved the state $25 million, I ask him two questions. 'Where is it? And
who's got it?'" Everywhere he went, Smith drew large crowds, even in
upstate New York, and it was apparent that the independent vote was
favorable to his candidacy. As the campaign heated up, all sorts of extraneous matters were introduced, but Smith, with his customary keenness, was able to keep three issues uppermost: water power (he favored
public ownership and development); home rule, particularly as regards
public utilities (he supported a wide extension); and the state reorganization which the Reconstruction Commission of 1919 had carefully designed.

Proskauer, as Smith's manager, used his customary tactic of simplifying issues and focusing on them sharply. In an interview a week before the election he declared that "the two main lines of attack on Governor Smith have failed completely. The first was an endeavor to portray Governor Smith as a 'good fellow' who was handing out favors to special groups. . . . The second line of attack was Miller's economy claim." The first was answered by a recital of Smith's "substantial and far-reaching accomplishments" as governor; the second, by exposing Miller's coolness toward "reconstruction and retrenchment." Miller's claim of economy was "merely an excuse to cover [his] destruction of the non-partisan plan to reconstruct the state government." So well did Proskauer's plan work that on the eve of the election the betting odds on Smith rose from 6 to 3 to 3 to 1. Proskauer predicted a Smith landslide and election with a plurality of more than two hundred thousands votes.

Proskauer was right about the first, but wrong on the second. Smith's plurality in New York City was 478,700 and in the state 390,000. Copeland won by 259,000. A Democratic state Senate was elected and the Republican majority in the Assembly was whittled down to a splinter. Smith won the large upstate cities of Buffalo, Rochester, Albany, and Syracuse (which was Governor Miller's home town). Smith's victory was "an extraordinary personal triumph," stated the New York *World*. "Again he has shown himself stronger than the boss of Tammany Hall and the bosses of the Democratic state machine. When Murphy died in 1924, Smith's personal loyalty to the man who had aided but not hampered him was now ended. He was at last his own master and, in fact, the master of the sachems of Tammany Hall. For it was Smith who insisted in 1925 that Hylan be denied the mayoral renomination and that Senator James J. Walker be picked to replace him in New York's City Hall.

Smith was aware of Walker's weaknesses. As the Josephsons have put it, "Walker seemed made to be an ornament of public life, but the governor knew that his protege was pleasure-loving, a romantic playboy, that he had a taste for champagne and nightclubs and pretty girls." Proskauer and Moses warned Smith, stating that Walker was a man of light character who never had taken his public responsibilities seriously. The Citizens Union was even more suspicious. Walker had been inclined to make "cynical deals" which, if he were elected mayor would "tolerate vice . . . and leave the city wide open." They were right and Smith was wrong. Proskauer, after the Walker debacle, could only comment wryly that Smith "trusted overmuch the integrity of some of the men who served under him."

Proskauer performed one other important service for Governor Smith. He helped him extricate himself from the messy Prohibition quarrel. The Eighteenth (or Prohibition) Amendment had been ratified and became the law on January 16, 1919. It declared the manufacture, sale, or transportation of intoxicating liquors for beverage purposes to be illegal, and gave the

Congress and the several states power to enforce the amendment by appropriate legislation. Congress had done so through the Volstead Act which, among other things, authorized search and seizure. New York's legislature had passed a similar measure in the Mulligan-Gage Law March 4, 1921—that is, during Governor Miller's administration. The Republican Party, having in mind that the temperance movement had its great strength in the rural areas of the country, generally supported Prohibition. The northern Democracy, with its power concentrated in the industrial centers and drawing its support largely from the workers and the lower middle class, favored the mitigation of the law to allow the manufacture, sale, and importation of beers and wines.

The defenders, the so-called Drys, believed that the outlawing of the manufacture and sale of liquor was worth the heavy price of the enforcement of what had obviously become an unpopular law. It prevented, so they claimed, wholesale drunkenness, decreased misdemeanors, improved morals, and supplied the work of probation officers. The Wet opponents pointed to the illegal traffic which had been taken over by organized syndicates and the gang wars that had ensued. They emphasized the wide corruption of the enforcement agents and police and the moral dilemma in which good, social-drinking citizens found themselves.

On May 4, the last day of the 1923 session, the New York legislature, its lower house controlled by the Republicans, passed the so-called Cuvillier Bill, repealing the Mulligan-Gage Law, and Governor Smith was caught in the kind of trap good politicians always seek to avoid. He had thirty days to make up his mind. On the one hand, Tammany Hall, spokesmen for the American Federation of Labor, workers generally, and his own inclinations, all favored the legalization of wine and beer. On the other hand, Smith's gubernatorial reelection had made him a national personage and a possible presidential candidate. Thus, signing the repealer and flouting federal law (as Franklin D. Roosevelt reminded him) might well destroy his chances for the Democratic nomination. He could not overlook the powerful, fanatical Dry support that came from the Southern Democracy.

Constitutional questions, of course, also were raised to make the governor's decision harder. President Nicholas Murray Butler of Columbia University, a "moderate Wet," writing to Proskauer on May 8, and favoring the repeal bill, did so on the ground of the "double jeopardy in which citizens have been placed . . . by the existence of both state and federal statutes for the enforcement of the prohibition amendment." In fact, the United States Supreme Court, in the so-called Lanza decision on December 11, 1922, had held that punishment in a state court would not prevent a federal court from enforcing penalties for the identical offense.

Professor Felix Frankfurter of the Harvard Law School, writing to Dr. Henry Moskowitz, Belle's husband and a friend of Smith's, argued in opposition. "Smith's disposition of the Mulligan-Gage repeal will show the mettle of the man," said Frankfurter. "The Eighteenth Amendment *is*" and therefore the issue was simple: "either nullification or enforcement." "Concurrent jurisdiction," a horror to one learned man, was thus a blessing to the other. As Frankfurter added, the State of New York would deal "with purely local violations" while the federal government would restrict itself "to interstate infractions and foreign importations." His advice to the Governor, therefore, was to veto the repeal bill, state candidly his opposition to the Eighteenth Amendment, call for its repeal by constitutional amendment, but have the state by adequate machinery engage in concurrent enforcement. Meanwhile, Governor Smith was being bombarded by all sorts of committee groups and by the press. The New York *Times,* noting how numerous were the demands for repeal, warned him that he would be committing political suicide, if he *did* sign the Cuvillier Bill.

Smith kept his own counsel. On May 31 he held a public hearing and listened impassively for five hours to all manner of exhortation and veiled threats. But he was committed to signing the repeal measure from the very start—in fact, he did so on the very next day. Proskauer, who had agreed with him, prepared a 4,500 word statement, setting forth the legal (and personal) reasons for his decision, and Smith affixed his signature to it. The document described the dilemma in which Smith was caught—but he believed in states rights. A state was not required to duplicate a federal law; repeal meant the elimination of double jeopardy; federal statute and enforcement were still the law of the land and offenders could be brought to book. He and New York State would continue their cooperation with federal agents and courts. "I yield to no man in respect for the Constitution," he added. He warned the Wets on this score and on the other assured the Drys that the saloon would not return.

> Much has been said with respect to the effect my action on this bill may have upon my own political future [he continued]. I have no political future that I am willing to attain by the sacrifice of any principle or any conviction of what in my mind is for the welfare and the benefit of this state and nation.

At the time that Proskauer was being so involved with Smith's political fortunes, he was also tending to his own affairs. His senior associate, Elkus, who was being called upon to undertake all sorts of public missions, was virtually retired, and had fallen ill. The other partner, Carlisle Gleason, without public involvement, was not only staying away from the office but maintaining no contacts with clients new or old. As Proskauer recalled later: "Elkus became a very sick man, and my partner, Carlisle Gleason, was a man of great ability, but he didn't want to work very much. And I found myself running the office, doing practically all the trial work, and bringing in most of the business and sharing equally with him."

There was time, nevertheless, for public and civic duties. In fact, this

was a continuing pattern of Proskauer's life and one that came to be accepted by his younger partners. He believed that a citizen had to assume
responsibilities, to serve in professional associations, and on civic bodies,
and to work actively with philanthropic organizations. The Bar Association of the City of New York took a good deal of Proskauer's time. In 1920
he was a member of a number of committees; in 1921 he consented to become a member of its Executive Committee. The work of the Citizens
Union, that watchdog of public morality and down-to-earth crusader for
good government, was always close to his heart. He had first become
active in it when a struggling young lawyer; now that he was successful and
very busy, he was happy to serve in its upper reaches where policy was
being made and public positions taken. In 1919 he was a member of its
City Committee, the governing body of the Citizens Union, its Executive
Committee, its Committee on Legislation, and its Campaign Committee.

Proskauer was particularly interested in seeing that judicial appointments and nominations were freed of the taint of politics, for the state's law
courts exercised great power, not only in the determination of complex
criminal and civil suits, but also in matters affecting large and valuable
property rights. Tammany Hall, as has been stated, had always wanted
the control of the courts, particularly for the latter reasons. The Bar Association and the Citizens Union constantly worked to have an independent
judiciary chosen for ability, probity, and unquestioned honesty, all to be
elected on a nonpartisan basis.

As a consequence, both bodies scrutinized judicial candidates, made up
lists of satisfactory aspirants, and carried on active campaigns before
primary elections took place, putting voters on notice regarding well-fitted
nominees. Proskauer was a leader in a joint activity of this kind of the two
organizations in 1920. And so effectively did they labor that in the two
state judicial districts serving New York City, only one out of some twenty
nominations turned out to be unsatisfactory. Obviously, none of this sat
well with Murphy of Tammany Hall and Samuel Koenig, his Republican
counterpart. As well, Murphy was being compelled to settle for the increasing independence of Governor Smith, when judicial vacancies, which
he could fill, occurred; for a gubernatorial interim appointment meant, at
least, another primary contest for the nomination for the full term.

And this is what happened to Proskauer. Smith kept on offering such
appointments to him and he kept on refusing. Proskauer later recalled
what took place in 1923:

> Smith called me one day and said: 'Now, every lawyer wants to be a judge
> sometime. This is your last chance. There's a vacancy on the Supreme Court
> and you can take it or leave it.' So I said to myself: 'If I take it I'm certainly
> under an obligation to stay at least half my term, seven years.' So I finally
> decided that I'd take it as a painless exit from a very difficult situation in
> which I found myself personally.

Smith therefore appointed Proskauer on June 9, 1923 to fill a vacancy on the Supreme Court, First District, as the result of a resignation. It was understood that he would stand for the full term in the following November elections. Congratulations poured in from all sides. The Citizens Union spread on the minutes "their appreciation of the high ideals of public service that have led him to accept the position of a Justice of the Supreme Court." Proskauer received the "hearty endorsement" of the Bar Association. The New York *Times* was lyric:

> The new judge has the heartiest endorsement of the members of the bar, and is recognized by all who know him as a man who in point both of ability and character is eminently fit for the bench. . . . It is to insist betimes upon the choice of judges who, like Judge Proskauer, have had such and have demonstrated the possession of such high personal qualities as to make it certain that justice will be administrated with all desirable promptness, with sound reasoning in the law and with a judicial integrity above suspicion.

The New York *World* was equally generous:

> [Not often had such a judicial appointment been] greeted with more hearty and general approval, from those best qualified to judge of its fitness. [Proskauer] is an able lawyer and an energetic and devoted citizen of community, whose energy and breadth of view have made him deservedly prominent in good works of a public and semi-public nature. . . . [He] would make a very able and distinguished judge.

One piece of ceremonial was necessary. Governor Smith telephoned Proskauer that "Mr. Murphy, the leader of Tammany Hall, was very generous in his attitude toward your appointment. And I think—he is an old man—it would be decent for you to go in and just shake hands with him." Proskauer went—with a bee in his bonnet. "Commissioner," he began, addressing Murphy by the title of the office he had held some thirty years before, "the Governor has told me that you were very gracious in endorsing my appointment to the bench and I've come here to say I appreciate it." Said Murphy: "Judge, you never belonged to the organization, but you've been very valuable to the party and to Smith, and I told Al that I thought he was entitled to give you anything that he wanted and you wanted."

What Proskauer wanted was to appoint his own confidential secretary as well as his law clerk (his young associate J. Alvin Van Bergh) to political plums that Tammany always looked on as its very own. Proskauer later reminisced about what ensued:

> One of my closest friends on the bench had a plumber as his legal secretary. So as I sat there talking, I turned to Murphy and I said 'Commissioner, the presiding justice has told me that for certain practical reasons he would like me to make my two confidential appointments immediately, and I'm here to

tell you that for one of these jobs I'm going to appoint my present secretary, who is an expert stenographer. In the other place I'm going to appoint a young lawyer in my office, who I think is a brilliant lawyer. If you have anything to say to me on that subject, say it now.'

Murphy, recalled Proskauer, looked at him as though "he had suddenly been kicked in the stomach." "Judge," said Murphy, "I have nothing to say to you on that subject, except that I hope you'll like your life on the bench." Proskauer made the appointments and in November, as has been noted, was reelected for the full fourteen-year term, serving only half of it, as he had promised himself when Smith named him in 1923.

PROSKAUER AS JUDGE

Joseph Proskauer, the fierce competitor, the bold and stalwart adversary, who delighted in matching wits with men at the bar and who took pleasure from the chase as much as from the catch, discovered early in his career that the law had its prosy side. From the view of the bench, dispensing justice had to do, more often than not, with poorly trained lawyers who often brought up unnecessary suits only because the world was filled with litigious people. These delays frequently stretched out into boredom and mental fatigue.

Patience and confidence were the required virtues that in the end brought the just and honorable man his deserts and the guilty and deceiver *his:* all because, presumably, impartial arbiters and deliberative and evaluative magistrates presided at the proceedings. Now and then out of the bumbling, stumbling contention an imperishable principle would emerge, recognized and hailed by a wise judge and followed by others: until it was replaced by another imperishable principle. But Proskauer was not a patient man; and it is doubtful that sitting on the bench gave him real pleasure. When he discovered that he was no longer the magistrate, but was rather, unconciously, reverting to his former role of the adversary, and when he found he was suffering from a lingering, nagging occupational malady (the tedium had got the better of his excellent health and fine physical shape) he resigned from the bench in 1930, after a little less than the seven years he had promised himself.

In his last private case of record before ascending the bench, Proskauer was counsel with Sullivan and Cromwell in an action for an accounting brought by the British Government against the defendant, the agent in World War I for the Remington Arms Company. It was being claimed that in the particular purchase involved, a contract coming to $60 million, false and fraudulent statements, showing costs to Remington greatly in excess of their true amount, had been rendered and restitution was being sought. His Majesty's Government was represented by glittering counsel; Proskauer on the other side was in a similar company. The defense triumphed when the court failed to find evidence of fraud and Proskauer received the plaudits and the rewards that came with the victory.

The contrast with the first three cases that came before him as judge was startling. In his initial opinion from the bench in October, 1923, in the case of *Catherine Haiss, Plaintiff,* v. *Charles S. Schmukler, Defendant,* Proskauer granted a motion for summary judgment against the defendant, the vendor of a piece of real estate, refusing to relieve him of his contractual obligations. Since the plaintiff, the vendee, was not required to take title subject to any tenancy, she recovered her down payment of $1000. In his second case, he rendered the opinion that the Commissioner of Public Markets had the right to fix fees for the occupancy of stands without the necessity of securing the assent of the Board of Estimate and Apportionment. And in his third, a suit brought against a steamship company, he declined to dismiss the complaint which alleged consummation "of a scheme by which all assets of the Federal Steamship Corporation were illegally divided among the individual defendants, intent to continue the business . . . without disclosure of such conduct to plaintiff, who has recovered judgment for breach of a contract thereafter made."

Before Proskauer had time to settle into his new life (to grow to like it and then be openly disappointed in it) he was readying himself for his election in his own right. This was to take place in November, 1923. He knew, of course, that Democrats would be cool to him because his association had been exclusively with Al Smith. He was no party man and he needed both the endorsement and the active support of Tammany to win. By October 1 it was known that he would be on the Tammany ticket, but now the Republicans balked. They would not make his nomination concurrent, as they did in the case of two other judges running for election. However, independent groups, the Citizens Union, the Bar Association of the City of New York, the New York County Lawyers Association, and the League of Women Voters, all announced their support. So did the New York *Times,* the New York *World,* and the New York *Post.*

Opposition came from a powerful quarter, the New York *American* and New York *Journal,* both owned by the very rich, quarrelsome, and dangerous William Randolph Hearst. Hearst's feud with Alfred E. Smith had become almost legendary. Smith had stood in Hearst's way to achieve a public career at too many points; he had, in effect, read him out of the Democratic Party; and Hearst's hostility spilled over on to the chief adviser and intimate friend of his enemy.

Dubbing Proskauer the "Murphy-Foley candidate" and a "Murphy jurist," Hearst's *American* and *Journal* opened the attack on him towards the end of the campaign. The *American,* on October 22, 1923, published a "revelation" purporting to demonstrate a "new striking instance" of the close relationship of Wall Street bucket-shop operators to the "Tammany bosses' " judicial candidate. It alleged that, without being an attorney of record in any open court proceeding and "after he had actually taken his place on the bench," Proskauer had been representing Charles A. Stoneham, owner of the New York Giants Baseball Club, who was then under indictment for perjury. Stoneham was at that moment also further involved in a pending and complicated creditors' action arising from an earlier transfer of the brokerage accounts of a former company he had headed, to E. D. Dier & Company, a bucket-shop which in turn had gone bankrupt. Trustees were apparently seeking to establish the degree of Stoneham's liability in the Dier failure (which had resulted in great part from the questionable solvency of many of the transferred accounts), based upon how many creditors' releases he could secure and how many settlements his attorneys could effect. The newspaper charged that Leo J. Bondy, Stoneham's lawyer and an intimate friend of Tammany Hall's Thomas F. Foley, had engaged Proskauer to act in his client's behalf, and that the judge had not only done so, but had held a conference in his private chambers while two cases in which he was sitting went unfinished. Wrapping within this allegation another, Hearst additionally depicted Proskauer as having drawn pay from June 9 to October 1 "without having done any work as Supreme Court Judge."

The more basic charge, however, visibly nettled Proskauer. He gave a statement to the New York *Times* on October 21, vigorously denying that he had advised Stoneham. It was "wholly false," and he had never seen Stoneham in his life. He had been called in by Bondy, he said,

> long before my appointment, to advise with the attorney as to one narrow technical matter in reference to a dispute as to the meaning of the word "creditors" in an agreement and order purporting to settle the claims of the Dier trustee. The trustee contended that it meant only creditors whose claims had been allowed in bankruptcy. The other side claimed that the work meant all creditors. As a result of my advice another agreement was made.
>
> After I returned from Europe this fall the lawyers on both sides sought an interview with me, and while I consented to see them, I immediately told them they would have to settle that matter among themselves, that I had been appointed a Justice of the Supreme Court and I would have nothing further to do with it. This is what occurred and all that occurred.

The *American* took his statement from the *Times* and endeavored to discredit him by innuendo, extrapolation, and inference.

Proskauer knew the brawling language of political in-fighting, too, and traded Hearst blow for blow. Hearst was a "political blackmailer" and "that low demagogue," he told a cheering audience of 1500 Bronx Democratic women leaders at the Concourse Plaza Hotel on November 5. "I am proud of his attacks," he added. "They are characteristic of one who had denounced Cleveland, McKinley, Roosevelt, Smith, and anyone else whenever he thought to gain some scrap of political advantage for himself."

If Hearst achieved anything, it was to cause Proskauer's admirers to close ranks. A nonpartisan lawyers' committee to aid Proskauer's campaign, which read like a who's who of the profession, had been organized on October 14. Now, additional lawyers continued to join and 150 met on October 22 at the Hotel Biltmore to volunteer for an active canvass. On the heels of this came endorsements from Nathan Straus, Louis Marshall, Rabbi Stephen S. Wise, and George W. Wickersham; and from a group of leading social workers, including Lillian D. Wald and Mary K. Simkhovitch. The last declared he had "applied his extraordinary legal abilities in the cause of the Forty-eight Hour Week for Women, the Minimum Wage Law, and in the movement to safeguard the right of Free Speech and Free Assembly.'' They cited his efforts in resisting the ouster of the Socialist assemblymen and seeking the repeal of the ''notorious Lusk Laws.'' If re-elected, this would be a justice ''whose decisions would be in line with changing industrial and social conditions.''

Hearst was not one to cry quits readily. Whatever he could not achieve publicly, for all the evidence pointed to Proskauer's growing popularity, he was prepared to do by intrigue and chicanery. Enlisting the support of a Tammany leader, James J. Hines, who felt he had a grievance against Governor Smith, Hearst started a movement in the Democratic clubs to dump Proskauer at the polls. Proskauer, to counteract this, made the rounds of the club houses, and when he got to Hines's own bailiwick, the Monongahela Democratic Club of the Eleventh Assembly District, he confronted Hines personally. Proskauer in his *Reminiscences,* forty years later, reported the meeting in these words:

> 'I'd like to have a talk with you.' He took me into a room, and I said, 'Where were you last Thursday,' at a certain hour. He said, 'I don't know. What do you mean?' I said, 'You know damned well where you were. You had a conference here at a certain hotel with the Hearst people, and you entered into an agreement with them to scratch me in the election. Now, it's no use denying it.' 'Ah,' he said, 'somebody is always shooting at me.' 'Yes,' I said, 'I'm going to follow the returns in your district, and if I run behind the ticket, I'm going to make it my business to get your political life.' Al Smith's nephew was with me and he said, 'Look out, they throw you out of a window here.' I said, 'This damned yellow dog won't lay a finger on me.' I told him, 'This is the end between you and me, Hines.'

When Proskauer informed Smith about this, the Governor said, ''You lay off, don't do anything about it. I'll see that he is scotched.'' When Proskauer next had occasion to talk to Murphy, the Tammany boss told him, ''I picked that matter up. They denied it. The election is over.''

And so it was. Proskauer was easily elected, coming in a good third behind Justices Mahoney and Levy, but trailing Justices Gavegan and Bijur, who had the endorsement of both parties. This was a particularly stinging rebuke to Hearst, who had come out for the eight Republican candidates and had savagely attacked the entire Democratic slate. All eight were defeated and Hearst's meddling had only led to his being paid off in his own coin.

Governor Smith was to continue with tokens of his friendship. In mid-December 1926, when it was announced that two justices of the Appellate Division of the Supreme Court were scheduled for retirement, he offered one of the vacancies to Proskauer. Proskauer accepted and assumed the position of associate justice January 1, 1927, to the pleasure of New York's bar, among them Elihu Root, Samuel Seabury, and George W. Wickersham. The *New York Law Journal* declared it a good appointment, because of Proskauer's "peculiar fitness for the consideration of complicated legal questions where wide knowledge of the law must combine with common sense and an acquaintance with human nature."

Proskauer, already restive, had begun to range widely and, using platforms whenever they were offered, had taken to speaking up about the law's dragging its feet and the delays that plagued the work of the courts. His new position added to his authority. He accepted an invitation to deliver a major address before the Association of the Bar of the City of New York on February 2, 1928. He called it "A New Professional Psychology as an Essential for Law Reform." Even now, years later, one reads it with a start, for his remarks have become today a matter of the utmost urgency, involving the best legal thinking, even to the United States Supreme Court. In this address Proskauer called upon lawyers to take an oath, comparable to the physicians' Hippocratic Oath, somewhat as follows:

> I will join with my adversary in waiving a jury trial wherever and whenever it can possibly be done without the sacrifice of a fundamental right. I will join with my adversary in supporting a trial justice in fair comment upon the evidence and reasonable direction to a jury on the facts. I will not put an adversary to his proof in respect to facts whose existence my client admits. I will refrain from merely formal or technical objection to the admission of evidence. I will co-operate with the trial justice and my adversary to secure a speedy, prompt and complete presentation of the facts of the case. I will neither make nor oppose interlocutory motions unless they are of real and practical importance. I will take no appeal unless I am satisfied that substantial error has been committed and that a new trial should reasonably give a different result.

Workable law reform, in his opinion, depended largely upon "a fundamental change in the group psychology of the legal profession towards its function and of the lay psychological attitudes toward the administration of justice," rather than just upon specific changes in statute and rule. He questioned the "baseless reverence" in this country of the jury trial in all types of cases, maintaining that in civil contract cases it had been transformed into "a wasteful, ineffective and outworn fetish." He cited his own judicial experience:

> We observe daily the spectacle of twelve perfectly honest jurors, untrained in the analysis of evidence, ignorant of the subject-matter of the litigation . . . , sitting through a long, complicated trial, with scores of documents and letters and accounts in the evidence, vainly endeavoring to interpret that which they can barely understand. We know the waste of time consumed in reading to a jury hour after hour and day after day written evidence which can be handed up to a trial judge and absorbed by him in a few minutes; and we know the frittering away of time in openings and summations.

Indeed, he observed, this reverence was the result of a popular misconception of the historic origin of the jury in civil cases. He reminded his audience that jurors had originally been of the vicinage, at least five or six in number, chosen in order to inform the court. They knew about the litigants and the litigation, "a notion as far removed as the poles from our present-day conception of a jury of twelve disinterested citizens acquainted neither with the parties nor with the subject matter of the litigation." Jurors, he added, were selected not because they know the litigants or the controversy, but because they did *not* know them!

Proskauer did not downgrade the role of the judge, however. Earlier, in 1926, he had criticized American lawyers at a Columbia Law School alumni gathering as being remiss in their duty for permitting long trial procedures and had urged reforms to end the congestion in the courts. Now, he was understandably irked that in most states, including New York, the judge was forbidden to help the jury by commenting on the evidence. He called upon the profession to "restore to the judge his power to function as a minister of justice and not as a mere presiding officer." He also gave disconcerting statistics of what this "same formalism" had produced in the functioning of the Appellate Division, First Department—a mass of cluttering appeals. "We are appeal mad! We have got to see to it that we get good judges and let them function," he warned lawyers and laymen alike.

Proskauer demanded that the American psychology of distrust of the magistrate end. But he also felt impelled to criticize "the psychology of the profession," its lack of give and take, its over-contentiousness, its unwillingness to be practical and save time and get results. His auditors were greatly impressed by his remarks and at the conclusion of his address adopted a resolution to submit his new credo to bar associations. On April 10, 1928 the Bar Association of the State of New York, Charles E. Hughes, presiding, adopted a resolution endorsing the spirit and purpose of Proskauer's remarks (which Chief Judge Benjamin N. Cardozo of New York's Court of Appeals called "fine and stirring") and requested the appointment of a special committee to encourage its implementation.

Proskauer pursued his proposals for law reform into his own court. To ease calendar congestion he almost single-handledly persuaded the Appellate Division to permit the trial of auto accident cases without a jury, if the lawyers so stipulated. The Appellate Division created a new part for this purpose and Proskauer was asked to head it. This practice, he observed, cut trial time by perhaps two-thirds. In the first month there came before him ten such cases; in the second, thirty; and thereafter they continued to increase rapidly.

On February 19, 1929, in an address over Radio Station WJZ, Proskauer moved out further. He sought to enlist the lay public in his crusade and for the first time he examined the status of criminal law. Calling upon recent thinking and research in psychology and sociology, he dealt with the nature and problem of punishment. Saying that the "layman had a part in law reform" (the title of his discourse), and looking at punishment, he said:

> The idea that increased severity alone will meet the situation runs directly counter to the opinions of those scholars who have given the subject patient and painstaking research and there is a strong group in this country today which holds the opinion that we must re-examine and revamp the very basis of society's attitude towards crime.

Rather than being sentimentalists for questioning increased severity as the solution, such persons, himself included, were actually the reverse, he declared. "There is nothing sentimental about the proposal that society does not adequately protect itself against the criminal by ignoring the facts of modern science and continuing blindly along the paths which were marked out in ignorance of what we now know."

Proskauer did not overlook the deterrent effect of punishment and believed that it should be retained. He believed it rested not primarily upon the length of the sentence, "but upon the swiftness and certainty of trial and conviction." Therefore, crime detection and the arrest of the offender had to become more efficient. If penology's first problem was to protect society from the criminal, it also had a second problem: to reclaim the criminal for society, if possible. Thus, vengeance in criminal law should give way to protecting society and rehabilitating the offender. The role of the psychologist, the sociologist, the social worker, and other specialists was consequently established. To Proskauer's highly logical mind, this exploration of the convict's entire personality, condition, and situation helped penologists to determine whether he could safely be returned to society or whether, as a hardened, experienced and unregenerated criminal, he "might find himself restrained for life exactly as we restrain for life a dangerously insane person."

This led Proskauer to take another giant step forward. The problem was daily evident to Proskauer in the treatment in courts of insanity as a defense. He cited [J. P.] Bishop on Criminal Law (1923) who had noted that now American jurisprudence was replete with cases of insane persons being executed as criminals. "And on the other hand," Proskauer continued, "we have constantly released into freedom men suffering with dangerous or harmful psychoses." He disclaimed championing any specific program or categorical formula, but he expressed his concern over "artificial legal definitions of insanity largely out of accord with modern medical concepts."

This was followed up by an address before the New York City Conference of Social Work on May 22, 1929, at which time he told his listeners that true justice needed less law and more psychiatry, thus inviting psychiatrists into the fraternity of psychologists, sociologists, and social workers to subserve the law. In calling for the reclamation of the criminal, he revealed a profoundly humane side to his character. He maintained that the criminal was more important than the crime. Without having named it, Proskauer was actually inveighing against the so-called M'Naughten Rule, handed down in Britain's House of Lords in 1843, which held that the accused was a responsible person and was largely sane, if he knew what he was doing and knew the difference between right and wrong.

If Proskauer was years ahead of his time, he enjoyed the satisfaction of seeing some enlightened progress. In 1965 the Bartlett Act amended liberally the M'Naghten Rule in the State of New York. Then, on February 28, 1966, the United States Court of Appeals for the Second Circuit further modified the rule in *U.S.* v. *Freeman* in a decision binding in New York, Vermont, and Connecticut; and in June, 1966 the State Supreme Court of Wisconsin in the Shoffner case, provided an alternative to the rule for defendants who plead not guilty by reason of insanity. Simply stated, both of these courts turned to the American Law Institute's 1962 definition of criminal responsibility which was broader, more scientific, and a long step forward: "A person is not responsible for criminal conduct, if at the time of such conduct as a result of mental disease or defect he lacks substantial capacity either to appreciate the wrongfulness of his conduct or to conform his conduct to the requirements of law." Thus, a disturbed defendant could avail himself of the option that Proskauer had fought to create, a mental hospital or a prison.

Although Proskauer was on the bench for a comparatively short period, he handed down an unusual number of important decisions. He confessed, however, his basic personal dilemma as a judge. In his autobiography, he wrote:

> [The judge] listens to an unending succession of accident cases. Alone, he encounters a monotonous parade of applications involving technical practice questions. Even in the equity term, the daily grind too often lacks dramatic interest. But occasionally a matter will come before him that poses problems of vital human or social concern. Semi-bored competence then gives way to a warming sense of being able to do an interesting and fruitful job, one that may even make its impact on the life of the community.

One such opportunity arose in February, 1926, when New York City was confronted with the prospect of a paralyzing strike in the dress industry, an arena where the Association of Dress Manufacturers and the International Ladies Garment Workers Union were constantly at loggerheads. This latest struggle threatened to tie up a thousand or more shops through a walkout of about twenty-two thousand workers on Monday, February 15. The manufacturers had sought an injunction, but Proskauer invited both sides to confer with him. Proskauer told them he did "not care to act as arbitrator in a labor dispute," but he believed that there must be some feasible way of repairing the existing agreement machinery so that it would work satisfactorily and avert a disastrous conflict. "It is not a matter of dollars and cents," he maintained, "but of flesh and blood and human lives." He was willing to sit up with the contending attorneys and their clients "until the sun rises, if necessary."

Actually, it was not until a week later that his mediation bore fruit. "Jurist Stops Strike In 1,000 Dress Shops," announced the New York *Times*. Through Proskauer's efforts it was agreed, on February 23, that an impartial chairman was to be appointed immediately to settle disputes which could not be resolved by direct negotiation or collective bargaining (long sought after by the union), and for the reiteration of the no-strike clause (favorable to the industry). This intervention led to a long peace in the industry, one that has been maintained right into the present time.

Honest and successful labor relations demanded impartiality. It was just as necessary to protect workers' rights in their unions as it was in their industry. In a case that came before Proskauer, members of a trade union had brought suit against the union's officers, charging misconduct and harassment. The workers had been accused of various derelictions, were tried and expelled from the union. They sought reinstatement in the courts; the ousted workers were the plaintiffs and the union officials the defendants. Proskauer found for the workers in these words:

> The great importance of labor unions in contemporary life requires that, for the sake of the public, of their own members, and of the institution itself, their affairs should be conducted with decent regard for the rights of their members. The procedure of these defendants was tyrannical and sinister. Instead of meeting the charges against themselves, they tried to destroy these plaintiffs for their temerity in making the charges. Equities most persuasive in plaintiffs' favor prompt the court to find a legal ground upon which to give redress.

His reputation for fairness led to at least one case whose outcome had an amusing and ironical twist. In an action involving discrimination by an Adirondack hotel owner in rejecting a would-be Jewish guest (a violation of the New York State civil rights statute, which imposed a penalty for such behavior) both sides waived a jury trial. Proskauer called both counsels to the bench and told the defendant's counsel that he should permit him to send the case to another judge, because the plaintiff was a Jew and that he, also a Jew, had strong feelings on the subject. "To my surprise," Proskauer concluded, "he insisted on my retaining the case." On the stand the defendant corroborated the plaintiff, but blamed his other guests for compelling him to violate the law. He realized that Proskauer would have to find against him. When the plaintiff told Proskauer he wanted no profit from the suit, only the vindication of a principle, and his lawyer stated he would be satisfied with a nominal fee, the judgment was for $100. The defendant's counsel then came to the bench and startled Proskauer by saying, "I told my client that if he had gone before any other judge it would cost him $1,000, but that I was sure you would let him off with $100."

If the law brought its satisfactions, it also imposed one of the "saddest duties" of Proskauer's judicial career: his decision in January, 1925 that Murray Hulbert had instantly forfeited his presidency of the New York City Board of Aldermen by unwittingly accepting an honorary appointment from Governor Smith as a member of the Finger Lakes State Park Commission. Section 1549 of the Greater New York City Charter forbade this kind of conflict of interest, even though the second position was honorary and unremunerative. By chance, this inadvertence had come to the attention of Hulbert's political foe, Comptroller Charles L. Craig, who ironically had been launched on his own political career by his quarry. Craig had then withheld Hulbert's monthly salary check and the latter had begun a mandamus action to compel payment. When the request for this peremptory writ came before Proskauer, he had no choice but to vacate the luckless Hulbert's presidency. Citing many precedents, he acknowledged the hardship inflicted and the relator's unselfish desire to contribute additional public duty. But the law demanded in behalf of the city "the undivided public service of its officers. It is self-executing," he declared. "When an officer transgresses its provisions he shall be deemed thereby to have vacated his city office." There was some speculation that Governor Smith might reappoint Hulbert to his office, but he failed to do so. Proskauer, however, derived gratification when Hulbert later became a "distinguished judge" of the United States District Court for the Southern District of New York.

Particularly complex as a category were those cases involving financial and fiduciary matters. Two such especially significant examples came before Proskauer. The first, *People ex rel. Broderick* v. *Goldfogle,* popularly known as the "Moneyed Capital Tax Case," arose in 1924 when a dozen individual suits were commenced by capital-handling firms, ranging from pawnbrokers' shops to national banks, to determine the validity of a state law passed in 1923 seeking to tax at the rate of 1 percent of the assessed value, moneyed capital that was being lent in competition with national banks. This act had been designed to overcome a State Court of Appeals decision, invalidating an earlier state law of 1922 taxing the stock of national banks, since federal statue forbade such an assessment at a higher rate than was imposed on other "moneyed capital." A congressional amendment subsequently provided that this investment capital was not to be exempt from the federal statute's prohibition. If the new state statute could stand, the state would then tax the national banks.

Proskauer heard the twelve test cases. Representing the several litigants were twenty-nine prominent lawyers, whose roster included John W. Davis, George L. Shearer, Jacob Gould Schurman, Jr., Edward S. Seidman, Sullivan & Cromwell, Martin Saxe, and other distinguished members of the bar. To John W. Davis was given the task by associated counsel of seeking to prove the new law unconstitutional. This was his last case before he became the Democratic candidate for the presidency in 1924. After a good deal of research, Davis was ready to present the common cause.

On July 15, 1924 Proskauer decided that in only one case, brought by a private banker, Dallas B. Pratt, was the assessment by the state valid, because of being in competition with national banks, and he then vacated the assessments against the other eleven plaintiffs. He went on to declare the 1923 state law constitutional. So knotty and complex were the issues that the decision was said to puzzle even bankers and brokers. They besieged the lawyers who had taken part in the suit for clarification. One of these, Edward S. Seidman, actually provided an explanation of the case in laymen's language for the New York *Times*. Since the way was now open to tax national banks, these institutions appealed Proskauer's decision, but it was sustained by the New York State Court of Appeals. The banks sued in federal court on the ground that the state statute in question did not meet the requirements of the federal statute. The United States Supreme Court so held, and many millions of dollars in taxes were saved to the national bank stockholders.

In the second case involving financial institutions, Proskauer handed down a notable decision in March, 1926. It dealt with a voting trust arrangement by the Bank of America, founded in 1812. The bank's voting capital had been increased on December 31, 1924 from $6,500,000 to $8,000,000 and placed as a block by its officers in the hands of trustees (albeit a number of the officers and trustees were the same) for a term of ten years, in order to prevent certain outsiders from gaining control of the venerable institution. The possible new owners had reputedly been planning to merge it with the much younger Manufacturers' Trust Company (founded in 1914), which in turn had been buying up several other banks, and they now obtained a temporary injunction to restrain the officer-trustees from voting the new stock. The Bank of America postponed its transfer vote, while the judge considered an extension of the injunction pending litigation.

On March 9, 1926 Proskauer declared this kind of voting trust illegal and void. State law and public policy, according to the court, were opposed to such naked trusts, even for the reasons believed, and banking officers could not act as proxies for the stockholders at a meeting. There were other means by which the capital could be increased, if it were desirable to do so. The Appellate Division, however, reversed Proskauer, but he had the ultimate satisfaction of seeing the Court of Appeals sustaining his judgment.

Other cases were less technical or complex but involved matters of some public concern or attracted popular interest. One such suit of more than passing notice arose between the well known theatrical producers, Marc Klaw and Abraham L. Erlanger, whose partnership had been dissolved in 1919. Although they were estranged, they remained lessees of the Gaiety Theatre. The lease, however, allowed the owner to sell his property (including the theatre site), which would thereupon automatically cancel the lease. The owner died in 1921 and Erlanger, confronted with an opportunity to buy the entire property for $3,000,000 or see the lease cancelled upon sale to someone else, requested Klaw to contact his father, then in Europe, and learn his wishes in the matter. Apparently, Klaw either was not notified or declined to commit himself. Erlanger, to protect himself, bought the property. This cancelled the lease, but Erlanger offered his former partner a half interest, which was turned down both then and during the subsequent trial.

Klaw brought suit against Erlanger for an accounting, charging that he had been defrauded of his share of the beneficial value of the lease that had still six years to run, and which was $20,000 below the prevailing market price for similar properties. Erlanger proved that he had notified Klaw of the impending sale, but still offered him a half interest in the property. Klaw refused. As a result, Proskauer was sharp with Klaw and ruled against him: plaintiff had been offered a half interest in the purchased property, and if he refused it, judgment would be entered for Erlanger. And Proskauer made this comment in his autobiography:

> If neither Klaw nor Erlanger bought the property they would have been out of possession at once. Erlanger's obligation to Klaw did not require him to sacrifice his own rights in the lease or his right to buy the fee merely because Klaw saw fit to do nothing. Klaw frankly testified that he did nothing because he believed that if Erlanger bought the property he would be under a trust obligation not to cancel the lease. What this means practically is that he was willing that Erlanger should buy the property, take all the risk of loss on the transaction and still permit him for six years to enjoy one-half of an expiring lease with a rental $20,000 under the market. This inequitable position strains the formulae of trust relationship beyond the breaking point. To hold that Klaw could follow his do-nothing policy and then require Erlanger substantially to allow him to benefit to the extent of $10,000 a year by reason of this advantageous lease, would be to convert the familiar doctrine of equity from a shield against over-reaching into a weapon of oppression.

Proskauer included another favorite case in his *A Segment*. . . . While sitting in the Appellate Division, he handed down a significant decision in June, 1929 in a complicated libel action arising tangentially out of the tragic breaking apart of the naval dirigible, the U.S.S. *Shenandoah* (ZRI), in a violent storm over Caldwell, Ohio on September 3, 1925, with a loss of fourteen lives. Mrs. Margaret Ross Lansdowne, the widow of Commander Zachary T. Lansdowne, made certain accusations of politicking against the Department of the Navy that ultimately resulted in a naval court of inquiry, which dismissed her charges. Subsequently, Mrs. Lansdowne's public accusations that Judge Advocate Captain Paul Foley had attempted to influence her testimony at the inquiry brought about his trial, and his exoneration. The New York *World,* in its coverage of these proceedings, was sued for damages by Foley for editorial remarks he considered to be libelous. The newspaper, in its defense, divided its accounts into statements of fact which it maintained were true, and into expressions of opinion which it averred were "fair comment, made in good faith, without malice, upon the said facts which are matters of grave public interest and concern."

Proskauer noted that this plea was "entirely novel" in American libel law, and thus arose the assignment to him of writing the opinion in support of the *World's* argument. The court followed the thinking of the English courts in this matter, holding that "the publication to be justified must contain no imputations of corruption or dishonorable motive, except in so far as they are an inference which a fair-minded man might reasonably draw from the facts truly stated and represent the honest opinion of the writer. If the imputations are thus inferable and honestly stated, the publication is justified. . . ." The court aimed at preserving "a fair balance between the social interest in free comment upon public affairs and the interest of the individual in the preservation of his good repute." The adoption of the 'fair comment' rule, which added still another milestone to the tradition of freedom of the press in America, Proskauer said, "was hailed by textbook writers as a forward step in the development of the American law of libel."

In reciting some of the causes that came before him as a trial judge and his reactions to them, Proskauer engaged in an interesting speculation in his autobiography. It indicated that his restless mind sought to find some satisfaction from what he was doing, despite the long stretches of trivialities and boredom.

> A judge in a trial court has always to meet the problem of determining how his own sense of justice shall prompt him to influence the presentation of a cause [he wrote]. Judge Charles M. Hough, of the U. S. Circuit Court of Appeals, surely one of the greatest jurists of my era, once related this anecdote. A young district judge came to him one day and said: 'Congratulate me, I've been on the bench a year today and I have never been reversed.' The reply was: 'Not so loud, young man, someone might hear you.' The strong judge risks error at times to achieve equity. One of the poorest judges I have ever appeared before had one of the best statistical records for affirmances. He achieved it by unduly urging the settlement of difficult cases and, failing success in that attempt, producing a mistrial. His charges to juries were colorless and left a jury floundering without adequate direction. He committed a few errors because by abdicating his powers he ran few risks of error. The great trial judge has the courage to risk error in his endeavor to guide a trial to a just conclusion. He will therefore with discretion comment on the evidence. He knows that if he errs, there is an appellate court to correct his

mistakes. He will not deliberately err. But he will fashion his action by taking no counsel of his fears of possible reversal. He may not do what he
believes to be just even though the heavens fall. But he will, fashion his
action by taking no counsel of his fears of possible reversal. He may not do
what he believes to be just even though the heavens fall. But he will, short of
that, try to make a jury understand the equities of a cause, and in any trial,
jury or non-jury, do all that in him lies to make law and justice synonymous.

Proskauer's elevation to the Appellate Division involved him in the work
of an extremely busy court. It brought him very close to colleagues who
had "poise and personality, and we lived together during those three years
of service as a reasonably happy family." This was a more prestigious
court and it demanded more from its judges. While only the Court of Appeals could lay down rules of law, Proskauer observed that his new court in
many cases had the final review of the facts. It imposed an "almost
monastic" routine upon him.

> For two weeks in every month [he wrote] I would sit on the bench Tuesday
> to Friday afternoons and spend mornings and evenings, as well as weekends
> in an unceasing examination of records and briefs. On Monday was the court
> conference, where every case argued and submitted during the previous
> week, with rare exceptions, was reported, discussed and decided. The rest of
> the month was allotted to the writing of opinions and some relief from the
> exacting grind of the previous two weeks.

Proskauer had the highest regard for the law and he served it with devotion. His judgments and opinions mainly sustained the mandate of the statutes which were relevant, unless constitutionality was involved. Popularity,
public desire, and political considerations never entered his mind. He was
hardly a revisionist and, while he was not the perpetual crusader, he did exhibit concern for less fortunate beings. "It was meaningful to me," related
Judge Irving Ben Cooper in 1963, "because Judge Proskauer was concerned
with humanity in other than legal channels. He flung himself into causes
with his tremendous vigor and logic to help others." He dealt with the
championship of causes rather than the championship of business or ven-
tures, Cooper said, adding,

> Who can refill their vessel of inspiration except someone who can feel the
> same way in a like cause? It is usually a holy thing. There is no money in it.
> It takes a Proskauer to say to others, 'Don't give up!' It reaffirmed my own
> determination and conviction that what I was about was right and solid,
> despite odds. That was a common reaction to all who listened to him. He
> held the torch high. It was stirring. He has a combination of an educated
> mind and an educated heart, and that's a rare combination!

This leavening of justice with his own sense of compassion marked Proskauer as anything but harsh for harshness' sake. Rather, he was a stern,
correct, and upright judge who could be biting and devastating in his com-

ments but who never lost sight of the end he sought. "He was sharp," according to Cooper, "and impatient with lack of preparation and of uncertainty in presentation. He was impatient with fumbling. He evinced it. A lawyer had to be on his toes before him. Proskauer threw himself into every case." Proskauer always hated incompetence or mediocrity. Lawyers who imposed upon the court's patience found him with but little of it himself. His style was simple, clear, and direct. Consequently, not all lawyers loved him. But those who understood that his irritability was mainly caused by his passion for justice regarded him with affection.

By holding to the proposition that justice delayed is justice denied, by being impatient with the law's postponements and procrastinations, and by being willing to take the harder path readily, Proskauer was able by such high standards for himself to influence a host of lawyers. He had contempt for judges who were afraid to take a position or influence a cause or who sought to avoid reversals at all costs. Reversed in about 20 percent of his decisions, he was too forthright and courageous to let reversals dominate his thinking. He was, in short, a judge's judge, and Justice Cooper summed it up by calling him "a thundering giant."

Proskauer's lack of patience and gruff manner could on the other hand mask a thousand kindnesses. Justice Cooper, as he recalled, as a young lawyer, "was practising by myself and there were few clients and I was trying to make a go of it and thrashing about." In one very complicated case that meant much to him, dealing with trespass in real estate, the original ruling was in his favor. His adversary, however, moved to re-argue the case and the judge split the decision which meant that Cooper's client would have to stand trial. Cooper, in turn, took an appeal to the N. Y. Supreme Court which agreed with the split decision. Cooper asked it to reconsider and he re-argued the case, whereupon the court reversed itself. His adversary then appealed and the case came up to the Appellate Division where Proskauer was sitting. Cooper was ready. He and his adversary were each allowed twenty minutes. Cooper got only one sentence out of his mouth, when Proskauer interrupted to ask: "Counsellor, isn't the crux of your argument this?" and then proceeded with the gravamen in a couple of sentences. "Thank you, your Honor, I have nothing more to say!" replied Cooper, and wisely sat down. Proskauer's analytical comment resulted in a complete victory for Cooper that day, and he recollects that Proskauer's sharpness of mind "just floored me."

Also greatly impressed by Proskauer's keen intellect was John M. Harlan, later Associate Justice of the United States Supreme Court. Harlan, who had opportunity to observe Proskauer at close range, when he served as counsel for the New York State Crime Commission, and Proskauer was chairman, on many occasions paid high tribute to his quality as a judge and a lawyer, his integrity, his image to the profession, and to his sharp tongue and even sharper mind.

Proskauer had early suffered from "misgivings" (as he said later) and an inner, nagging uncertainty about remaining on the bench, but he was intensely loyal to Governor Smith and believed that he was morally bound to stay at least half his term before coming to a final decision. Almost from the beginning of his judgeship a violent digestive disorder began periodically to assail him. His doctors found no organic cause for the condition and "ultimately diagnosed it as a psychosomatic disturbance" and left it up to the patient to overcome his ailment. Proskauer recalled: "During my entire seven years of judicial service I thereupon actually willed myself into health, but never for a moment was I unaware of the struggle involved."

This awareness was heightened when he found himself subtly intervening in the trial of a case where one side was badly outclassed in legal talent and the true facts were therefore not being brought to light. The able attorney on "the wrong side," who happened to be a close friend, came up to him later and inquired, "Why should my client hire me and pay me a fee when the other side gets you for nothing?" Proskauer never forgot this. A doer rather than an arbiter, he realized that instinctively he was an advocate for what he thought was right, whereas a conscious effort was always required for him to keep within the confines of judicial conduct.

But when Proskauer began to watch the courtroom clock, he knew that the time had come to consider resigning. Weary of the general runs of cases coming before him and welcoming the end of the working day, he desired to make the break. He again took counsel with his friend, Morgan Joseph O'Brien, whom he had consulted when originally offered the appointment to the bench. O'Brien had told him to accept and had promised to tell him, when the time came, to resign. Yes, said O'Brien, the time had come.

One afternoon, while listening to some half dozen accident cases, Proskauer scribbled these verses on a pad:

> By a ship door a stevedore's beheaded;
>   A small boy has fractured his skull;
> And by *"res ipsa loquitur"* steadied,
>   Recovered his damage in full.
>
> A girl had her womb retroverted
>   As though she's been gored by a bull;
> But her pain into money converted,
>   She can pleasures of marriage now cull.
>
> This verdict is grossly excessive;
>   That charge of the judge is too vague;
> These permanent wounds are progressive;
>   That plaintiff has lied like the plague.

> And the clock moves around - O, so slowly,
> And my mind roams from Rome to old Prague;
> Oh! Oh! for the life of the lowly
> And a stiff drink of good Haig and Haig.

When court rose that afternoon, March 10, 1930, he submitted his dog-gerel to presiding Justice Victor J. Dowling and announced that he had decided to resign.

There was no uniformity in the reaction to the Judge's decision. Judge Benjamin N. Cardozo, soon to become an Associate Justice of the United States Supreme Court, wrote him, "First, for the love of you, I must wish you happiness. Then, for the love of my profession, I must cry alas! and beat my breast. But you have made a noble record."

Walter Lippmann expressed an opposite opinion:

> I do not know why you have decided to leave the bench. I do know that the news has been received with great regret. And yet, in my own mind, while I know that the state is losing one of its most distinguished judges, I feel there may be compensating advantages. You will be freer to devote yourself to those public causes which you invariably serve so well. In any event, my warmest greetings and every good wish.

In his *A Segment* . . . Proskauer made his shrewd observation on his two-sided career by comparing the advocate and the judge:

> The advocate draws his strength from the more vivid traits of personality that guide him to and fit him for the conflict of the forum. The judge finds his power in the more sober elements of personality that give him delight in the joys of the study and the irenic determination of conflict. . . . Advocate and judge each has his mission to secure justice by the processes of our law. The qualities of mind and spirit with which they are endowed lead them to play very different roles in the drama of the courtroom. But each of them in his own way serves his mistress—the law—and thus serves one of the noblest purposes of mankind.

Phillip A. Haberman, Jr., who was to become a younger associate of Proskauer when he set up his own law office, and, like him, a man who loved the bar, came across this passage in Lord Cockburn's *Life of Francis, Lord Jeffrey* (1852), which hit off Proskauer equally well:

> The questionable thing about his judicial manner consisted in an adherence to the same tendency that had sometimes impaired his force at the bar—speaking too often and too long. He had no idea of sitting, like an oracle, silent, and looking wise; and then, having got it all in, announcing the result in as many calm words as were necessary, and in no more. Delighted with play, instead of waiting passively till the truth should emerge, he put himself, from the very first, into the position of an inquirer, whose duty it was to ex-tract it by active processes. His error lay in not perceiving that it would be

much better extracted for him by counsel than it generally can be by a judge. But disbelieving this, or disregarding it, his way was to carry on a running margin of questions, and suppositions, and comments, through the whole length of the argument. There were few judges in whom this habit would be tolerated. It is disagreeable to counsel, disturbs other members of the court, and exposes the individual to inaccurate explanation and to premature impression. But, as done by Jeffrey, it had every alleviation that such a practice admits of. It was done with great talent; with perfect gentleness and urbanity; solely from an anxiety to reach justice; with no danger to the ultimate formation of his opinion; and with such kindly liveliness, that the very counsel who was stranded by it liked the quarter from which the gale had blown. Accordingly, he was exceeding popular with everybody, particularly with the bar; and the judicial character could not be more revered than it was in him by the public.

Thus did Proskauer step down from his judgeship. Immediately thereafter, on March 11, 1930, he formed the firm of Rose and Proskauer, later to be called Proskauer, Rose, Goetz, & Mendelsohn. With this firm he was to be actively associated for more than forty years, in fact until his death.

THE PRESIDENTIAL CAMPAIGNS OF 1924 AND 1928

8

Proskauer was not on the bench a full year before he was again involved in Al Smith's political fortunes. Smith's engaging personality, his proved capacities in public office, his commitment to administrative and social reform, his forthrightness about the failures of Prohibition—qualities in which Presidents Harding and Coolidge had proved themselves to be singularly lacking—had attracted national attention. Even more important, as a political campaigner and a vote-getter, his ability to capture the large cities of New York in the face of powerful Republican organizations held out the promise of the recreation of the national Democratic Party. In short, Smith had become presidential timber, and his popularity was quickly demonstrated in early April, 1924, when the Wisconsin Democratic primary showed him running far ahead of the putative favorite, William G. McAdoo.

This was a stunning upset, for McAdoo stood for all the things Smith did not. Born in Georgia, he had come to New York to make his fortune as a lawyer and successful financial promoter. He had become the son-in-law of Woodrow Wilson and his Secretary of the Treasury, and had then moved to California. His background was rural. He was the darling of the Drys, not publicly hostile to the Ku Klux Klan (which was wielding political power in the South and the Middle West), and he had the friendship and political backing of William Randolph Hearst. In his way stood Alfred Emanuel Smith, product of the cities, a member of New York's Tammany Hall, a Wet, and a Roman Catholic. To anticipate, Smith, although himself unsuccessful at the 1924 Democratic convention, had ended McAdoo's aspirations. But McAdoo and his friends and the lost causes they represented had their revenge in 1928 and 1932.

Smith obtained the endorsement of the New York State Democratic Convention and auguries further promised well, when the Democratic National Committee chose New York City for the gathering of the nominating convention and Franklin D. Roosevelt consented to become Smith's campaign manager. Roosevelt had had a minor public career, but he bore a magical name, was a high-born New Yorker, a liberal and independent anti-Tammanyite in politics, and he had begun to show qualities, despite his physical handicap, of courage and high spirits, if not political astuteness. Friends rallied around and admired him. He set out at once to organize the "New York State Citizens Committee to Promote the Candidacy of Alfred E. Smith for President" and in a short while had gathered together about three hundred prominent persons in public and civic life to work with him. Judicial propriety forbade Proskauer's participation, but he, as well as his associates, Belle Moskowitz and Robert Moses, was constantly at Smith's elbow. During May and June it became increasingly clear that Smith would enter the convention with a large body of the instructed votes as one of the frontrunners—hence, the struggle between him and McAdoo was destined to be long and severe. To hold the Smith supporters and to win the wavering, the strategists decided upon boldness on touchy issues. The Volstead Act was not to be attacked, but saloons and hard liquor were. Smith was to favor the sale of beer in those states which had voted it, but he was to come out unalterably opposed to the Ku Klux Klan, whether or not the party platform supported it. When the question of putting Smith's and Roosevelt's names in nomination came up, it turned out (ironically, for he had never liked Roosevelt) that Proskauer was responsible—for, not only did he suggest Roosevelt, but he also wrote the "Happy Warrior" speech with which, thenceforth, Roosevelt was always to be associated.

In his *Reminiscenses* Proskauer described the colloquy between him and Smith, when the latter asked one day who was to be his running mate and he was told that it would be Roosevelt.

> The Governor asked: 'For God's sake why?' I said: 'Because you're a Bowery Mick and he's a Protestant patrician and he'd take some of the curse off you.' Smith thought a minute and said: 'Maybe you're right, let's go and talk to him.' Roosevelt had a little room in headquarters up across from the Biltmore where we had an extra office. We went in and Al said: 'Frank, Joe and I have been talking this over and I've come here to ask you to make the nominating speech.' 'Oh, Al,' he said, 'I'd love to do it, but I'm so busy here working with delegates I have no time to write a speech,' and he turned to me and said: 'Joe, will you write a speech for me?'

Roosevelt's biographers have been cavalier about Proskauer's help in pushing their hero into history. Prior to 1924 Roosevelt's career had been undistinguished. He had been leading the life of a wealthy gentleman farmer in the Hudson Valley, and had no need to practice law (he had also been an indifferent student in the Columbia Law School). Such forays as he had made into state politics had left the hard-bitten leaders of the New York Democracy unimpressed. Tammany Hall, as did Smith and Proskauer, looked upon him as a dilettante who played his politics by hunches and, as Proskauer put it later, suffered from an inability "to think consecutively." His disabling illness—at age 39 in 1921, he had been stricken with poliomyelitis—and his long and brave struggle to recovery had attracted sympathy, but none of the political movers and shakers in the Democratic Party had considered him a man with a political future.

Proskauer and Smith gave Roosevelt a rostrum in a hall on which all eyes in the nation were focused, for the embittered contest between Smith and McAdoo represented more than just the usual quadrennial convention spectacle. It was the last open effort at the domination of the Democratic Party by the rural populist American for which William Jennings Bryan had been the spokesman since 1896, and whose disparate elements had been held together by a common fear and hatred of strangers and outsiders: the foreign-born, Roman Catholics, Jews, organized workers, middle-class intellectuals—the dwellers, in short, of cities and their sybaritic ways.

Smith, by stopping McAdoo, now their spokesman, defeated them in their effort to use the party to hold back the forces in America responsible for its great industrial growth and its social development. The Democratic Party from that year on was transformed: Smith was the catalyst but, ironically in this case, the agent paid a heavy price. For the defeated host brought him down in 1928 and 1932. Strangely enough, the Roosevelt whom Smith made and followed in his footsteps as governor of New York in 1929-1932, sought and obtained the help of Smith's enemies, McAdoo and the Southern leaders, to prevent Smith from getting the nomination in 1932.

In his *A Segment*... Proskauer wrote nothing of his authorship of the Roosevelt speech. Much as he came to dislike Roosevelt he remained silent as long as Roosevelt also did. But he was piqued into telling the whole story, in 1961, when he dictated his *Reminiscences* for the Columbia University Oral History Project, as a result of two occurrences. The first was the appearance and great popular success of Dore Schary's *Sunrise at Campobello* (1958), initially as a book, then as play and motion picture. Shary had gone out of his way to play down Smith and make Roosevelt the shining knight. In the play Schary put the relationship of the two men in this fashion, concerning the nomination:

> *Smith:* I'll want to have a look at what you're going to say, and Joe Proskauer may have an idea or two. He's a good phrase-maker.
> *FDR:* I won't mind the addition of a few phrases. But Al, what I say will have to be what I want to say.
> *Smith:* Yes, Frank, you have made that quite clear....

The second was a characteristically patronizing story printed in *Time* on April 18, 1960. Called "The Defeat of the Happy Warrior," it was designed to speculate whether a Roman Catholic could be elected to the presidency in obvious anticipation of the likely candidacy of another Roman Catholic, John F. Kennedy. *Time* alluded to the famous end of the Roosevelt speech, which Proskauer had built about the central theme of the poem called "the Character of the Happy Warrior," written by William Wordsworth in 1807, whose closing couplet was "This is the Happy Warrior; This is he/That every man in arms should wish to be." And then *Time* added this in a footnote:

> Whether or not the tag helped Smith, it did help Roosevelt: he became known as the man who called Al Smith the Happy Warrior. But Roosevelt deserved little credit. The Wordsworth couplet... was written into the nominating

speech by its principal ghost writer, New York Judge Joseph M. Proskauer. Roosevelt accepted the idea reluctantly, argued that the flourish was too literary for hard-headed convention delegates.

Time, which prided itself on its careful researching, should have known better and got the whole story straight. In a book about her father, published in 1956, Emily Smith Warner wrote:

> The arduous task of writing the speech was another matter, and Judge Joseph M. Proskauer, assumed that responsibility, though many conferences were held to decide what the speech should contain. Because of his long and intimate acquaintance with Father and with Father's political accomplishments Judge Proskauer was entirely at home in outlining many highlights, but the speech he wrote was much more than an account of Father as a politician. It was a masterpiece of its kind and the judge wrote every word of it, crossed every *t* and dotted every *i.*

And Rexford B. Tugwell, in his biography of Roosevelt, *The Democratic Roosevelt* (1957), added, "Something has been made of Roosevelt's not having written this himself—Judge Proskauer, Smith's mentor, seems to have been its author—but politicians seldom write the speeches they deliver."

Proskauer continued in his *Reminiscences:*

> After an interval of about a couple of days I sent him [Roosevelt] the 'Happy Warrior' speech, essentially as it was finally made. He telephoned me and asked me to stop in and talk to him. I did on the way home one evening. He said: 'Joe, I can't make that speech, it's too poetic. You can't get across Wordsworth's poem to a gang of delegates. I wrote another speech,' and showed me the draft of a speech that was conventional. I said, 'Frank, there's no use you and me debating the merits of your brainchildren. Let's get somebody who has good publicity sense and he can tell us which is better.' 'Well, who do you suggest?' I said, 'I don't want to make a suggestion. You name him.' He said, 'What kind of man?' And I said, 'I'm thinking of somebody like Herbert Swope,' who was then the managing editor of the *World,* which was then a great Democratic newspaper. He said, 'What could be better?' So he called up Swope and that night Swope and I went up to the Roosevelt house. We explained the situation to Herbert, and we handed him these two speeches without telling him which was which. He read the Roosevelt speech first, and then looking at me he said, 'Joe, this speech you wrote is lousy.' Then he read my 'Happy Warrior' speech and he said, 'Frank, this is the greatest nominating speech since Cleveland was nominated by Bryan. This is historic.' And Roosevelt kept arguing. And about midnight, I said to him, 'Frank, the time has come for a showdown. I wrote this "Happy Warrior" speech for Smith and its purpose is right, and you're going to make that speech, or you're not going to make any.' And he said, 'All right, if you feel as strongly as that about, I'll make it.'

The Democratic Party platform was a patchwork of compromises and equivocation. The anti-Klan forces, led by Bainbridge Colby, failed to put through a resolution openly denouncing the organization—it was opposed by an alliance of Bryan-McAdoo delegates, 546.15 to 541.85. A plank endorsing the League of Nations (Wilson had died recently) lost resoundingly. The Republicans were attacked for corruption, their protective tariffs, their wish-washy foreign policy, and their failure to enforce Prohibition.

The balloting began on June 30, with the Democratic Party still committed to a two-thirds vote of all the delegates for a nomination. On the first ballot the vote was McAdoo, 431½ and Smith, 241, with seventeen other nominees trailing behind. Ballot followed ballot with neither McAdoo nor Smith yielding to the other. On the sixty-fourth ballot McAdoo got 439, Smith 307, and a new dark horse, John W. Davis of West Virginia, 123 votes. After the sixty-ninth ballot, when McAdoo had drawn ahead to 530, which represented almost one-half of the votes, Smith and his advisers realized he could not win and they proposed to McAdoo they both withdraw. As Smith later wrote: "I suggested to Mr. McAdoo that we both withdraw our candidacies. I admitted that I did not believe I could be nominated and I was satisfied that he could not be. In the interest of party harmony, I suggested that we both remove our names from consideration, throw the convention into the hands of the delegates themselves, and let them make the choice." McAdoo was amenable, but with one unacceptable condition—the dropping of the two-thirds rule. This meant that he would have a veto over the naming of a candidate, since he had the greatest number of votes to release. So the struggle continued.

On the seventy-sixth ballot Smith's vote went on to 368. On the eighty-seventh he passed McAdoo, 362 to 315. On the one-hundreth Davis crept up to tie McAdoo, while Smith had 351. The heat and exhaustion were wearing the delegates out and on the night of July 9 McAdoo yielded to an agreement which Smith had already publicly accepted: both were to release all delegates and quit the race. On the one hundred and third and final ballot, John W. Davis, now an outstanding New York City lawyer who had been a very good ambassador to Great Britain in the Wilson Administration, received the nomination, with 844 votes.

The cause of the Democracy was doomed. Despite Davis' ability, he was generally unknown to the American electorate; the vice-presidential nomination went to Charles W. Bryan of Nebraska, of no help either. Two other factors presaged defeat. The first was the appearance of a third-party ticket, the so-called Progressive Party, made up of Senators Robert M. La-Follette and Burton K. Wheeler, which was bound to gain in the cities and among liberals at the expense of the Democrats. And the second was the Coolidge era of prosperity, already in full swing. The rout was really a complete one. Davis carried only the Solid South and Oklahoma with 136 electoral votes; LaFollette got only his own State of Wisconsin with 13 votes. Coolidge received 382—his popular vote was greater than the combined votes of his two opponents.

To help the Davis candidacy in New York, Smith consented to run once more for the New York governorship, his Republican opponent this time being Theodore Roosevelt, Jr. Smith won easily, although Davis lost New York by 850,000 votes, and Smith went on to his third and fourth gubernatorial terms.

The usually astute Al Smith made one monumental blunder which long plagued him politically. Boss Murphy had died and Smith, as he himself had proclaimed it, was the head of the Democratic Party in the State of New York, including New York City. He was therefore responsible for the choice of James J. Walker for the mayoralty. Proskauer recorded that he had sought to dissuade Smith from this action, questioning its propriety. But Smith replied that Walker had solemnly sworn by the memory of his dead mother that he would reform and seriously undertake an efficient administration and "would work hand in hand with Smith to that end. Smith could not believe that such an oath would be broken."

After Walker was elected and Smith had begun to regret his error, he approached Proskauer and asked whether he would resign from the bench and become corporation counsel of the city, in order that Smith could establish some control over the Walker administration. Proskauer asked, "Al, what makes you think that Jimmy Walker would ever appoint me as his corporation counsel?" "Because I'd tell him to," Smith replied. Said Proskauer, "You've got another think coming." And he was right. Once Walker was in office, as Proskauer stated in his *Reminiscences,* "Al could never talk to him on the telephone. He just went his own way." And on to disaster—to embarrass Smith in 1932.

Smith's continued fine record in Albany and all those natural qualities of leadership and achievement he possessed and continued to exhibit made him the Democracy's outstanding contender for the presidential nomination of 1928. He had defeated McAdoo and his curious congeries of supporters in 1924. America had accepted his city (and purposely exaggerated) ways and his forthright opposition to Prohibition. But there *was* a fly in the ointment. To many of the older-stock Protestant Americans, as wrote William Allen White, editor of the Emporia [Kansas] *Gazette,* a thoughtful and an honest man, Smith represented a threat to "the whole Puritan civilization, which had built a sturdy, orderly nation." All this may be summed up in the fact that Alfred E. Smith was first and always a devout, church-going Roman Catholic.

This distrust, even fear, came out in the open in April, 1927, when there appeared in the *Atlantic Monthly* "An Open Letter to the Honorable Alfred E. Smith," written by Charles C. Marshall, an Episcopalian and a retired lawyer. Could a Roman Catholic, in the light of his church's history, truly accept the "American constitutional principles" separating church and state? Smith's conduct had convinced Marshall that Smith was a dangerous man. Even in his few words of praise for Smith, Marshall complained of a "note of doubt, a sinister accent of interrogation, not as to intentional rectitude and moral purpose, but as to certain conceptions which your fellow citizens attribute to you as a loyal and conscientious Roman Catholic." Marshall continued by stating that recent encyclicals of Popes Pius IX and Leo XIII had inferred the supremacy of the Roman Catholic Church over the secular state. And he supported his argument with examples of all sorts of interferences by church authorities in lay matters outside the purely ecclesiastical concerns.

The editor of the *Atlantic Monthly* had sent a proof of the article to Franklin D. Roosevelt with the suggestion that Smith, or someone on his behalf, might want to reply. Roosevelt had earlier proposed to Smith that he defend his patriotism in the weekly *Independent,* but Smith had indignantly replied that he saw no need to do so. Roosevelt forwarded the proof to Mrs. Moscowitz and she also had sought, but in vain, to convince Smith that a reply was necessary. Next, she turned to Proskauer who immediately saw the urgency of her appeal. He reported the affair, in essentially the same language, in both his *A Segment . . .* and his *Reminiscences.*

He and Mrs. Moscowitz asked the editor of the *Atlantic Monthly* to hold space in the next issue open for a limited time for Smith's reply. Then, Proskauer called on Smith, and their conversation ran somewhat as follows:

Proskauer: When are you going to work on your answer to this?
Smith: I'm not going to answer the damn thing.
Proskauer: You have to answer it, Al. Here's a man who throws down the challenge to you that your religion makes it impossible for you honestly to be sworn in as President of the United States. You owe it to yourself, your party, and to your religion, to answer it.
Smith: 'I don't know how to answer that sort of stuff. I've been a devout Catholic all my life. I never heard of these damned bulls and encyclicals. I don't know what the words mean; they've got nothing to do with being a Catholic. You answer it.' I said, 'Well, that would make a great hit. A Protestant lawyer challenges a Catholic candidate for the Presidency, on this issue and you want it answered by a Jewish judge. Where the hell are your brains?' He looked at me a minute and said, 'Joe, of course you're right. Honestly, I don't know how to answer it. I just know it ain't so. You've got to take the contract' . . . and I said, 'Oh, that's a different story. I'll take the contract. A lawyer can brief anything. Give me a priest.' He said, 'You can have the whole diocese. I just want one priest and I know the one I want.' He said, 'Who do you want?' I said, 'This is going to leak. I want the priest above all others whose patriotism is not subject to question and that's Father [Francis P.] Duffy. He's not a great scholar but he can put me on the track of what I've

got to know.' So he said, 'You know him. Call him up.' I said, 'Say, I'm not running for the Presidency, Al, you are. You call him.'

Proskauer and Duffy proceeded to work out an appropriate reply and Proskauer wrote the article. The finished product was taken to Smith in Albany where he, Proskauer, and Mrs. Moscowitz reviewed it carefully. As Proskauer reported in his *Reminiscences,* this conversation took place:

> *Smith:* Thank God, that job is done. Shoot it.
> *Proskauer:* Now, wait a minute.
> *Smith:* What's the matter now?
> *Proskauer:* Al, this has turned out in my mind so damned good that I'm afraid we may have said something in here which will give offense to Catholics and before you release this I want to show it to the Cardinal [Hayes].

Smith agreed and telephoned the Cardinal and Proskauer took the train that evening with his manuscript. The following conversation ensued:

> *Hayes:* Judge, I'd give my right hand to see Al Smith President, but I will take no part in politics.
> *Proskauer:* I think your Eminence doesn't quite grasp the significance of my question. I'm not asking you to take any part in politics. I came here as a messenger from a communicant of your church and I ask you to tell me whether there is anything in this document which offends the dogma of the Catholic Church and you can answer that question and no other.
> *Hayes:* I think that document violates no dogma.

Proskauer's article, "Catholic and Patriot: Governor Smith Replies," appeared in the *Atlantic Monthly* in May, 1927. It carried of course Smith's name. It came to the question of loyalty at once. "These convictions [about the Two Powers] are held neither by me nor by any other American Catholic, as far as I know," Smith said. "I should be a poor American and a poor Catholic alike, if I injected religious discussion into a political campaign. Therefore, I would ask you to accept this answer from me not as a candidate for any public office but as an American citizen."

> Moreover, I am unable to understand how anything that I was taught to believe as a Catholic could possibly be in conflict with what is good citizenship [Smith continued]. The essence of my faith is built upon the Commandments of God. There can be no conflict between them.
>
> Instead of quarreling among ourselves over dogmatic principles, it would be infinitely better if we joined together in inculcating obedience to these Commandments in the hearts and minds of the youth of the country as the surest and best road to happiness on this earth and to peace in the world to come. This is the common ideal of all religions.

Nor did Proskauer allow Smith to dodge the problem of dogma. The encyclicals Marshall had made so much of were not articles of faith, he wrote for Smith. They had no dogmatic force, as Cardinal Newman himself had held. "Nor can you quote," the article continued, "from the canons of our faith a syllable that would make us less good citizens than non-Catholics." When Marshall and Smith recited the Lord's Prayer, they prayed "not to 'My Father,' but to 'Our Father.'" Many of the quotations and charges alleged against the Roman Catholic Church applied "only to the complete Catholic State," and then only that of the past. Roman Catholics believed in the separation of church and state, as Cardinal Gibbons had flatly said. "With these great Catholics," Smith declared, "I stand squarely in support of the provisions of the Constitution which guarantees religious freedom and equality." The article went on to say that Smith had never been under any religious pressure, clerical or lay, in the administration of any office he had ever held. Nor had he showed any "special favor to Catholics or exercise discrimination against non-Catholics."

> I summarize my creed as an American Catholic [Smith concluded]. I believe in the worship of God according to the faith and practice of the Roman Catholic Church. I recognize no power in the institutions of my Church to interfere with the operations of the Constitution of the United States or the enforcement of the law of the land. I believe in absolute freedom of conscience for all men and in equality of all churches, all sects, and all beliefs before the law as a matter of right and not as a matter of favor. I believe in the absolute separation of Church and State and in the strict enforcement of the provisions of the Constitution that Congress shall make no law respecting an establishment of religion or prohibiting the free exercise thereof. I believe that no tribunal of any church has any power to make any decree of any force in the law of the land, other than to establish the status of its own communicants within its own church. I believe in the support of the public school as one of the cornerstones of American liberty. I believe in the right of every parent to choose whether his child shall be educated in the public school or in a religious school supported by those of his own faith. I believe in the principle of noninterference by whomsoever it may be urged. And I believe in the common brotherhood of man under the common fatherhood of God.
>
> In this spirit I join with fellow Americans of all creeds in a fervent prayer that never again in this land will any public servant be challenged because of the faith in which he has tried to walk humbly with his God.

The two articles, particularly the Smith reply, generated national interest. Smith was deluged with correspondence and congratulations. Newspaper editors generally agreed that his answer was honest and explicit and that the issue was settled. Not so with Marshall, however. It was evident from his subsequent conduct that his *bona fides* was questionable, for he sought to keep the debate alive. He wrote a "Rejoinder" and he published a pamphlet in which he raised other questions, indicating that the answers to his charge of the "Two Powers" did not satisfy him or other non-Catholics. "May your disclaimer mark the beginning of the era when the [Roman Catholic] Church may so redress her historic claim that the whole Christian world may be one with her and her polity be brought into harmony with the modern State," he concluded.

Marshall did not have to stir the embers to keep the fires alive. Smith knew well enough that many Americans were using his Catholicism as pure politics, creating general distrust. He knew he had to face the issue sooner or later. In a speech in Oklahoma City in 1928 he deplored the injection of "bigotry into a campaign which should be an intelligent debate of important issues." "Here and now, I drag them [these prejudices] into the open and I denounce them as a treasonable attack upon the very foundations of American liberty. I have been told that politically it might be expedient for me to remain silent upon this subject, but as far as I am concerned no political expediency will keep me from speaking out in an endeavor to destroy these evil attacks."

The boom for the Smith nomination by the Democracy in 1928 got under way early, despite the bitter smear campaigns waged against him by fundamentalist ministers, Drys, and the remnants of the now discredited Ku Klux Klan. By March 17 Smith had 140 delegates committed to him, many from states which had opposed him in 1924. Enthusiastic support came from all parts of the country. A month before the convention (which was to be held in Houston, Texas in June) Smith was regarded as certain of victory. Three weeks later his lieutenants claimed 686 of the 1,100 delegates. Proskauer, committed to his conception of judicial propriety, permitted himself to work only behind the scenes, but his activities did not go unnoticed. The New York *Times* described him as "the diplomat of the Smith camp [who] is regarded as being largely responsible for the conciliatory attitude which the Smith workers have adopted toward the Drys and anti-Catholic leaders of the party." Contenders who had been groomed to stop Smith—Senator Thomas J. Walsh of Montana (a Roman Catholic but a Dry) and Governor Albert C. Ritchie of Maryland—dropped out of the race before the convention opened. All that seemed to remain were the formalities.

When the convention was brought to order on June 26, Proskauer, despite his protestations in *A Segment* . . ., came out in the open. He commenced work with the chairman of the Resolutions Committee to see that a platform was devised to suit Smith. As he put it, "I simply did some drafting with [Senator] Pittman and tried to hammer out a Jeffersonian Democratic platform." Apparently, he was doing much more. He was striving to control the New York delegation, including many Tammany Hall stalwarts, who had begun to see themselves pushed into the background and denied direct access to Smith who was still in Albany. Smith had named a convention manager to speak for him but he and the other Tammany leaders, Boss Olvany, Mayor Walker, and Surrogate Foley, who were on the Smith board of strategy, found that the only direct telephone wire to Governor Smith was in Proskauer's room. A story pointing out the distaste of the professionals for the amateur was leaked to the New York *Times,* stating that Proskauer "attempted to decide matters without full consultation and that generally he carried things with too high a hand . . . [and that he] showed lack of tact in dealing with delegates from other states." In any event, the telephone was moved, ruffled feelings were smoothed out, and Proskauer thereafter devoted himself exclusively to the platform.

On June 27 Franklin D. Roosevelt again placed Al Smith in nomination. Once again, "amid wild cheers," said the New York *Times,* Roosevelt used the magic slogan that had become his hallmark as well as Smith's: "Victory is his habit—the Happy Warrior." Only seven state delegations, six of them from the South, refused to join the demonstration that followed. Smith received the nomination on the first ballot, with 849⅔ votes out of 1,097½ cast. The next day Senator Joseph T. Robinson of Arkansas, a Protestant and a Dry, was named Smith's running mate. Earlier, the Republicans had picked Secretary of Commerce Herbert Hoover as their candidate. As for Proskauer, the press reported that he was considering resigning from the bench in order to take an active part in the Smith campaign. As it turned out, he did not—but there is no doubt that until November he was one of its most active participants.

Second only to Smith himself, the person in the Democratic ranks who attracted wide attention was Smith's campaign manager and chairman of the Democratic National Committee, John J. Raskob. Like Smith, he was a Roman Catholic of humble origin and with no formal education. But he had climbed by his own efforts the steep path of success in the fields of corporation organization, management, and finance. In fact, he was immensely wealthy, and, as an associate of the DuPonts, had played a leading role in the acquisition and rehabilitation of General Motors Corporation. As a bold operator in the stock market, he was one of the prophets of the new age of Prosperity Everlasting. His enormous charitable donations to the Roman Catholic Church had been duly acknowledged by the conferring of a papal knighthood on him by Pius XI.

Had Raskob been a member of a political party, he would doubtless have been Republican. However, he was a conservative and an intimate of the industrial greats of the country. He had privately admired Herbert Hoover's acceptance speech, but he had had no previous experience with politics. Yet, Al Smith chose him for a key post in his campaign. Why? Was it defiance of the populist, fundamentalist, anti-Catholic South and West? Was Smith nailing his colors to the mast? Was it for campaign financing?

The Josephsons, in their biography of Smith, expressed another explanation, one which carries credibility.

In the later stages of his career Alfred Smith's political friendships shifted perceptibly [they wrote]. Formerly he had relied for a flow of ideas on his [Albany] Kitchen Cabinet... as well as the group of intellectuals and ghost writers made up of Mrs. Moskowitz, Moses and Proskauer. But toward 1925 and 1926 a different breed of men began to figure prominently in his inner circle, those Ed Flynn [Tammany Boss of the Bronx who followed the star of FDR after Smith's defeat in 1928] called his 'golfing cabinet.' Among these was a new-rich group of native New Yorkers... [made up of] William F. Kenny..., James Hoey..., George Getz..., James Riordan.... All these joined in making generous contributions to Smith's campaigns. A new and impressive figure appeared in the Governor's golfing cabinet around 1926: John J. Raskob....

It may very well be that the conservative bent of Smith's later thinking after 1930, and particularly as the basis of his hostility to the New Deal, derived from his association with these new companions. The Josephsons believed so, but Smith and Proskauer were closer to the bone. They were shocked by what they considered Roosevelt's disloyalty to Smith in 1932. Proskauer was franker than Smith: he always held Roosevelt in low regard and said so: he was "cynical, opportunistic, willing to enjoy the labors of others and lacking in Smith's uprightness." One should observe that Roosevelt's New Deal had serious faults and committed outrageous errors, to be sure, but its humanity cannot be denied. The attitude taken by both men led them into strange political adventures, the most futile and foolish of which was participation in the Liberty League.

The strategy of the 1928 Smith campaign was devised by many persons the more important of which, declared *The New York Times Magazine,* September 23, 1928, were Proskauer, Henry and Belle Moskowitz, Robert Moses, Raymond V. Ingersoll, Professor Lindsay Rogers of Columbia University, Roosevelt, Herbert Lehman, and Colonel Frederick Stuart Greene. Proskauer and Mrs. Moskowitz were described as the "intellectual godfather and godmother" of the Governor. There is no doubt that Proskauer had his hand in the writing of every one of Smith's major speeches (including the one of acceptance) and in his every important campaign decision.

Proskauer went with Smith on his tour of the West in the summer of 1928 where at least one of the Governor's key addresses, that on farm policy, was prepared under Proskauer's careful eye. He and Smith had often discussed the farm problem. Smith admitted his unfamiliarity with its national aspects and asked Proskauer to take the "contract" for studying and instructing him on this vital national issue. One of the distorting aspects of the prosperity of the 1920s had been the malaise that had hit American agriculture with resulting decline in farm income, notably as regards the large growers of the agricultural staples of wheat, corn, and cotton. Export markets for American crops had dwindled to the accompaniment of sharp drops in prices at home as well as abroad. Congress had sought to come to grips with the crisis and twice had passed the so-called McNary-Haugen Bills, only to have them turned back by presidential vetoes. Hoover, in his campaign speeches, had nothing to offer the farmers. Thus, the way was open for Smith to try to win the Middle West and the Far West, enemy territory, indeed, for a Roman Catholic and a Wet.

Proskauer went to work with meticulous care. He brought into his preparations George N. Peek, a recognized national authority on farm programs, as well as Lindsay Rogers.

> [The three men] immediately consulted a large number of Grange leaders, presidents, officers of farm organizations. We drafted a program which was based mostly on the old McNary-Haugen Bill [Proskauer declared in the *Reminiscences*]. It proceeded on the conclusion that it was absolutely impossible to control agricultural production. Plowing up the third row and killing little pigs wouldn't do it because God Almighty controlled production, sunshine and rain—man partly with fertilizers. We came to the conclusion that the way to help the farmer was by a systematic and reasonable planning of distribution. When we finished that job of preliminary investigation, we went over it with the Governor. He called a meeting at Albany of a large number of leaders of farm organizations and had almost a whole day session with them. He said to them, 'Gentlemen, I'm not here to tell you. I'm here to learn. These suggestions have been made and I want to get your reaction to them.' The reactions were uniformly favorable.

Raskob, wanting an examination of the plan by a competent economist, suggested Professor Edwin R. A. Seligman of Columbia University. Since both Proskauer and Seligman were friends and both had homes in Lake Placid, the draft program was sent to Seligman there and Proskauer "went over to his camp one evening and spent the whole evening there, and he gave it his blessing." The speech went off well. Smith boldly approached the question of farm surpluses (from which Hoover was shying away)—and in Omaha he was received by Nebraska farmers in friendly fashion. Well-disposed commentators declared that the speech, delivered on September 18, would win Smith the farm vote.

Smith faced up to the open intolerance which greeted his efforts everywhere. As a result, the 1928 campaign was one of the meanest ones in American presidential contests. As his train proceeded southward to Oklahoma City, where he was to speak September 20, Proskauer recorded in his *A Segment...*, "we could see the fiery crosses of the Ku Klux Klan burning in the countryside, and as we stepped down from the cars we were confronted by thin-lipped, evil-looking sneering men, and we heard rumors of violence." A vicious underground press, of newspapers, handbills, pamphlets, a good part circulating nationally, had been steadily pounding a drumbeat of hatred and vilification, which not only attacked Smith's New York origins and Catholicism but as well the Jewish advisers in his entourage.

Some who heard and watched Smith in Oklahoma City sensed his un-
easiness in the presence of a hostile and strange audience. However
skilled he was in give and take exchanges with audiences, he was not
accustomed to open hatred. In fact, he was advised not to speak out. But
he did, attacking the bigotry and intolerance of his listeners:

> I drag them into the open and I denounce them as a treasonable attack upon
> the very foundations of American liberty. I have been told that politically it
> might be expedient for me to remain silent upon this subject, but as far as I
> am concerned no political expediency will keep me from speaking out... I
> attack those who seek to undermine [our institutions] not only because I am a
> good Christian but because I am a good American and a product of American
> institutions. Everything I am, and everything I hope to be, I owe to these
> institutions.

He openly attacked the Klan. He mentioned the Grand Dragon of the
Realm of Arkansas who had called for his defeat because he was a Roman
Catholic:

> The world knows no greater mockery than the use of the blazing cross [he
> said], the cross upon which Christ died—as a symbol to instill in the hearts of
> men a hatred for their brethren, while Christ preached and died for the love
> and brotherhood of man.

But his honesty and fearlessness did not help. The day before the Oklahoma newspapers had announced that former Senator Robert Owens (of
that state) was bolting the Democratic Party because of Smith. The day
after his speech, in the same Oklahoma city auditorium, possibly before the
same audience that had come to hear Smith, Dr. John Roach Straton, a fundamentalist preacher, delivered a discourse on "Al Smith and the Forces of
Hell."

The election returns were not even close. Smith did not do so well as
Cox had in 1920 and Davis in 1924: he received 87 electoral votes to
Hoover's 444 and carried only eight states, six in the Deep South, plus
Massachusetts and Rhode Island. Five Southern states, Virginia, North
Carolina, Florida, Tennessee, and Texas (which the Democrats had carried
since 1876) voted against him, as did the Border states Kentucky, Mary-
land, Delaware, and Missouri, which had usually gone Democratic.

A harder effort on behalf of Smith in 1928 might have produced happier
results. Smith had run powerfully in the industrial East, particularly in the
country's biggest cities, and he had obtained 40.8 percent of the popular
vote as against Cox's 34.1 percent in 1920 and Davis' 28.8 percent in 1924.
An interesting analysis of the 1928 voting, as revealed in Ruth C. Silva's
Rum, Religion, and Votes ... (1962), shows Smith's impressive strength,
despite the "noble experiment" of Prohibition and Hoover's "everlasting-
prosperity" talk.

> Not only did he [Smith] carry 8 states with 87 electoral votes, but he also led the Democratic Congressional tickets in 16 other states having an additional 201 electoral votes [wrote Silva]. Thus he was strong enough to either carry the state or lead his Congressional running mates in 24 states having a total of 288 electoral votes, or 22 votes more than the 266 necessary for victory.

Silva also found that Smith in this respect did better than the Democratic candidates, Parker (1904), Bryan (1908), Wilson (1912), Cox (1920), Davis (1924), Truman (1948), Stevenson (1952 and 1956), and Kennedy (1960), each of whom trailed farther behind their Congressional running mates than did Al Smith in 1928.

The reason for Smith's defeat and sinking star, at least the one offered here, was the deep-seated enmity of the Democratic Southern leaders, who feared that the ''New South'', which they had mislead since 1876, was now really being threatened. As a result, they failed to stand by their party's choice. Their conduct in 1924 and 1928 lost Smith the 1932 nomination and the presidential election. And to this should be added their plotting (along with Franklin D. Roosevelt's) to shelve Smith and get the nomination for Roosevelt. For Roosevelt was an available candidate. He had been elected governor of the State of New York, when Smith had lost it, and he had set about dismantling Smith's organization in the state government and skillfully chopping away at the Smith image of the ''Happy Warrior.'' In fact, Roosevelt himself began to look like the ''Happy Warrior.''

THE CAMPAIGN OF 1932 AND OTHER POLITICAL ENCOUNTERS

Proskauer's devotion to Al Smith made him fall into a fatal error: he saw Franklin D. Roosevelt through Smith's eyes, instead of his own. As a result, both men underestimated Roosevelt's capacities, political skills, and driving ambition. Roosevelt had won the governorship of the State of New York in 1928 and Smith, in the same year, had lost his bid for the presidency. From then on Roosevelt thought only of his own chances for being elected to the highest office in the land.

Smith had asked Roosevelt to run in 1928, not because he had demonstrated any particular acumen or administrative ability, but because of his name. Smith assumed, and Proskauer agreed, that Roosevelt, now elected, would be happy to have Smith's advice and guidance. In 1928 Roosevelt had pledged to carry on in his distinguished predecessor's footsteps. He stated that he would complete Smith's program—the development of waterpower and rural resources, reform labor legislation, and exercise the executive's role in budgeting and financing. Smith had trained a loyal group of workers, including his cabinet and his "kitchen cabinet," along these lines. Once Roosevelt was installed in office, Smith offered him his services, even suggesting that Roosevelt might wish to retain at least two of the members of the Smith "kitchen cabinet"—Secretary of State Robert Moses and Belle Moskowitz, his confidential aid.

Politely but firmly, Roosevelt turned down the offer. Smith, hurt by the decision, moved on in 1929 to the new job Raskob had made for him. He quickly settled down in New York City into a different sort of life, one that offered him ease, comfort, and security (or so it seemed, as we shall see.) He was now too busy to give much thought to Roosevelt, except to wonder over his slights and to note that Roosevelt was not doing well in Albany. And when the depression began in 1930 and Smith's job was becoming almost unmanageable, he had other things on his mind than Roosevelt and presidential politics. Towards the end of the year, when Smith at last began to assert himself politically, it was too late.

The fact is, Roosevelt was not getting very far in Albany. The Republican Party controlled the legislature and when it pressed hard, Roosevelt yielded. According to one historian, during his first term Roosevelt "appeared willing to settle for half a loaf, and the legislature, recognizing this fact, was inclined to give him just that." Commentators were not impressed. Walter Lippmann thought Roosevelt was merely a pleasant man, and shrugged him off. *The Nation* stated that "his weakness and readiness to compromise have been as evident as his personal charm and absolute integrity."

Perhaps, Smith did not realize that, even then, Roosevelt had his eye on the White House. Roosevelt knew that Albany was the road to it, as it had been for his predecessors, Grover Cleveland and Theodore Roosevelt. The fact that Smith thought that his nomination again in 1932 was his due was irrelevant to Roosevelt's ideas.

Roosevelt had to plan carefully for this campaign. He had to build up a personal organization loyal to him and to keep its members about him with political jobs; he had to develop a position, an association with policy, that was completely unlike Smith's; and he had to come to an understanding with those forces in the Democratic Party which had rejected Smith in the 1928 election. Perhaps this was treachery to a friend, or double-dealing, but it was politics, Roosevelt's notions about politics, at any rate, and he did not hesitate to use it.

Roosevelt dropped Belle Moskowitz, replaced Moses with Ed Flynn, Democratic boss of the Bronx, and named Louis Howe, his personal friend, as his confidential secretary. And as his "roving ambassador" he picked James A. Farley, an Irish Catholic and a power in Democratic state politics who came from Rockland County and not from Tammany Hall.

Roosevelt's personal style of operation was revealed in his first message to the legislature. He talked of the plight of the state's farmers, their need for better marketing and credit facilities, and their unequal place in the economy of the commonwealth. In short, he was moving into what had been Smith's enemy-country and shifting his accent from industry to the rural country and its small farm operators. He knew that they, in addition to being cultivators of the soil, were also for Prohibition, hostile to immigrants, the cities, and Roman Catholics, and, generally, were fundamentalists in their Protestantism. In short, Roosevelt, the New York patrician, was fast turning to populism and away from industrial liberalism as a way of rebuilding the Democratic Party. Populism really meant more than ruralism: it meant class hostilities and turmoil, the cleavage between the rich and the poor; and suspicion of corporations and of banking and international finance which, presumably, stood in the way of the legitimate credit needs of consumers and producers. Only a government's "honest currency" could meet these credit needs. Populism continued strong in the South and West.

The way Roosevelt came to accept this political position (which was the theoretical basis of his so-called "New Deal") may be seen in his key address of his presidential campaign, delivered before the Commonwealth Club of San Francisco, September 23, 1932:

> Our task now is not discovery or exploitation of natural resources, or necessarily producing more goods. It is the soberer, less dramatic business of administering our resources and plants already in hand, of seeking to reestablish foreign markets for our surplus production, of meeting the problem of under-consumption, of adjusting production to consumption, of distributing

wealth and products more equitably, of adapting existing economic organizations to the service of the people. The day of enlightened administration has
come.

Such were the broad elements of the Roosevelt masterplan to gain the
Democratic presidential nomination. At once he and his intimates began
working on it, never faltering from the primordial theory.

Raskob, a rich, skilled, and imaginative businessman, had thought he
was providing a sinecure for Al Smith, as a result of one of his coups. He
and a group of friends acquired the old Waldorf-Astoria Hotel on Fifth
Avenue and Thirty-Fourth Street, razed it, and announced that on the site
they would erect the tallest commercial structure in the world, topped with
a gigantic mooring mast and to be named the Empire State Building, in
honor of Al Smith. Smith was to be the president of the corporation, supervise erection of the building, and rent its offices to all the great corporations seeking new and modern headquarters in the city. This was not an
onerous assignment in the palmy days of 1929. His salary was to be
$50,000, plus extra allowances, and he was to have plenty of time to keep
his hand in politics, looking toward 1932.

The Great Depression changed all these hopes and expectations. The
Empire State Building was constructed, but it turned out to be a white
elephant. More than half of it remained unrented, while Smith was
spending all and more of a normal working-day, seeking tenants and
financing to meet the bills. Even Washington was approached. Smith
wanted to see some of the city's federal offices housed there. Along with
these headaches was Smith's concern over the troubles of some of his
friends who had established a new bank, which had failed, and because
they were on the Board of Directors they had become personally involved.

It was not until the November, 1930 elections, when clearly a Democratic
tide had set in, that Smith began to be his old self again. There were many
Democratic victories throughout the states, including Roosevelt's reelection in New York. The Democrats captured the lower house of Congress and, with the help of Republican insurgents, could now look forward
to controlling the Senate. It was not too early to begin thinking of 1932.
Soon, Smith got in touch with Raskob, chairman of the Democratic National
Committee, and Jouett Shouse, its executive director, to start planning the
grand strategy for the next national election. When the committee met in
March, 1931, Smith proposed that it take a forthright position on at least
one important issue, that it favor the repeal of the Prohibition Amendment.
Much to his shock he learned that Roosevelt had long before prepared for
this move and that the resolution was doomed because Farley had lined up
enough Southern votes in the committee to defeat it.

Here were Roosevelt's new allies, determined to "kill off" Al Smith at
any cost, as one of their leaders Cordell Hull of Tennessee brutally put it.

And Roosevelt was the man to do it. Roosevelt, on his part, sold his birth-right for a mess of pottage. He hoped (to change the figure of speech) that when the crunch came, he could wiggle out of it with all those skills of in-direction of which he was a master. He agreed, as Oscar Handlin pointed out, that "between conventions, the spokesmen on policy matters are, pri-marily, the Democratic members of the Senate and the House [and this meant] the permanent surrender to a bloc of Southern senators of an effec-tive veto over national legislation."

One may ask why Smith failed to become alarmed in 1931 and early 1932. Was it because of his emotional involvement in his own and his friends' troubles? Was it personal pride? Was it his persistent refusal to take Roosevelt seriously? Why did he not object, when his personal friend, James Hoey, and his political cronies, Ed Flynn and Herbert Lehman (now Roosevelt's lieutenant-governor), told him they were going to support Roosevelt? It has been said that Smith was told that Roosevelt had been ad-vised to see him—but Roosevelt never got around to it. Handlin put Roose-velt's failure to do so purely on temperament:

> It was not in Roosevelt's temperament to confront such a situation squarely. Then and later, for all his charm, he was awkward in the inability to look those to whom he could not be graciously acquiescent directly in the eye. He lacked the incapacity for the straightforward no. . . . He could not look Smith in the face and say, it ought to be me, not you.

But it must be remembered that Handlin was writing when he was still under the spell of the Roosevelt personal charm. Now, at the distance of forty years, should not a spade be called a spade? Roosevelt was using treachery to kill off his friend. Approaches were being made to and bar-gains struck with all sorts of unsavory figures in the Democratic Party world, while nasty rumors were being circulated. Dan Roper of South Carolina, Tom Heflin of Alabama, and William Randolph Hearst (now of California) each had his political clout in the populist cane brakes and piney woods. There were visits and bargains with them, and, in the urban Democracy, with Jimmy Hines, the disreputable Tammany Hall district leader, and Jim Curley, once mayor and later jailbird of Boston. There were also mean and frightening tales: that DuPont, Raskob, and Smith were the agents of a Wall Street plot to stop Roosevelt; that the Vatican was going to try again, through Smith, to make the United States a political appanage; and that the liquor interests were again stirring restlessly.

Smith, at last shaken out of his lethargy, made his move with the open-ing of 1932. He delivered a number of speeches in January. In February he announced his candidacy for the nomination but, he added, he would not make an active campaign for delegates. He would run, if named by the convention. That was his fatal error. The dice were loaded against him. He had no political organization and no bottomless purse to draw on. He had no platform from which to speak regularly, formally and informally, nor a public office from which there could pour an endless stream of trivia, chitchat, and interviews. Worst of all, he could not do anything about Roosevelt's plots and strategems; that is, the louder and louder talk that no Roman Catholic could ever be elected to the presidency.

When the Democratic convention opened at Chicago on June 27, Smith had only one-half as many as the pledged delegates as had Roosevelt. So well had Farley and his coworkers labored that almost the entire Roosevelt following came from south of the Mason and Dixon line and west of the Mississippi. On the first ballot Roosevelt's vote was 661 and Smith's 201; Roosevelt needed 100 more for the required two-thirds majority. It became apparent after the next two ballots that the convention would be deadlocked and that Roosevelt could not win, unless he had the votes of Texas and California and these were pledged to John N. Garner of Texas, speaker of the House of Representatives, who in his person and career epitomized all those animosities that spelled hatred of Smith.

Early in the proceedings Smith had anticipated such an outcome and had discussed ways and means with McAdoo (now Hearst's personal agent) much as they had in 1924. Certainly, they agreed to talk again, if the Garner votes were in danger of swinging over to Roosevelt. Smith reported to Joseph Proskauer, and this presumed "understanding" guided the conduct of his managers on the floor of the convention. As a result, they were not on guard against undercover deals and not alert enough to protect themselves against the machinations of men such as Roper and Curley.

Eventually, the Roosevelt men got to McAdoo and Hearst, both of whom had too many scores to settle with Smith, and these or their emissaries struck a bargain with Garner. The Garner votes would switch to Roosevelt, assuring his nomination, if Garner were assured of the vice-presidency. By this move the Smith forces were taken unawares and on the fourth ballot Roosevelt was nominated. Said Handlin: "The West and South had won no greater victory since 1912."

From then on it was downhill for Al Smith in politics, with Proskauer always the *fides Achates,* trailing along. Both men were unhappy about what was taking place in Washington in the New Deal. They did not quite know why, except that the increasingly powerful central government evolving was alien to Jeffersonian and Wilsonian ideas. But, Jeffersonianism, too, had been hostile to urban growth and development and suspicious of the people who lived in cities, and neither Smith nor Proskauer was sympathetic to that. They could sense, however, that the economy was out of kilter; that, despite all of the strenuous and often ingenious efforts at reform, massive unemployment of men and disemployment of capital continued; and that the New Deal, with its talk of a more equitable distribution of wealth, was more rather than less likely to pit class against class. But of one thing they were certain: they could not trust Roosevelt. This suspicion soon became an active and deep-seated dislike. And as a result, Smith and Proskauer and many others who believed similarly joined in August, 1934 to form the American Liberty League.

This organization was chartered in the District of Columbia by a mixed company. In it were great corporation executives, bankers, lawyers, and sometime powerful Democratic politicians who now were on the outside; among them were John W. Davis, Al Smith, Irenee DuPont, John Raskob, Jouett Shouse, Frank L. Polk, and Joseph Proskauer. On its executive Committee were seventy presidents or directors of corporations. Its legal department, including many outstanding members of the bar, was headed by Davis. Its president was Jouett Shouse, whom the Democracy in 1932 had ditched along with Raskob and Smith.

If the American Liberty League had stuck to a straightforward economic analysis—that the New Deal instead of rescuing the American economy was sinking it deeper and deeper into the mire and that its populist doctrines, by attacking capital, was preventing recovery—then a meaningful debate might have taken place. Instead, it talked the artificial language of the slogan makers and sought to unseat the President by vague charges of threats to traditional American freedoms. The organization was skillfully outmaneuvered and in the end could say nothing in reply to the clever jibes that it was made up of "economic royalists," was "a drum with a noisy tympanium covering an empty void," and that it was a cabal of rich men with whom Al Smith had allied himself in order to block the great social reforms of the New Deal.

At a banquet in the Mayflower Hotel in Washington on January 25, 1936 before about two thousand men and women Smith made a speech that turned out to be a disaster. He rambled, he made gauche witticisms, and he seemed to believe that the New Deal had really turned socialist. He said: "It is all right with me, if they want to disguise themselves as Norman Thomas or Karl Marx or Lenin, or any of that bunch, but what I won't stand for is allowing them to march under the banner of Jefferson, Jackson, and Cleveland." And he ended with a threat: when the November elections came, he and other Democrats of like mind would probably "take a walk."

And this is precisely what Smith and Proskauer did in the Democratic National Convention, when Roosevelt was named for a second term by acclamation. They "took a walk" and turned around and supported the candidacy of Alfred M. Landon, the Republican nominee. Smith and Proskauer were welcomed. They had built up honorable records in the 1920s and could claim every right to be designated "liberals." But the ragtag and bobtail, the "lunatic fringe" that came along with them and the obvious reactionary line of the American Liberty League were too embarrassing for Landon and the Republican National Committee. The latter ended by asking the newcomers not to endorse its ticket.

The American Liberty League did not survive the elections of 1936, but this did not prevent Smith and Proskauer from engaging in other political adventures. In 1940 came the threat of a third term for Roosevelt (who openly manipulated the convention, much to the distress of good party members like James A. Farley) and Smith and Proskauer "walked again." In fact, Proskauer pulled out all the stops. Even before being approached by Wendell Willkie, he telegraphed him:

> I ask to be enrolled for active service as a devoted supporter of your candidacy. As a Southern-born Democrat, I take this course because you are defending the democratic principles against those who have taken the name and violated the traditions of democracy.

Proskauer took the stump, was named a Republican presidential elector and was consulted frequently. Willkie did not make a particularly good candidate and his defeat was early foreseen. Proskauer, in looking back on the episode was forced to say, "This, my last political venture, was doomed to failure." Smith, meanwhile, had retired into complete privacy and, unlike Proskauer, had sought a reconciliation with Roosevelt. In 1942 Smith and Roosevelt met and spent the time pleasantly talking of earlier days and their growing families of grandchildren. Two years later Smith was dead tired, and almost forgotten. The times had passed him by.

During the early 1930s, when he was working hard and successfully to reestablish a private law practice, Joseph Proskauer had been pitched twice into the hurly-burly of politics because of the interests of a client. He had crossed swords in public controversy with Governor Franklin D. Roosevelt and with Mayor Fiorello H. LaGuardia. In both incidents he had successfully defended his client, but he had come off second best in politics. Despite his great skills in advocacy he realized that he was no master of the guile and trickery of the dog-eat-dog contests of the public forum. This was the chief reason why Roosevelt and his friends got the best of him and Al Smith in 1932.

In 1930, when he had just come off the bench, Floyd L. Carlisle, chairman of the Niagara-Hudson Power Company, telephoned him to ask him to represent the company before the St. Lawrence Waterway Commission. As Proskauer wrote in his *Reminiscences,* the following colloquy took place:

> *Proskauer:* Floyd, I'm a struggling new young lawyer. It's a great retainer, but I can't take it.
> *Carlisle:* Why not?
> *Proskauer:* I'm in favor and I'm on record as being in favor of public ownership of the dam site.
> *Carlisle:* That doesn't need to deter you. We'll stand for that, if you can negotiate any kind of decent arrangement with the State of New York.

Proskauer got in touch with Julius Henry Cohen, counsel to the Commission, which was headed by Professor Murray Haig of Columbia University. The Commission, whose task was to draw up plans for the development of hydroelectric power on the St. Lawrence River, had grown out of legislation long agitated for by Smith and finally enacted by the legislature in 1930. Proskauer recalled that Cohen considered it fortunate that he was to represent the power company before the Commission, saying it was "something of an advantage to the State . . . [for he] could not very well act as counsel to Carlisle and turn his back on the principles for which Al Smith and he had stood."

Using the Port of New York Authority as a model, Governor Smith in 1926 had proposed a St. Lawrence River power authority, a state-owned corporation, to develop, generate, and transmit hydroelectric power. Smith's intention was for the state to construct and own the plant and to sell the power to private transmission companies. He believed that such an authority could do its work effectively and at the same time remain independent of politics. As his adviser, Proskauer had helped Smith work out the plan and the rationale behind it, to wit, that "the water powers of this State are the property of all the people, and that, when developed, the people should be the beneficiaries."

This was a far cry from the stand taken by the Republicans, both in the nation and in New York. In 1921 the Republican state legislature had passed the Water Power Act (modeled upon the federal Water Power Act of 1920 and signed by the Republican Governor Nathan L. Miller) which permitted the private development of water power, for as long as fifty years after being licensed. Smith, Miller's successor, had consistently disregarded the mandates of this legislation. The public interest, to say nothing of the conservation of New York's natural resources, demanded state ownership and regulation, even to the supersession of the cities in the overseeing of utilities operations. And Smith had finally won, with Roosevelt inheriting his policies.

Proskauer was in an interesting position. The Niagara-Hudson Power Company had been formed in 1929 and was one of the three largest public utility holding companies in the State of New York. In the northwest region it was virtually a monopoly; therefore, competitive bidding was impossible. It was up to Proskauer to get the best price by contract for the services of his client while, simultaneously, operating within the context of his commitment to the idea that the power belonged to the people. All concerned, the state commission and its attorney, the company, its president, and its attorney, were prepared to work together, amicably. Cohen later declared that Carlisle cooperated in "a most loyal and public spirited manner," that he and Proskauer "clicked," and that the discussions were apparently achieving a "common denominator." Cohen said that all involved "were pathfinders of a new trail." In retrospect, Proskauer stated that they agreed on the "course of procedure which settled the very difficult legal questions that were involved—who really owned the water power?—some of a number of engineering difficulties." And, he added, they got to the point where all they lacked was the consent of the federal government.

At this juncture, in the spring of 1931, with the commission's report in proof, Proskauer and Roosevelt met at the executive mansion in Albany to discuss the proposed contract with the Niagara-Hudson Power Company. Proskauer later told the story of the meeting, describing in detail how Roosevelt jettisoned the program. His account is largely substantiated in Cohen's *They Builded Better Than They Knew,* published in 1946:

> I walked into the mansion, sat down and had tea. I said, 'Frank, this report has great kudos in it for you. It will enable you to say that you're the first governor who ever got a great utility company to agree to public ownership of a dam site. But more important than that is the contractual control of resale rates of power so that the company is restricted by contract instead of having to go through all this complicated rate-making process. If that's enough for you, I think we can get federal consent and you can mark your governorship as the beginning of a great development of water power on the St. Lawrence River. But if for any reason you want to keep this thing in politics, you wink your right eye and I'll promise that this conversation never happened.' He looked at me a minute and said, 'Joe, you know me too well for that. I'm under a debt of great personal gratitude to you and Floyd'—Carlisle was an important upstate Democrat—'and the state is under a great obligation to you for the broadminded way in which you've approached the solution of this problem.' I said, 'Well, that's fine, but what did you want to say to me?'
>
> 'Oh,' he said, 'I just want one change in the bill they are drafting or suggesting. I want it to provide that the state should have the right to build a statewide transmission system.' I said, 'What? Do you know what it would cost?' He said, 'No. I haven't the foggiest notion.' Well, I said, 'My vague guess would be between a quarter and a half a billion dollars. It would ruin every utility company in the State of New York. The whole object of this agreement was to avoid the State going into this business of furnishing power to the consumer.'
>
> 'Oh,' he said, 'Joe, it's a gesture. Nobody is ever going to build.'
>
> 'Goddam it,' I said, 'I asked you whether you wanted to play politics with this and you told me no. Now you're suggesting the damnedest, dirtiest politics I ever heard of, Frank, and if you're looking for a fight you've got it.'
>
> 'You're always getting excited,' he said, 'let this thing rest. I'm coming down to New York . . . and I want you and Floyd to come up to the house and sit down with Haig and Cohen, and we'll talk this thing over quietly.' And I said, 'Yes, but how about publicity over the weekend?'
>
> 'Not a peep,' he said. 'We'll be absolutely quiet until we meet.'
>
> I came back and reported and on Monday night he transmitted that report [just prior to the day of Roosevelt's suggested conference] to the legislature with a message that asked for this change suggesting somewhat indirectly

that it would be used as a club over the Niagara-Hudson Power Co., in its negotiations with the state. I met him up at his house on Tuesday night and I confess to the use of scathing profanity. His whole commission arose in arms against him. He had a statute passed legislating them out of office as though he had appointed every damn one of them, created a new commission with a fellow who came here from Kansas. . . . That was the end of a perfect friendship. That colored my relationship with Roosevelt for all the years to come.

This is what had happened. As the Republican legislature played along, Roosevelt got his bill (which put an end to the Haig-Cohen commission) passed and replaced it with a State Power Authority, invested with the responsibility of the development of the St. Lawrence River, including its hydroelectric power potentialities. The bed and waters of the river within the borders of the state and the power and power sites were to remain forever an inalienable right of the people. Power, when developed, was to be primarily for the use of home and rural consumers, but the State Power Authority was also to make power available to municipalities at "reasonable cost."

Aside from the thorny and unanswered questions of costs and financing, construction, pricing, and "fair competition," there was the matter of agreements with the Canadian Government and the Province of Ontario. President Hoover was disposed to move warily, but Secretary of State Stimson did hold discussions with the Canadians which culminated in an international treaty, signed in July, 1932. But the Senate did not ratify it until 1954. Roosevelt's openly partisan biographer, Bernard Bellush, ends his recital of this bizarre episode with this remark in his *Franklin D. Roosevelt as Governor of New York* (1955):

> As Roosevelt prepared to transfer his activity to the nation's capitol, Carlisle's Niagara-Hudson was seemingly the victor in New York's power struggle. However, the obstructionist, short-sighted tactics of Carlisle and his Republican cohorts in Albany and Washington insured the setbacks they would receive in years to come.

In 1935 Proskauer had a somewhat similar experience with New York City's equally hard-bitten and worldly-wise politician, Mayor Fiorello H. LaGuardia. It involved another contest between public authority and a public utility company. Proskauer was the counsel of the Consolidated Gas and Electric Company, of which Floyd L. Carlisle was chairman of the board of directors. Late in 1934 the company submitted a bid of $10.5 million to supply the city's electric needs for the streets, parks, and public buildings for 1935. In the spring of that year, LaGuardia, regarding the bid as "excessive and exorbitant," formally rejected it. Then, after getting the company's consent, he announced that the City of New York would readvertise for bids and that the company would have another opportunity to resubmit. This was the agreement, but LaGuardia's sudden declaration that he meant to propose that the city erect its own power plant, at a cost of $45 million, was contrary to it.

A storm naturally broke over the city. Early in June the Board of Estimate voted down LaGuardia's proposal. Proskauer attacked the plan in a radio debate, warning New York's citizens to beware of public officials who offered "something for nothing." Maurice P. Davidson, LaGuardia's commissioner, defended it on the ground that only through a "yardstick" which offered public competition with privately owned utilities, such as the Tennessee Valley Authority, could the consumer obtain a fair deal in rates. On June 19 LaGuardia got an all-day public hearing on his proposal before the Board of Estimate. Leading the opponents was Joseph Proskauer. Such charges as "petty politics," "fantastic dreams," and "misinformation" flew thick and fast. Finally, it came out that the crux of the whole issue was in the financing of the municipal yardstick plant; and that the new State Power Authority Roosevelt had created was going to act as intermediary in the seeking of a federal loan. A compromise resulted with the passage of a local bill which called for a referendum on the city power plant. This meant that the heat and obfuscation marking such discussions on intricate matters would continue for another several months.

Mayor LaGuardia's case was technically weak. His plan did not clearly provide for the financing of the project, except that an authority was to be created to issue bonds on a plant whose land the city did not own. But the cause was a popular one and largely because of that Proskauer had to carry on an uphill fight. He pursued LaGuardia in the courts and LaGuardia berated his persistent antagonist in the public press.

The climax came in a confrontation of the two champions, LaGuardia and Proskauer, before an audience of a thousand women at the clubhouse of the American Woman's Association on the night of October 21, 1935, a debate sponsored by the League of Women's Voters and the Women's City Club. On the morning of the meeting LaGuardia informed the chairman that he would not speak, if Proskauer had the opportunity to answer him. Proskauer replied by saying that the Mayor could both open and close the debate. But the Mayor would not settle for that. "He says," reported the now distraught go-between, "that the only concession he'll make is that he won't come on the stage while you're speaking so he can't answer you either." Proskauer describes the story in his *Reminiscences:*

The Chairman: Well, that's ridiculous. Oh, please don't let us down. We've got an enormous crowd coming. Everybody is interested in this.
Proskauer: All right but on one condition. And that is that I have the right to tell the audience what the Mayor has said.
The Chairman: I agree you have the right.
Proskauer: All right, I'll speak, but I don't want you to think that I'm naive. The Mayor will come on the stage while I'm speaking but I'm ready for that.

That evening, before a large gathering, Proskauer explained what had transpired. He said he had thought that he and LaGuardia would meet face to face to debate the issues. He warned his listeners that, since La-Guardia was "not always strictly accurate in his accounting of facts," he, Proskauer, had rented the same auditorium for a week hence and, if the Mayor said anything which required answering, he would be there then to do so.

No sooner had Proskauer begun speaking than LaGuardia walked out on the stage and the following exchange took place, to the delight of the audience.

> *Proskauer:* Mr. Mayor, I just finished telling these ladies and gentlemen that you refused to speak here tonight if I had any opportunity to answer you.
> *LaGuardia:* That's as accurate as the Consolidated Gas ever gets anything.
> *Proskauer:* (To chairman) You're the chairman of this meeting. Do I correctly state what the Mayor told you and what you repeated to me, coupled with his pledge not to come on the stage while I'm speaking?
> *Chairman:* (unhappy) Yes, that's correct.
> *Proskauer:* (to LaGuardia) Do you challenge her veracity?
> *LaGuardia:* Oh, go on with your speech.

Proskauer proceeded, presenting his argument and adding that LaGuardia had been responsible for the referendum fiasco, not the utility, for he had failed to put a single penny of the city's money or credit behind the plan, all of which was in violation of the city's charter and the laws of the State of New York. LaGuardia then took the floor, rattled off reams of figures and ended by promising that the municipal plant would meet all expenses, charge low rates, and pay taxes as well. At this point his audience apparently lost patience, for the hall was filled with cries of "How? How?" One listener asked him to repeat his figures.

The Mayor, having lost control, declared, "That is typical of the Consolidated Gas. I apologize to the other ladies present." Proskauer, seizing his opportunity, wanted to know whether his opponent was implying that the company had brought "a claque" to the meeting. Mayor LaGuardia, protesting that he had not interrupted Proskauer, paced back and forth a few steps, shaking his head, and said: "This isn't strange to me. I'm used to it." Proskauer retorted: "Mr. Mayor, it's true, I did interrupt you, sir, but I didn't insult a lady." And so it went, with mounting confusion in the minds of the audience. Mayor LaGuardia was obviously discomfited.

All of this may be put down as entertainment, rather than civic enlightenment. Meanwhile, the courts were passing on the original injunction Proskauer had obtained to stop LaGuardia. Finally, the Court of Appeals agreed that the Mayor's plan for a municipal yardstick plant was in violation of the city's charter.

The love-hate, attraction-repulsion relationship of the two men continued. In 1934 the state legislature authorized LaGuardia to set about creating a Charter Revision Commission to draw up a modern frame of government for the city. The Mayor's initial effort to choose its members—Al Smith was to be its chairman and Judge Samuel Seabury its vice-chairman—quickly collapsed. He had sought to get working together too many divergent interests, with the result that Smith and others withdrew. He tried again in 1935, and this time he gathered together a distinguished body of New York's citizens who were prepared to work together in the city's interest. Thomas D. Thatcher, once United States solicitor-general, was named the chairman, and other members were Thomas I. Parkinson, president of The Equitable Life Assurance Society; Charles Evans Hughes, Jr., also a former solicitor-general; S. John Block, former chairman of the New York State Socialist Committee; Joseph D. McGoldrick, a former city comptroller; Mrs. Wiliam P. Earle, a former president of the League of Women Voters; and Justice Frederick L. Hackenburg of the Court of Special Sessions. Counsel to the commission were Professor Joseph P. Chamberlain of Columbia University and Lawrence A. Tanzer, a specialist in the law of municipal corporations. It was this body that LaGuardia proposed to Proskauer that he join and Proskauer, having never forgotten the earlier knock-down-and-drag-out about the Consolidated Gas Company, refused. Promptly, Thatcher got in touch with Proskauer and asked him to meet with him and LaGuardia in the latter's office. Proskauer recalled this meeting in these words:

> Joe, there are many reasons why I want you on that Commission. And I've asked Tom to come here and I want to repeat in his presence the pledge I made to you that I will not raise any question about utilities and Con Edison or anything of that sort at all.

With this assurance and a witness present, Proskauer yielded. Public hearings were held, experts were consulted, and civic bodies gave the Commission's work wide publicity and their cooperation. In 1936, after a year and a half of intensive labor, the Charter Revision Commission presented a preliminary report and draft of the proposed fundamental law and a second round of hearings was scheduled. High in the new changes were the substitution of a council of twenty-nine members to replace the Board of Aldermen; election to the council by proportional representation; a capital outlay budget on a city-wide basis (with the downgrading of borough autonomy); and city-wide planning. The charter was to be submitted to a referendum for voter consideration at the November elections. Proskauer, in both the preliminaries of preparation of the document and its formal defense against its opponents, was of great help.

The record showed, for example, in May, 1936, a four-hour meeting, in a Bronx County building, chaired by Thatcher with Proskauer very much in evidence. The defenders of borough autonomy pressed hard. Organized-labor spokesmen, complaining of the absence of a minority report and of specific mention of the industrial relations of the city, were equally critical. In a turbulent session in Queens, Thatcher and Proskauer again had to meet the onslaught of the borough-autonomy spokesmen. There were other meetings in the other boroughs. In all of these were the particularly vocal leaders and members of the Tammany Hall clubs throughout the city, many of whom were on the public payrolls and aware of the jeopardy their jobs were in as a result of the proposed consolidation of municipal offices and functions under a centralized mayoral authority. Not content with the give-and-take of these hearings and the long hours spent in them, Proskauer spoke over the radio a number of times, the last of his speeches occurring October 20, which he called "A Long Step Forward." Here he made a strong appeal for citizen approval in the referendum on the ground of fiscal integrity, saying: "The new charter contains numerous changes which would improve the financial affairs of the city, and provide for the introduction of a pay-as-you-go plan, by such gradual stages as to permit it to be effectively realized, and thus save the payment of heavy interest charges."

To prevent Mayor LaGuardia from setting up irresponsible fiscal authorities similar to the one he had proposed in the case of the municipal yardstick plant, the new charter contained the same prohibitions of the old one against capital projects requiring the marketing of bonds without the city's endorsement and pledge of financial backing. Proskauer tells of the Mayor's last-minute intervention in his *Reminiscences:*

> We met one night at the Bar Association for the final meeting of the commission to pass a formal vote to file the Charter. [At this point] Thatcher sheepishly told me: 'I have a letter from the Mayor. He is demanding that this clause be eliminated.' I said: 'Tom, you know that the Mayor promised me that he would not raise this question. Even if it were added, there would still be the identical provision in the State's General City Law. [Proskauer suggested that Thatcher phone the Mayor] and tell him I'm trying to obviate the necessity for controversy in this. And I'll go along if we put in a clause that his section of the Charter should be inoperative if the General City Law was changed.'

Thatcher telephoned at once and reported back to the meeting: "No, he's obdurate."

Proskauer, with the acuteness that made him such a formidable trial lawyer, saw at once what LaGuardia was up to, and he trumped his trick. Proskauer told the Commission, as he recalled it in his *Reminiscences:*

> 'It's perfectly obvious what his strategy is. He wants to eliminate this section of the Charter and then he'll go to the legislature and say that the people have eliminated this in the Charter so they ought to eliminate it in the General City Law. I'm on the spot. I'm going to withdraw from this meeting.

If you comply with the Mayor's request, I shall resign immediately and have a statement in tomorrow morning's newspapers, and I'll be outside this room waiting your call.' I left the meeting and after a while, young Charlie Hughes came out . . . and said, 'My colleagues have unanimously voted to sustain you and not the Mayor.' So the Charter was filed, whereupon Tom Thatcher got a letter from the mayor saying that when he appointed this Commission he thought he was going to get a Charter and now he's got an abortion. And unless we recalled it and took that clause out, he was going to fight the Charter. And Tom politely told him to go chase himself and then he came out for the Charter.

The revised and final version of the Charter was proposed on August 14, 1936, with two questions to be submitted to the voters on November 3. One was whether to approve it, and the other was whether the new councilmen should be elected under a system of proportional representation. Coming into the homestretch—and showing Proskauer's indefatigable energy—Proskauer and Hughes were scheduled to speak before the New York City Advertising Club on October 8. Proskauer also debated James J. Lyons, Bronx borough president, at a symposium luncheon of the Grand Street Boys. He addressed a large audience in Temple Emanu-El of Borough Park in Brooklyn, and he spoke over Station WEVD on October 30, specifically refuting charges again made by Louis Waldman that the Charter was inimical to the rights of labor. Lined up in opposition were the solid cohorts of Tammany Hall and all its allies in the sister boroughs.

But that hard work on the part of the members of the Commission, notably the clever campaigning of Proskauer, Thatcher, and Hughes, was crowned with success. The referendum vote on the new Charter was 950,305 in favor to 596,440 opposed. That on proportional representation also won, this time by an even larger majority, 923,186 to 555,127. The new government would be installed on January 1, 1938. So hard did the Commission labor that many of the fundamental changes it effected have continued to survive, (or so it seemed until the unhappy year 1975). The distinctive feature of the new law was its brevity and clearness. The Commission, as Proskauer put it in *A Segment* . . . "had drawn a short, clear, businesslike and workable Charter that would tend to destroy inefficiency and waste, and provide New York City with a better government than it had ever had before."

LaGuardia, as clever an infighter, as peppery, quick-tempered, vocal, and, when the occasion demanded, as voluble as Proskauer, was also an honest man. He recognized the great merit of the work done and, in a public ceremony at City Hall on November 23, he lauded the members of the Commission, expressed the city's gratitude, and awarded them certificates of merit.

TRIALS WITHOUT JURIES 10

When Joseph Proskauer announced his intention of resigning from the bench and resuming actively the practice of the law, all sorts of approaches from existing firms began to appear. Some he considered and for one reason or another rejected, one of them on the insistence of his wife, who said it would not measure up to his standards of legal conduct. He was also sounded out by Alfred L. Rose, partner in the firm of Paskus & Rose, successor of Rose & Putzel which had been founded by William R. Rose in 1880 and had played an honorable part in New York's legal annals. Thirty years earlier, when Proskauer had started out looking for work, he had called on Rose & Putzel, but had been turned away by Gibson Putzel: "I'd like to give you a job," Putzel had said, "but we just took in a boy who impressed us here and we have only room for one clerk." The "boy" was Benjamin G. Paskus who, in time, became the elder Rose's partner; and, in turn, Alfred, the son of William, began to knock on doors himself.

In 1908-1910, when Alfred Rose was attending New York Law School, his family firm thought some down-to-earth law experience would be helpful toward the bar examination. Would James, Schall & Elkus, where Proskauer was clawing his way upward as a junior partner, take him in? Then, for a year and one half it was a Rose who attended a Proskauer, accompanying his senior by a decade to court and doing the fetching and carrying "boys" or "clerks" were expected to do. When Alfred was admitted to the bar in January, 1911, he left Elkus-Proskauer to join Paskus & Rose. By 1930 Paskus had been ailing, the elder Rose was virtually retired, and the firm was now largely made up of Alfred Rose and Norman S. Goetz who had been taken in in 1926.

It was the younger Rose who started the ball rolling. He talked it over with Paskus and Goetz and they deputized Rose to sound out Proskauer. Rose called on Proskauer in his chambers. Yes, it was true: he was thinking of resigning. Well then, said Rose, "I'd like to carry your brief case again. Neither Paskus nor my father can be active again; the fact is, we need a boss." Would Proskauer consider being that?

Proskauer knew of the firm's excellent reputation; its work was largely that of solicitors. It had good clients among corporations and estates, and very little of its work took it into court. But Proskauer hesitated. He had no stomach for managing a law firm, as he had done for Elkus, and he was concerned about his ability to bring in new business after seven years on the bench. Rather, he preferred court work. He could see his fitness for playing the part "of counsel"—being brought in by other firms—and this required no elaborate organization. While thinking it over he and his wife went on a cruise. Upon their return he told Rose he would join forces with him—and then began a close friendship that lasted for more than forty years.

The new firm of Proskauer, Rose & Paskus (later Proskauer, Rose & Goetz) made its appearance on March 21, 1930 and for a brief time continued at its old office, with Proskauer taking the room that had been occupied by the elder Rose. In six months a move to larger quarters was necessary. Rose was as good as his word: as new business came, he protected Proskauer from the annoyances and inconveniences of office management. As Rose recalled it, Proskauer gave him "a lot of headaches . . . because of his irascibility, his sharpness, and his abruptness."

> And yet [he added] he and I have now been associated since 1930 and I have never had any words of unpleasantness or even disagreement with him on a personal basis. He might come storming into my office about something, and I would say: 'What the hell, Joe, I'll look into it,' and that would end it.

The fears of Rose's friends were unfounded. To Rose and his associates the Judge (as Proskauer was thenceforth called) was actually "very softhearted and basically a very kind individual." He was the soul of loyalty and generosity to his friends, although his irascibility often antagonized them. The result was that he was admired but not liked, largely because Rose protected him. Rose respected Proskauer's distaste of trivia and he knew how to harness his impatience. For instance, Rose recalled, he saw Proskauer one day pacing up and down, and muttering to himself: "Nobody ever pays any attention to me, nobody ever pays any attention to my matters." Rose put his arm around him and said: "Joe, if you don't go into your room, I'll throw a net over you." Proskauer stood still, looked intently at Rose, smiled, and retreated into his office without another word. Proskauer described this as an example of "the happiest of professional relationships."

One consequence of this pleasant partnership was the accelerated growth of their law firm: in 1971, forty years later, it consisted of thirty-nine partners. As Rose noted it:

> . . . its practice spread especially in the field of litigation; the representation of national companies either as general counsel or as special counsel in particular matters; substantial growth in estate and tax work; the development of an entirely new department devoted to labor relations, all of which required greatly increased firm membership and office personnel.

Proskauer was now in his element. Among his very first cases were two which were far apart in professional significance, but each revealed something of his skills in the courtroom. The first dealt with his representation of the executors of an estate which was suing to recover certificates in a cemetery corporation, but where his only real witness had died. He had been able to secure a photostat of an agreement between the decedent and

the two defendants, one that would win the case if only it could be introduced in evidence. Unfortunately, however, the document was on two
separate sheets of paper. The second contained the agreement's form-
closing and the three principals' signatures only. Thus, it was up to Proskauer to establish the relationship between the two pieces of paper. After
cross-examining the chief, or first, defendant, Proskauer confronted the
witness with the second page over which he had superimposed a sheet of
yellow paper in which he had cut slits that disclosed nothing but the signatures. Exhibiting it to the witness, Proskauer later wrote, "I inquired
whether that was his signature. He was clearly amazed at our possession
of the photostatic copy. He stammered and said he did not know whether it
was his signature. The trial justice turned to him with the admonition that
there was no jury, that he was an experienced and educated man, and that
he must know whether it was his signature. He admitted finally that it
was. I offered the entire photostat in evidence." It was accepted subject
to connection. But, meantime, Proskauer noted that the second defendant
was evidencing discomfort: his eyes were bulging and perspiration
streamed from his brow. Permitted to withdraw the first witness, he suddenly called the co-defendant:

> *Proskauer:* Is this your signature?
> *Witness:* Yes.
> *Proskauer:* Did all you three men sign this paper with the first page annexed?
> *Witness:* Yes.
> *Proskauer:* This was the agreement between you?
> *Witness:* Yes.
> *The Court:* Do you mean to say that after you three men signed this paper
> and the testator of these plaintiffs died, you two men purloined those certifi-
> cates?
> *Witness:* I told my co-defendant that I would stand by him till I went on the
> witness stand, but I wouldn't commit perjury for him.

The next morning counsel for the defendants withdrew his defense and
consented to judgment.

The second case, his initial major litigation under the new regimen, hap-
pily placed Proskauer in a role of special counsel for John A. Garver, senior
partner of the prominent law firm of Shearman & Sterling, which represented the National City Bank of New York (NCB). In June, 1930 Garver
wrote Proskauer that his firm was in terrible distress in a Russian ruble
litigation. "Will you come down here and lead a rescue party?" he asked.
Proskauer accepted and soon found himself senior counsel in a highly complex lawsuit involving $50 million deposited in two branches of The Nation-
al City Bank in Czarist Russia. The Russian Communists, upon seizing
control of the state apparatus of Russia, had closed the bank's offices and

confiscated the assets held against deposits. The suits originated when depositors brought their claims against the bank into the New York courts. In the preliminaries the courts had been finding against the bank, but when the case was brought before the State Supreme Court Proskauer was successful in securing a reversal because of errors committed in the trial. But, as he wrote in his *A Segment . . .*, larger issues were involved:

> The problem confronting us was how to handle the entire situation. The strategy indicated was to temporize as far as possible until such time as our government might recognize the Soviet government. Time, political and economic changes were helpful to us. We therefore had to institute what military men call a series of delaying actions, to hold off definitive and conclusive judgments until the action we expected took place. There ensued a long series of trials and settlements until finally, a year later, the courts decided that thereafter the bank was not liable.

In short, Proskauer's cause was saved by the *de facto* recognition of the Soviet Union by President Roosevelt on November 16, 1933, following Foreign Minister Maxim Litvinov's promise that there would be negotiations to settle claims and debts. That these failed of fruition did not alter the new and fortunate status of the bank in this litigation.

American recognition of Russia also inspired another lawsuit involving NCB, Shearman & Sterling, and Proskauer, who served as trial counsel. The Russo-Asiatic Bank had long been conducting business in Czarist Russia. It had opened an account of several million dollars with NCB prior to 1917. After the first Russian revolution and the creation in March of that year of the Lvov-Miliukov provisional government to be succeeded in July by that of Alexander Kerensky, (which was recognized by the United States), it marketed an issue of millions of dollars of its treasury notes in the United States. Within five months, on December 27, the Communists (now in power) abolished the Russo-Asiatic Bank, sequestering its functions, assets, and liabilities and repudiating its treasury notes. At the time there was a balance of $2½ million in the Russo-Asiatic account with NCB.

Upon recognition in 1933, Soviet Russia assigned to the United States its own claim against NCB for this balance. Three years later the United States Government, in turn, demanded payment by the bank. Upon being refused, it commenced suit. By that time the bank held $4½ million of the treasury notes. It countered Washington's claim by maintaining that the Soviet Union had been within its proper rights in seizing Russo-Asiatic and its assets, but had also become obligated for the liabilities of the prior provisional government, including the treasury notes. The United States, suing as the assignee of the U.S.S.R., had assumed these obligations; but the bank asserted that it was entitled to offset the $22 million owed on these treasury notes. The case was tried in the spring of 1950 in the United States District Court before Judge Simon H. Rifkind. Inasmuch as there had been a similar suit brought against the United States Government by the Guaranty Trust Company (in which Rifkind had found against the bank), Shearman & Sterling considered it would be unwise to bring their case, which Proskauer was managing, before the same judge. Proskauer disagreed and, according to him, this colloquy took place between him and Phillip A. Carroll, a Shearman & Sterling partner:

> *Proskauer:* Let me see the record in the Guaranty case and Rifkind's opinion. . . . I think I find certain factual differences, that would seem to me to distinguish that case from ours. I'll try this case with you on one condition, that you stipulate to try it before Rifkind.
> *Carroll:* Are you crazy?
> *Proskauer:* No. Any other judge taking this case would say: 'I'll follow Rifkind.' Rifkind is the only judge to whom I can argue: 'Showing the absolute correctness of your decision in the Guaranty case, we have these differences which turn the balance in our favor.'

Proskauer's risk paid off. Rifkind found for the bank on all counts and the government did not appeal from the decision. Proskauer estimated that he had helped save the bank at least two million dollars.

Proskauer also served Shearman & Sterling in at least three other related ''rescue'' operations in behalf of NCB. One of these, known as the Gallin Case, was of more than passing interest, because not only the bank and its affiliate, the National City Company, were involved, but, indirectly and severally, twenty-five of the bank's directors. The case had to do with a suit, brought by a bank stockholder, Celia Gallin, against all the parties named, on her own behalf and for all other stockholders, charging mismanagement of the corporation's affairs. Initially, it was brought in the New York Supreme Court on February 9, 1933. Such a ''class-action suit'' (then unique but now a commonplace) had fascinating aspects. If the plaintiff won, any monies recovered went to the corporation. The only benefit to the complaining stockholder, if successful, lay in the increase in the assets of the corporation to the extent of the damages recovered from its directors. If unsuccessful, she was to be virtually free of any penalty, costs, or expenses.

This litigation touched off a rash of like suits (including an amended complaint in the Gallin suit) until there were eleven plaintiffs. Typical of such ''class-action suits'' was the fact that, in this particular instance, the complainants held only 278 shares of NCB stock out of a total of more than six million outstanding. The bank and the company were formal defendants, as corporate persons. The magnitude of the litigation was seen in the fact that nineteen of the directors retained separate lawyers, comprising fourteen firms and one individual attorney, while the plaintiffs were represented by no fewer than nine firms and one attorney.

To expedite the proceedings and protect the interests of each litigant, all the suits were combined into one, that of Miss Gallin's amended complaint. And towards the same end both groups of lawyers agreed upon respective counselors to represent each faction in the preparation and conduct of the case. The plaintiffs retained Hays, Podell & Shearman, with David L. Podell as their counsel, and the defendants engaged John W. Davis and Joseph Proskauer as their spokesmen. It was apparent that the proceeds were going to attract wide attention.

The complaints and charges were grave. Attacking the integrity of the directors, the plaintiffs alleged "a variety of wrongful, improper, wanton, reckless and negligent acts resulting in the waste, expenditure, misappropriation, diversion and loss of funds belonging to the Bank and the Company." Damages requested came to more than seventy million dollars. All the lawyers were actively involved every step of the way. It was ironical, as Judge Edward S. Dore noted in his opinion, that the bank was not insolvent, but was rather a going institution with over one billion dollars in deposits, including an increase of $125 million in the first quarter of 1934. After the organization and the preparation of the case, the so-called "task force" took over for the defense—Porter R. Chandler for the Davis firm, J. Alvin Van Bergh for Proskauer, Rose & Paskus, with Walter F. Pease, of Shearman & Sterling, as coordinator of their efforts. Davis, Proskauer and various partners of the other firms for the defendants worked long and hard, writing briefs and holding conferences.

The trial, which lasted from March 22 until May 23, 1934, was held before Judge Dore in Manhattan without a jury. Proskauer's opening statement for the defense, recorded by Walter K. Earle, was regarded as a model of clarity and completeness. The result was a victory for the defense. There was no appeal. Judge Dore believed, however, that the high salaries, bonuses, and personal loans in which the bank's management had engaged warranted further examination, and he appointed a referee to hear evidence and report back to the court. While the directors had been exonerated, the referee found that the profit-sharing in which the bank's leading officers had participated had been devised by those who were to be directly benefited, and, therefore, a judgment was ordered against them. The court concurred. Wrote Proskauer in *A Segment. . . .*, "I recall with some amusement the comments of Mr. Davis that it was hard to realize we were congratulating ourselves on a judgment of $1,800,000 against our clients, instead of one for the seventy-odd millions originally demanded."

Shortly after their successful defense in the Gallin case, Davis and Proskauer again combined their talents to assist Shearman & Sterling and other firms in *O'Connor* v. *Bankers Trust Company,* a suit brought by the United States Comptroller of the Currency. Popularly known as the "Harriman Bank Case," it had risen out of the troubles of the Harriman National Bank & Trust Company in the early years of Roosevelt's New Deal. The bank had closed during the "Bank Holiday" of March 5-13, 1933 and, failing to reopen, had gone into receivership. Inasmuch as the bank was one of the twenty-one-member national banks of the New York Clearing House Association, the government charged that the other twenty were obligated to guarantee the deposits of its defunct member under terms of an agreement between the New York Clearing House Committee and the president of the Harriman bank. The government further held that, if the committee had not had such authority, the member banks individually should be held liable for breach of warranty of authority. As a result of such suits, the president of the Harriman bank and its receiver, and eleven other banks (including NCB) settled because of special circumstances, but the trial of the remaining nine proceeded.

The array of counsel on both sides was dazzling. Proskauer was called in for the defense by Shearman & Sterling to assist John W. Davis and representatives of the firms of Root, Clark & Buckner, and Curtis, Frederick & Belknap. On June 29, 1936 Justice Bernard L. Shientag handed down his decision against the plaintiffs, the government among them. The case went to the Appellate Division, which upheld Shientag, and finally to the State Court of Appeals. Here the defendant banks were represented jointly by Proskauer, Davis, B. M. Webster, Jr., Robert N. West, and others. Davis and Proskauer were the advocates before the court, while Webster and West prepared the cases and drew up the briefs. Again Davis and Proskauer were victorious, the judgment being affirmed without opinion on July 7, 1938.

These vindications of the banks did not preclude shareholders from bringing "class-action suits", and one was started against NCB (which had settled with the government) by three stockholders who owned thirty-three shares, but began suit on behalf of all the stockholders in 1940. They sued the directors, charging that they had "acted wrongly and recklessly and were personally liable to the bank" (and therefore to themselves, the plaintiffs, as stockholders) because they had settled the claims of the comptroller for $725,000. They sought to compel the bank's directors to reimburse the bank for that sum. Acting as the sole leader of all the defendants before the court, and associated with Shearman & Sterling's Robert O. West, Proskauer again successfully defended the bank and its directors. On June 5, 1940, in the Supreme Court, Judge Carroll G. Walter found the plaintiff's contentions "conclusively disproved by the evidence" and, hence, exonerated the defendants of wrongdoing.

In his *Reminiscences* Proskauer observed that "John Davis and I were joint counsel there. . . . He used always to say: 'I'm the pulling out and you're the bludgeoning.' And we were a good combination together. I was devoted to him; he was a great lawyer, a most lovable man, and the finest colleague one could have." Needless to say, Proskauer delighted in these experiences, for he was performing before a gallery of his peers as well as before some of the country's outstanding jurists. Therefore, he could frankly say, "I got great satisfaction out of my work as a judge, but I got rapture out of my career as an advocate."

In these earlier decades, when Proskauer had returned to active practice, the representatives of both old and new companies sought out his services. A long list of his clients included, among many others, American Metal Company, Bethlehem Steel Company, Cities Service Company, Loews, Inc., Radio Corporation of America (RKO), Sinclair Oil Company, the Texas Company, Universal Pictures, and Union Carbide and Carbon Company.

In his *A Segment*... and in interviews subsequently held with him, Proskauer singled out the Warner Brothers litigation as one of his favorite cases. The first of these, *Koplar* v. *Warner Brothers Pictures,* which was inspired in 1932 by a Senate committee investigation into alleged fraudulent practices of great corporations, was brought for the purpose of challenging the large compensation and bonuses given to the three principal executives of the Warner company, Harry, Jack, and Albert Warner. A highly favorable six-year contract had followed a series of coups the Warners had engineered, including the absorption of the large chain of Stanley Theaters and their leadership in the development of motion picture films with sound. A stockholder's suit, begun by a man named Koplar, sought to overturn this contract under which each of the Warners was to receive an annual salary of $500,000 as well as 90,000 shares of the company's stock. The inauguration of the suit precipitated a bitter but unsuccessful proxy fight which sought to upset the contract and to elect new directors to investigate charges of misconduct and mismanagement.

While this was unfolding, a second stockholder's suit was commenced over the same set of facts. The firm of Davis, Polk, Wardwell, Gardiner & Reed was retained to check into the propriety of the corporation's settlement with the Warners and, after a full investigation, this suit was settled out of court in 1935. Approved by the stockholders, it provided for the return of 100,000 shares of stock to the company, the *quid pro quo* being the release of any claim against the brothers. This failed to satisfy Koplar. He continued his claim, maintaining that the second settlement was not binding upon him and that the market value of the returned shares was but a fraction of their earlier value, when issued to the Warners.

Proskauer defended the Warners in the Koplar case. By developing the history of the company, he established that its success and survival in the Great Depression had been the result of the abilities, skill, and efforts of the brothers themselves. The defense further showed that the Stanley Theaters stockholders had been the ones who insisted upon the long-term contract, before agreeing to the absorption of their company by the Warners. The court agreed, finding that "under all the circumstances of this case the payment to the brothers of $10,000 per week and 90,000 shares of common stock did not constitute a waste of corporate assets. In view of the character of the personal services and of the financial assis- ance, past and future, rendered by the brothers, the payment was not ex- cessive and did not amount to waste."

The anticlimax to the Warner litigation occurred in 1940, when the U.S. Department of Justice prosecuted several film companies, including Warner, for violation of the Sherman Anti-Trust Law, charging them with engaging in both the production and the exhibition of their pictures in their own theaters, which thus became a guaranteed outlet. The case was tem- porarily terminated by a consent decree, and it was not reopened until the end of three years. The defendants won, but they were directed to dispose of all their theaters in which they owned less than 95 percent. This affected Warner Brothers hardly at all—but it did seriously harm their competitors, notably Paramount Pictures Corporation and RKO. The de- fendants were also to stop certain practices in the industry that aimed at eliminating competition.

In this long litigation, which saw appeals by both sides and a directed return from the United States Court of Appeals of the suit to the district court for a fresh examination of whether theater ownership had actually been used to violate the Sherman act, the immediate outcome was partial victory and partial defeat. The government was successful in appealing against licensing and for the sale of feature films to individual theaters by compulsory competitive bidding; but it lost on its appeal for the total sep- aration of film producers from the ownership of any theaters as being in restraint of competition. Ultimately, when the entire case came back for retrial, both Paramount and RKO entered into consent decrees which agreed to the separations. The other defendants, the Warners included, were ordered to do so after the retrial.

The government's victory turned out to be costly and damaging beyond anticipation. Among the many factors that later depressed the movie industry and caused so many theaters to close down, was without doubt this loss to the exhibitors of the financial resources and firm paternal sup- port of the large movie studios. This was a curious example of the misuse of the antitrust laws by the federal government. It demonstrated that big- ness in corporate organizations *per se* was no evil and that by threatening and obtaining consent decrees the United States Department of Justice could stifle growth in an industry where the enterprise of bold innovators performed important functions.

When Judge Proskauer wrote his *A Segment...*, he appropriately entitled the chapter dealing with his career at the bar, "The Art of the Trial Lawyer," for he had ranged widely. He successfully defended the Public National Bank, when it was charged with the illegal conversion of a large block of stock pledged as a security for a loan by Richard Whitney, president of the New York Stock Exchange. Whitney, later convicted and sent to Sing Sing Prison as a proved embezzler, was in this particular instance using stock for his loan belonging to an estate. The courts found for the bank, Proskauer's client, stating that the bank had accepted the securities in good faith for the estate's executors had endorsed them over in blank to Whitney. Proskauer also played a part in the sensational Ivar Krueger swindles. The Swedish promoter, through the companies he controlled and created, Krueger & Toll and the International Match Company, had involved in his machinations the Boston investment firm of Lee, Higginson & Company. When the Krueger house of cards collapsed, with losses running into the hundreds of millions of dollars for American investors, Lee, Higginson, among others, was sued as being party to the frauds. Proskauer represented the Boston firm and was able to prove its freedom of guilt; it had been as much the dupe and victim of Krueger as had all the other American banking firms caught in his toils.

Variety lent spice to Proskauer's legal life. He once unsuccessfully represented City Magistrate Francis X. McQuade who, in an obscure quarrel over its ownership, had sued Horace Stoneham, president of the New York Giants Baseball Club. He also represented, this time successfully, Mrs. Gertrude Vanderbilt Whitney, in the sensational family quarrel over the custody of her niece, Gloria Morgan Vanderbilt. Mrs. Whitney had charged Gloria's mother, Mrs. Gloria Laura Morgan Vanderbilt, with being an unfit parent and had sought permanent legal care of the girl. Mrs. Whitney had lost the first round in the lower courts and an appeal was pending. Her attorney, Frank D. Crocker, invited Proskauer to argue the appeal. Proskauer consented under the stipulation that Mrs. Whitney accept his terms in full; namely, that Mrs. Whitney give him permission to fish at all times for trout in the waters of Bog Stream which ran through her property! This is the way he told the story in *A Segment* . . .:

> Trout fishing was always one of my passions, and I would travel many miles in order to whip a good trout stream. Such a one was Bog Stream, located in the preserves of the Whitney family in the Adirondacks. For years I had been permitted entry, but shortly after I came off the bench this permission was revoked. I was disconsolate. Then one day my friend Frank Crocker, counsel for the Whitney family, asked me to argue this appeal for Mrs. Whitney. I told him I would argue it only if she met my terms in full. He stared at me in some astonishment. Unfortunately, I told him gravely, he was just thinking of money. What then was I thinking of? He demanded. Trout! I said. If I could fish Bog Stream, I would argue that appeal and he could fix the fee. . . . I have since been fishing Bog Stream.

Criminal practice held no attractions for Joseph Proskauer. He mentioned in his book only two instances of such retainers, in one of which he defended Henry A. Kahler, chairman of the board of the New York Title Company, after indictment for using improper advertising. A co-defendant, Frederick Fuller, president of the company, was defended by another outstanding lawyer, former Governor Nathan L. Miller. After a trial of more than two weeks the defendants were acquitted in a verdict that was rendered in the early hours of the morning. Proskauer resolved that thereafter "the strain of defending men of repute in criminal causes ought to be put on younger men."

His second reference to a criminal case in which he appeared consisted of a tale he told to illustrate one of the pitfalls inherent in cross-examination: in this instance, by asking one question too many. Proskauer and another attorney were defending two lawyers who had been indicted for conspiring with an assistant attorney to obstruct justice. The conspiracy had to do with an alleged bigamy and the complainant was a woman who had been gingerly cross-examined by Proskauer who was satisfied that he had laid the basis in the mind of the jury that the lady might have had a mercenary motive. Not so his colleague who, dissatisfied with Proskauer's cross-examination, began an inquiry into what had happened at various times and on various occasions. Finally, recalled Proskauer, he put the question: "Where were you on such and such a night?" The witness replied promptly and with devastating effect on the case: "I was in Westchester, in an automobile, with your client. He had asked me to go out with him and try to find a certain witness. Instead, he drove the car to a dark spot on a lonely road and insulted me." Later, Proskauer observed that he had spent a good part of his life in the courtroom, refusing to ask that final question which his less experienced juniors always urged upon him.

Proskauer, who could be Olympian, could also nod like Jove. Younger lawyers thronged the court when he was conducting a case. One of them recalled the following incident. As counsel in a bank case before Judge McCook, he was doing his usually impressive job. At one point he slipped, however, and engaged in an argument with the judge on the admissability of a certain piece of evidence. When McCook referred to another case, Proskauer replied, "Yes, I remember. We spanked you on that." McCook looked down on him and retorted: "Right now, you are before me as a lawyer and I am sitting as a judge, and the question of who is going to spank whom is going to change its character."

Proskauer knew all the tricks of the art, or craft, of handling a witness. Once he was trying a case before Justice Thomas F. Murphy, and this time he had on the stand a favorable witness. In order to impress the jury, Proskauer made the most of his opportunity by asking him to repeat again and again the same answer to the same question. Justice Murphy, becoming restive at the excessive delay, protested. Rejoined Proskauer: "I am having trouble hearing this witness." "Come now," said the Judge, "there is nothing the matter with your hearing. You can hear the grass growing, counselor. Please proceed."

Karl N. Llewellyn, formerly a professor of law in the Columbia Law

School and later in the Chicago Law School, also went to school to Proskauer. In his book, *The Common Law Tradition: Deciding Appeals* (1960),
he wrote admiringly of Proskauer's techniques in appeal proceedings,
listing him among "articulate artists" in the courtroom, along with John
W. Davis and Charles Evans Hughes. Llewellyn gave an example of Proskauer's handling of a very difficult case, on appeal, which had to do with
the harsh New York usury law. Proskauer was for the defense. The facts
seemed to indicate a clear instance of usury, but it was complicated by the
lender's insistance that the borrower incorporate before receiving the loan,
because a business corporation could not plead usury. The case ran its
course in the lower court, security was voided, and the court looked
through the "form" of incorporation in order to penalize the illicit
"evasion." Proskauer, the new counsel, appeared for the lender-"usurer"
in the final appeal before the Court of Appeals, and Llewellyn recorded that
he opened up an entirely novel and contrary line of argument:

> [He] persuaded the court to look rather at the loan market when times were
> bad and at businesses which needed rehabilitation but would be barred from
> credit by a 6 percent limit on return; reason was therefore clear, other end to;
> the legislature had carefully, almost explicitly, made the corporate device
> available for the very purpose of letting a businessman meet the business cost
> of a business loan for a prospective business profit.

Proskauer's brothers at the bar admired his skills in the courtroom, but
they also chose him to lead them in their professional associations. He was
elected vice-president of the New York County Lawyers' Association in
1943 and its president in 1947 and 1948. Earlier, in 1930, he had been
named vice-president of the Association of the Bar of the City of New York.
He felt such roles were important, for, in effect, they helped maintain the
vitality and self-discipline of the profession. As he wrote in *A Segment . . .,*

> The bar associations through grievance committees are an arm of the courts
> to cooperate in holding lawyers to the high and exacting standards of our call-
> ing. Disciplinary proceedings against lawyers are not numerous, but are
> sufficient to keep practitioners keenly alive to the obligations of trust and con-
> fidence to client and court.

PROSKAUER AND
THE JEWISH COMMUNITY

It took Proskauer almost two decades before he was able and ready to take on one of the obligations to which German Jews like himself committed themselves; this was active participation in philanthropic endeavor. The motives were clear enough. The interest in and the care of the unfortunate among themselves—side by side with the support of the synagogue—had always been one of the enduring bonds that had held together Jewish communal life through so many centuries in the Diaspora. To the "assimilated" German Jews the success of such activities was only further proof that they were on the right track: that they "could take care of their own": that they could smooth the processes of adjustment for the newcomers and those who fell by the wayside: that therefore a minority group was capable of successful adjustment to the mores of the dominant culture.

In consequence, German Jews like Proskauer worked hard at their charitable organization societies. Again, they sought to prove something: that those they founded and maintained were to be as good as those existing in the non-Jewish world: in the professional social work practices they employed, in the cultural programs for the young in settlement houses and the Young Men's Hebrew Association (YMHA), in the hospitals that were erected and the clinics and research laboratories they kept up so munificiently.

And for another two decades, Proskauer, in his philanthropic involvements, with such a rationale, followed this course. That side by side with it there existed another rationale—the one that guides the thinking and activities of many constituting the great majority of the Jews in the United States, those who were of East European origin—he only dimly understood.

The fact is, a minority in the United States can live apart from the dominant culture and both lead a full life and be American. In the case of the Jews, this was occurring in two ways. In the first, social cohesiveness could be based wholly on religious separation: religion not only as a ritual and a liturgy but also as a way of life. This required the creation of religious communities, as a subculture, right in the midst of the regnant one: where the devout lived together, maintained their own food markets and processors, supported and sent their children to their own separate schools, frequently worked together in their own industries. There always had been such religious communities in the United States—apart, sometimes at war with the greater society—the Mormons, the Amish, the Shakers, the Dunkers, come to mind.

Among Proskauer's co-religionists, there were the Chassidic Jews, who had been establishing such settlements throughout New York City and elsewhere in other urban centers. They were relatively few in number: however, their aspirations and activities—largely as these centered in their talmud torahs and Yeshivas—had the encouragement of many other Jews who were not only Orthodox but also Conservative in their rituals, who were native-born American Jews as well as the newly-arrived from East Europe.

Religious belief apart, there was a second way for the maintenance of the Jewish identity: and this was in the belief in or sympathy with the ideas of Zionism. Taking all its aspects together, Zionism held that the Jews were more than a people, the "people of the Book and the Law": they were a nation, always spiritually in being in the almost two milleniums when they lived in the Diaspora: held together by their Book, their Law, their religious leaders and scholars; by their common tragic fate of segregation, pillage, and murder; and their hope that they were fated to become once more a physical nation as they had been under the kings of Israel. Modern-day Zionism, after Theodor Herzl, therefore was more than messianic: it was secular and political in its conception and drive: and its belief that the Jews could establish—and it had to be in Palestine—a national homeland, in which all Jews could have pride did not vitiate their allegiance to the lands of their birth and residence.

Another idea about Zionism. Many became Zionists because of their feeling that the root problem of Jewishness—and that was anti-Semitism—was hopeless of solution without the achievement of full equality for Jews wherever they lived. A long step in that direction was the attainment of a national physical existence. By 1940, such a homeland—more and more Jews saw, Zionists or not—had to be in Palestine. It is important to our story of the life and education of Joseph Proskauer to understand that he, a German Jew, fully "assimilated" into the American mores, as he believed, a non-Zionist as well, came around to this position in the 1940s: and, as a consequence, was recognized as one of the important builders of the State of Israel.

Beginning in 1920 Proskauer assumed positions of leadership in many Jewish philanthropic organizations and, like all the things he undertook, he worked hard and usefully in them. The first was his acceptance of the vice-presidency of the Jewish Board of Guardians, a society having to do with juvenile delinquents, including the Hawthorne School, a correctional institution. In 1926 he became president of the YMHA. As such he successfully led a campaign for funds to erect for it a new building, handsome and functional. Both of these associations suited his interests, the latter in particular, for it has long played a vital role in the cultural life of New York City, serving as a poetry center, a leader in the development of the ballet, and an experimental theater.

In 1931, in the midst of the Great Depression and soon after he had returned to private practice, Proskauer assumed the presidency of the Federation for the Support of Jewish Philanthropic Societies, an organization which was, in effect, a "community chest" for raising funds for the support of nearly one hundred Jewish hospitals, homes, shelters, family-welfare centers and other social-service bodies. Proskauer, in *A Segment* . . ., described its role as a "model for the development of other philanthropic institutions." Many of its constituent societies were leaders in pioneer social work against which the performance of other public welfare programs could be measured. Proskauer's plea for the expansion of insurance programs, with public authority playing its part, was well taken and a good deal of modern development in the social services followed this direction. But in time public funding of such sophisticated welfare activities finally returned to private philanthropy. Proskauer and his colleagues had become too sanguine in assuming otherwise. Proskauer seems to have had a sense of this flow of events, despite his asseverations to the contrary, for in the 1930s and 1940s he gave more and more of his extra time to the American Jewish Committee.

The American Jewish Committee (AJC), founded in 1906 by a small group of well-to-do German Jews, had its immediate impetus in the atrocities visited on hundreds of Jewish communities in Russia, under the semi-official approval of the so-called Black Hundreds. The purpose of the AJC was "to prevent infringement of the civil and religious rights of Jews and to alleviate the consequences of persecution." The Committee did not claim to be a representative body, however. Members were elected by self-constituted district councils and it functioned through an Executive Committee of thirteen persons. Its work was that of a pressure group, not by campaigns of propaganda or public outcrys, but, rather, by efforts to exert influence in approriate places—for many of its members were influential people, well-known Reform rabbis, distinguished lawyers and judges, great bankers and merchants. Their avowed aim was to protest against the persecutions of Jews, particularly abroad, and to do something about discriminatory practices. In 1951 (after the Committee had widened its scope and became staffed with a permanent personnel), its then President Jacob Blaustein described its raison d'être to President Harry S. Truman: "Founded by a group of distinguished American Jewish leaders in 1906, the Committee is the oldest organization devoted to combatting bigotry, protecting the civil and religious rights of Jews, and advancing the cause of human rights throughout the world."

In its first twenty years of operation, the work of the AJC was actually the voice of its two presidents, both impressive men. The first was Judge Mayer Sulzberger of Philadelphia, a legal historian, who led it from 1906 to 1912. The second was Louis Marshall of New York, a highly regarded constitutional lawyer. He served from 1912 to 1929. In its inner circles were such well-known Jews as Rabbis Cyrus Adler and Judah L. Magnes,

Jacob H. Schiff and Felix Warburg, bankers, Adolph Lewisohn, indus-
trialist, and Julius Rosewald, merchant. Joseph Proskauer, who was
named to the select group in 1930 from New York, soon became a hard
worker and, as a result, was assigned to membership on the Committee's
two most prestigious groups, the Policy Committee and the Executive
Committee.

The Committee completed two characteristic projects during these years
that pointed up its limited objectives and methods. Operating on the assumption that a diplomatic affront to the Russian Government would force
it to curb "official" anti-Semitism, the Committee succeeded in obtaining
the consent of Congress in 1911 to abrogate the United States treaty of
commerce and navigation with that country. This because the Russians,
by refusing to give visas for travel in their country to foreign Jews, including Americans, was discriminating "on the ground of race or religion."
The second was the bringing to heel of Henry Ford, in his vicious anti-
Semitic campaign in the 1920s, at the very time when the members of the
AJC and all German Jews were under the impression that their plan of
proper assimilation into American society was working. A wave of isola-
tionism and nativism was also sweeping over the country, shaking the high
hopes of German Jews that, in the United States at any rate, anti-Semitism
was not to be their lot.

The reasons for these nativist manifestations were many. One was the
letdown after the failures of the Wilsonian moralistic diplomacy; others
were the severe postwar economic depression of 1920-1921, the "Red
Scare" with the survival of Communism in Russia, and the hostility of rural
toward urban America. The devices used to bludgeon America into com-
pliance were frightening. The Ku Klux Klan, with its hooded demonstra-
tions against and attacks on all "outsiders"—Negroes, Catholics, Jews,
immigrants, and all foreign-born—was revived and met with signal political successes in both the South and Middle West. There was a wide
circulation of hate literature in which many "patriotic" societies participated. Highly reputable universities, particularly their medical schools,
frankly admitted the establishment of quotas for admission, usually directed against Jews. "Outsiders," chiefly Jews, were finding entrance into
the professions and employment in corporations at middle-management
levels virtually closed to them.

Henry Ford, backed by his great financial power and magical name, used
his influence for the wide dissemination of the spurious *Protocols of the
Elders of Zion,* a document alleging the creation of an international Jewish
conspiracy which had been forged by Russian Czarists before World War I.
It had been translated into many languages. In the United States it was
seized upon by all sorts of agencies in their campaigns for immigration
restriction and the curbing of radicalism.

In his newspaper, the Dearborn *Independent,* Henry Ford on May, 1920 launched a wide attack on "The International Jew," printing the *Protocols* to "prove" that Jews controlled international business, finance, and public information media, and were allied with the Communists to destroy capitalism. The AJC, instead of mounting an organized campaign and using all the weapons of retaliation (for example, it refused to support a boycott against Ford products), stuck to its customary methods of polite rejoinder and private negotiation. The plan succeeded.

In 1927 Henry Ford admitted the error of his ways and in a letter to Louis Marshall publicly apologized and retracted his anti-Semitic statements. This was of course a victory for the AJC, but its effectiveness had been seriously impaired. Certainly, its leadership of American Jewry no longer remained unquestioned—largely because of the softness of its reply to anti-Semites and its equivocal attitude toward Zionism and Palestine.

Modern-day Zionism, the return of Jews to a national homeland, as has been stated, was the creation of the Hungarian-born journalist, Theodor Herzl, who after reporting the Dreyfus affair for a Viennese newspaper, in 1896, wrote his famous pamphlet, *The Jewish State*. In it he expounded the idea, entirely from a secular point of view, of the creation of a Jewish autonomous political state as the solution of the "Jewish question." The notion took fire at once and the first World Zionist Congress, meeting in Basel the next year, proclaimed as the aim of Zionism the establishment of such a homeland, "secured by public law." It was agreed that the place should be Palestine. Soon a world-wide organization sprang up, consisting of national federations with local societies. Herzl became the secretary of the Congress, its governing body, whose agitation gave Zionism wide currency, notably among East European Jews and other immigrants in the United States. Herzl lived until 1904. A year later the Congress, after a bitter wrangle, the majority again declared that a Jewish state should and could be established only in Palestine. The debate arose over an offer by the British Government of a Jewish homeland in its colony of Uganda in East Africa. The upholders of this minority position, the so-called Territorialists, were led by the novelist Israel Zangwell who felt that any refuge for persecuted Jews was an immediate necessity. They were also appalled by the Russian outrages, as had been the founders of the AJC, and thereupon withdrew from the Zionist movement. The remainder of the Congress and the world federation was afterwards supported largely by American Zionists who were by no means united and, like all such agitational and didactic movements, soon splintered off into various factions. A few Jews of German origin were attracted to Zionism. Some of them were members of the AJC. Later, Supreme Court Justice Louis D. Brandeis was to be their American spokesman.

With the outbreak of World War I (and the idealist motives of national determination for oppressed minorities Woodrow Wilson associated with it), Zionists put their hopes in an Allied victory. Now its leader became the

distinguished British Jewish chemist, Chaim Weizmann, with the organization's headquarters in London. This concatenation of circumstances
and the darkest days of the Allied cause prompted A. J. Balfour, the British
Foreign Secretary, to write a letter to Lord Rothschild which declared the
British Government's "sympathy with Jewish Zionist aspirations." He
also named Palestine as a proper homeland for those Jews who wished to
settle there. The so-called Balfour Declaration's operative statement ran
as follows:

> H. M. Government view with favour the establishment in Palestine of a
> national home for the Jewish people and will use their best endeavours to
> facilitate the achievement of this object, it being clearly understood that noth-
> ing shall be done which may prejudice the civil and religious rights of exist-
> ing non-Jewish communities in Palestine, or the rights and political status
> enjoyed by Jews in any other country.

The declaration was imprecise, for it incorporated two pledges, one to the
Arabs and the other to the Jews. But, in the case of the Jews, Balfour was
very clear (and here he had the concurrence of his Prime Minister Lloyd
George), for when he was asked in February, 1918 to clarify his own thinking, he said: "Both the Prime Minister and myself have been influenced
by a desire to give the Jews their rightful place in the world; a great nation
without a home is not right. My personal hope is that all the Jews will
make good in Palestine and eventually found a Jewish State." In 1921
Balfour and Lloyd George went even further: both agreed that the declaration was designed to give the Jews an opportunity to become a majority in
an eventual Jewish state.

In 1922 the Balfour Declaration was written verbatim into the mandate
given by the League of Nations to Great Britain: the Mandatory Power was
to govern Palestine, Jews were to have the right of immigration into it and
access to the land, as well as the right of autonomous development in their
settlements. Article II of the mandate made Great Britain responsible for
placing the country under such "political, administrative and economic
conditions as will secure the establishment of the Jewish National Home
. . . and the development of self-governing institutions." Thus, by a couple
of strokes, the once inchoate yearnings of the Zionists and Jews everywhere—those, at any rate, who had not been lulled into inactivity by hopes
of assimilation—had now become hard, political reality.

And the Balfour Declaration and its implementation drove a deep wedge
into the American Jewish community. American Zionism, and what in
effect grew to be its political organ of expression, the American Jewish
Congress, founded in 1922, became a powerful force. Lined up against it,
in opposition to the idea of a national homeland in Palestine, were Reform
rabbis generally and their association, the Union of American Hebrew Congregations. To Reform Judaism in the United States, "America is our
Palestine, Washington our Jerusalem." Also in opposition as it had been

since its founding, was AJC. In a statement written by Louis Marshall and approved by the Committee's membership in April, 1918, the Balfour Declaration was endorsed, with reservations. The Committee wrote its own definition of a "Jewish Homeland." It was to be a cultural and religious center, rather than a political state, and it was to strive to dissipate the suspicion in the non-Jewish world that acceptance of the idea of "homeland" meant the dilution of loyalty by Jews to the lands of their birth or adoption. It was, in short, a declaration once again in the belief and efficacy of assimilation. As Marshall described it:

> The Committee regards it as axiomatic that the Jews of the United States have here established a permanent home for themselves and their children, have acquired the rights and assume the correlative duties of American citizenship, and recognize their unqualified allegiance to this country, which they love and cherish and of whose people they constitute an integral part.
>
> This Committee, however, is not unmindful that there are Jews everywhere who, moved by traditional sentiment, yearn for a home in the Holy Land for the Jewish people. This hope, nurtured for centuries, has our wholehearted sympathy. We recognize, however, that but a part of the Jewish people would take up their domicile in Palestine. The greater number will continue to live in the lands of whose citizenship they now form a component part, where they enjoy full civil and religious liberty, and where, as loyal and patriotic citizens, they will maintain and develop the principles and institutions of Judaism. When, therefore, the British Government recently made the declaration the announcement was received by this Committee with profound appreciation. . . .
>
> The opportunity will be welcomed by this Committee to aid in the realization of the British Declaration, under such protectorate or suzerainty as the Peace Congress may determine, and, to that end, to cooperate with those who, attracted by religious or historic association, shall seek to establish in Palestine a center for Judaism, for the stimulation of our faith, for the pursuit and development of literature, science and art in a Jewish environment, and for the rehabilitation of the land.

There matters stood, with a kind of wary truce existing, in the relations between Zionists and non-Zionists. One step toward cooperation was taken in 1929 by the former in the establishment of the "Jewish National Home." This was the creation of the so-called Jewish Agency, designed to encourage the economic development of the region, to which all Jews, of whatever political affiliation, were invited to join. Louis Marshall helped in its formation and he sat on its first executive.

Joseph Proskauer, as a German Jew and a member of a Reform congregation, concurred in the decision of the AJC about Palestine, including the Jewish National Home. As for a Jewish political state, however, he said he would have no part of it, adding this special personal reason for his decision: two-thirds of Palestine's inhabitants were Arab. He could see no way of reconciling the different views and aspirations of two hostile religious and ethnic groups in the same land.

The 1930s were agonizing years for all Jews and, hence, it is doubtful that the AJC rose to its opportunities. Jews were living under a mounting terror in Germany. They were being harassed, their businesses closed, educational and employment opportunities denied them, and there was Nazi talk of mass extermination. Together, these compelled decisions by those anxious for their welfare and, in fact, their survival. One could follow the road of appeasement of Hitler's Germany, as the British and French governments did, or one could cry alarm, as did Zionists, socialists, and trade unionists in the free world. To add to the anxiety, there was the tightening up by the British in Palestine of restrictions on the development of their national home and the entry of Jewish immigrants. American Zionists and the American Jewish Congress called for bold measures and economic pressures, including boycotts, on Germany. The AJC, pleaded for nonintervention, restraint, and private negotiations on the ground that not only the safety of German Jews would be endangered, but also their own security in the United States.

A positive position had to be taken. The hand of the AJC was forced, when in 1937 a British Royal Commission, headed by Lord Peel, proposed partition of Palestine and the immediate creation of two states, one Jewish and the other Arab. The Committee now took a public stand, opposing a Jewish state. Discussions were entered into with American Zionists, but to no avail. In fact, joint action was becoming increasingly difficult with the introduction of side issues. The AJC insisted that all the talk of Jewish nationalism cast further doubt on the loyalty of American Jews to the United States and, according to its spokesmen, the Committee could never accept "abandoning our fundamental point of view—that we are Americans of Jewish faith, of American nationality, and that we can never permit anything that threatens to affect this status." Executive Secretary Morris D. Waldman, declaring that he personally raised no objection to an independent Jewish nation in Palestine, sought to shift the debate to something else: "We do reject Jewish nationalism, which means the organization of the scattered Jewry of the world into an international political unity or entity, and we object to the existence of the World Jewish Congress as the parliament of such an international political Jewry."

In these years Joseph Proskauer was a die-hard. He had no truck with the Zionists. Waldman, in his *Nor By Power* (1953), quoted Proskauer as saying,

> I am satisfied that from every point of view of safety for Jews in America there has got to be an open, vocal Jewish dissent from nationalism and political Zionism: and if the American Jewish Committee doesn't make itself the mouthpiece of this public position, some other organization will have to.

There was a brief let-up to the public bickering, when Nahum Goldmann, president of the World Jewish Congress, disavowed any intention to set up "a Jewish nation in the Diaspora, with political allegiance to any international Jewish authority." There were other quarrels, also, but now of little significance, except to reveal another facet of Proskauer's character—his hubris which would not permit him to suffer fools gladly and could turn him into a highly contentious man, when his foe refused to yield. On one point, in his quarrel with the Zionists, he would not give way: that was his opposition to the idea of a central authority that would speak for the Jews of the America and of the world.

As late as 1961, when he was dictating his *Reminiscences,* Proskauer was still angry at the attempt of the Zionists to "create a Jewish enclave either in America or in the world." And when he was president of the AJC from 1943 to 1949, he fought tooth and nail the attempt by American Zionist leaders, notably Rabbi Stephen S. Wise and Rabbi Abba Hillel Silver, to set up an American Jewish Assembly—to drown out his opposition by force of numbers. Proskauer was right. The influence of Jews in the United States and in the world generally, as well as the United States Government, vis à vis Palestine, would have been seriously compromised, had the whole of American Jewry become the tool of the Zionists. It is to Proskauer's credit that he did not turn into a vendettist. At the same time that he was carrying on this fight, he was working, as the spokesman of AJC, to include in the charter of the United Nations a "Declaration of Human Rights." His great abilities as a negotiator and parliamentarian attracted wide attention and was watched and applauded by the Department of State. It is not too much to say that, when the United States came to make its fateful decision about Palestine in 1947-1948, the fact that Proskauer and the AJC, just because they were non-Zionists and had supported the partition of Palestine but also the political recognition of the State of Israel, played a key role. Proskauer, by his earlier accomplishments in San Francisco, had established his *bona fides.*

In 1943 Proskauer had refused to accept the presidency of the AJC until it endorsed a statement of principles which correctly echoed his thinking. This "Statement of Views," which was adopted, did not pledge support to the establishment of a Jewish state. It reiterated the well-known position of the Committee that American Jews were American nationals and that there could be "no political identification of Jews outside of Palestine with whatever government may there be instituted." It called for Jewish-Arab collaboration and, at the end of the war, the creation of an international trusteeship in Palestine, to be responsible to the United Nations.

However, Proskauer was not content to let matters rest in this uncertain and unstable state. He was aware of the deep hostilities within the American Jewish community he had helped to create and he saw that the rehabilitation and reordering of the Committee was imperative if it was to play a role in the portentous events forecast by an Allied victory. With characteristic energy he moved swiftly. In 1944 the whole nature of the AJC was changed. It became a national membership organization whose members could form themselves into local chapters (thirty-five appeared almost immediately) and a positive program was pushed. The major struggle was to be against anti-Semitism: "... the problems of world Jewry cannot be solved by any single political panacea, but by concentrated activity toward the attainment of a secure place for Jews in all countries of the globe."

Proskauer's hand was writ large in all the new activities on which the Committee embarked. It obtained a new executive director, John Slawson, to replace the retired Waldman. With the title of executive vice-president, Slawson and Proskauer worked closely together on improving the image of the organization and launching the many fresh enterprises that kept its name in the forefront of the thinking and planning, going on about the postwar world. Proskauer did not stint of his time and energies. He continued as president of the Committee from 1943 to 1949 and, as he wrote in *A Segment...*,

> I found myself involved in endless delicate negotiations with governments and government officials of many countries, including our own; with unstinted endeavors to rescue European Jews from the expanding horror which beset them and to find for them places of refuge; to consider the explosive problems that arose in Palestine and from the activities of certain extreme Zionist groups; and to combat the creeping menace of new forms of anti-Semitism which the example of Hitler seemed to have brought to our own America.

His work, including his public statements, his appearances before legislative committees and governmental agencies, and his conferences in Washington, was facilitated and given sharp focus by that done under Slawson's direction. A Committee on Peace Problems and a Department of Scientific Research were established, the latter designed to combat anti-Semitism through the utilization of the social sciences. A Public Education and Information Department embarked on programs of work with organized labor, youth organizations, and veterans to fight bigotry, new offices were opened in Washington and London, and a publication, *The Committee Reporter,* was launched.

The action that flowed out of this new life was impressive. Four representatives of the committees toured displaced persons camps in Germany and Jewish experts were attached to the United Nations Relief and Rehabilitation Administration. Judge Simon H. Rifkind, a Jew, was appointed an adviser to the United States commander of the American Zone in Germany. Keenly aware of the cruel predicament of these stateless refugees in the camps, the Committee, both as an organization and through personal representations to President Truman and Secretary of State James Byrnes, not only urged that immigration into Palestine be eased, but also into the United States. With the latter President Truman concurred. At the same time there were other activities, all sponsored by the Committee. A conference on Jewish adjustment in America was opened and a magazine, *Commentary,* was founded, which quickly became an outstanding journal of opinion and critical discussion in the English-speaking world. Efforts were sponsored against anti-Semitism in Argentina, and Latin-American representatives were added to the staff of the organization.

As World War II was drawing toward a close, the American government, toward the blocking in of the terms of a settlement, established a Commission to Study the Organization of Peace, headed by Columbia University historian James T. Shotwell. With this body the AJC cooperated. Proskauer, in his presidential address to the Committee on January 30, 1944, proposed an international bill of rights to be included in a plan for the solution of postwar problems. At the end of the year he completed it as the "Declaration of Human Rights," a document designed to be incorporated into the Charter of the United Nations. The AJC issued it on December 15, 1944, with the endorsement of 1,326 Americans, including President Franklin D. Roosevelt. Roosevelt had seen Proskauer and Jacob Blaustein, the Committee's chairman of its Executive Committee, and suggested they go as consultants to the delegation in San Francisco, then working on the UN Charter. "Work to get these human rights provisions into the Charter so that unspeakable crimes, like those by the Nazis, will never again be countenanced by world society," Roosevelt had told them.

In laying down the broad principles assuring human rights, Proskauer's declaration stressed these international aspects of such a guaranty:

> That an international bill of human rights must be promulgated to guarantee for every man, woman and child, of every race and creed and in every country, the fundamental rights of life, liberty and the pursuit of happiness.
>
> No plea of sovereignty shall ever again be allowed to permit any nation to deprive those within its borders of these fundamental rights on the claim that these are matters of internal concern.
>
> Hitlerism has demonstrated that bigotry and persecution by a barbarous nation throws upon the peace-loving nations the burden of relief and distress. Therefore it is a matter of international concern to stamp out infractions of basic human rights....
>
> To those who wander the earth unable or unwilling to return to scenes of unforgettable horror shall be given aid and comfort to find new homes and begin new lives in other parts of the world. This must be made possible by international agreement....

The Department of State invited forty-two leading American organizations to send consultants to San Francisco to act as liaisons between the American people and their delegation, among them the AJC. Proskauer was named, with Blaustein as his alternate, and the two men arrived in San Francisco on April 28, 1945, only three days after the so-called Organizing Conference. They came prepared and their recommendations (to which they gave proper publicity) were to the point. They called for the creation of a "conference commission" to draw up an international bill of rights to spell out and supplement the preliminary draft that had been drawn up at

Dumbarton Oaks in 1944. They prepared another on "statelessness" to deal with the problem of European displaced persons, and a third to consider migrations in Europe, resulting from economic and social upheaval. Proskauer and Blaustein accepted their mandate seriously and soon compelled the American delegation to realize this. Shortly after the start of the conference, they began to meet every Wednesday and Friday afternoon with a member of the American delegation. Secretary of State Edward R. Stettinius, Jr., its head, frequently attended. If unable to do so, he sent a high-level substitute. There were almost daily conferences with other members of the delegation and with permanent officials of the Department of State. In between times, Proskauer was out seeking information, making friends, and sounding out the opposition for his pet project, a commission on human rights.

There was opposition. The Soviet delegation was cool—"very suspicious of any proposal which might eventually lead to interference with internal Soviet affairs." The same was true of the British, having in mind India and its far-flung colonial empire. The American delegation was split, as was the Department of State. The prospects for positive action, certainly in the American delegation, seemed remote. May 2 was the deadline for any amendment by a major power to the Dumbarton Oaks proposals. Early that day Dean Virginia C. Gildersleeve of Barnard College, an American delegate, told the consultants that it was unlikely that the delegation would propose any extension of the human rights provisions beyond those existing in the draft. This created a critical situation, but Proskauer met it at his best. Within a few hours, five consultants, including Proskauer, drew up a petition to Secretary Stettinius, carefully outlining the defects in the Dumbarton Oaks document, offering suggestions for its supplementation, and an argument in support of positive action by the American delegation. Signatures to it were obtained from twenty-one of the forty-two consultants (all who were reached). When Stettinius and his board of consultants met, they heard these suggested amendments to the Dumbarton Oaks Proposals:

1. That to its purposes in Chapter I be added: 'To promote respect for human rights and fundamental freedoms.'

2. That a new principle to Chapter II, be added, to wit: 'All members of the Organization, accepting as a matter of international concern the obligation "to defend life, liberty, independence and religious freedom, and to preserve human rights and justice in their own lands," shall progressively secure for their inhabitants without discrimination such fundamental rights as freedom of religion, speech, assembly and communication, and to a fair trial under just laws.'

3. Addition to Chapter V, Section B, 6, after 'economic and social fields': 'of developing and safeguarding human rights and fundamental freedoms.'

4. Addition to Chapter IX, Section D, 1, after 'social commission': 'A

human rights commission.'

Principles Involved

The ultimate inclusion of the equivalent of an International Bill of Rights in the functioning of the Organization is deemed of the essence of what is necessary to preserve the peace of the world.

a. The dignity and inviolability of the individual must be the cornerstone of civilization. The assurance to every human being of the fundamental rights of life, liberty and the pursuit of happiness is essential not only to domestic but also to international peace.

b. The conscience of the world demands an end to persecution and Hitlerism has demonstrated that persecution by a barbarous nation throws upon the peace-loving nations the burden of relief and redress.

c. It is thus a matter of international concern to stamp out infractions of basic human rights.

d. Therefore in the language of Judge Manley O. Hudson of the Permanent Court of International Justice: 'Each state has a legal duty . . . to treat its own population in a way which will not violate the dictates of humanity and justice or shock the conscience of mankind.'

Relevancy to the Conference

a. It is fully realized that the primary objective of this Conference is to devise the structure of the new world organization.

b. Nonetheless, it would come as a grievous shock if the constitutional framework of the Organization would fail to make adequate provision for the ultimate achievement of human rights and fundamental freedoms.

c. The Atlantic Charter, the Four Freedoms, the Declaration of the United Nations and subsequent declarations have given mankind the right to expect that the area of international law would be expanded to meet this advance toward freedom and peace.

d. Sponsorship of this project by the American Delegation would win the enthusiastic support of the American people, and speaking particularly for the organizations we represent, would command their hearty approval.

Conclusion

We therefore urge upon the American Delegation that in this vital field it take a position of leadership.

After an introductory statement by Dr. O. Fred Nolde, Proskauer spoke, saying, "If there is to be freedom in this world, and peace, human rights must be safeguarded and there must be machinery within the United Nations to promote such freedom, to make human rights a living reality." He then turned to address Stettinius directly:

I am bound to you by ties of personal friendship and official loyalty. But I am here to tell you that the voice of America is speaking in this room as it has never before spoken in any international gathering. And this is what it is saying to you: 'If you make a fight for these proposals and win, the bands will play and the flags will fly. If you make a fight for it and lose, we are still for you. If you lie down on it, there is not a man or woman within the sound of my voice that will have a word to say for your charter. You will have lost the support of American public opinion and I submit to you that you will never get a charter ratified.'

After a moment's silence he turned to his colleagues: "I've assumed to speak for the board of consultants, but if anyone here disagrees with my statement he can now register his dissent." Philip Murray, president of the Conference of Industrial Organizations, arose. "I can still feel the pounding of my heart," Proskauer recalled, "at the fear that he was going to dissent." Murray pointed a finger at Stettinius and stated, "Mr. Secretary, I didn't sign that paper." He then paused and Proskauer's heart pounded harder. The only reason he had not signed it, Murray admitted, was that "they didn't get it to me. I am here to tell you that I believe I am speaking not only for the C.I.O., but for all labor when I say that we are 100 percent behind the argument which has just been made."

Stettinius, as Proskauer recorded it later, was "visibly moved." He rose to his feet impulsively, confessed that he had no idea of the intensity of feeling on this matter, and declared he would immediately put the statement before the American Delegation. That night he did so and the Delegation voted to present the proferred amendments to the conference. As a result of the American initiative, the four major powers agreed to sponsor the amendments and Proskauer, to the plaudits of his friends and other onlookers, had the satisfaction of seeing their ultimate incorporation into the United Nations Charter.

Criticisms of the "Declaration of Human Rights," as they were subsequently developed, pointed to its weaknesses. They were in part justly put although, of course, post-hoc judgments. But its inadequacies were those of the Charter; indeed, fundamentally, inadequacies of the conception of a United Nations which had no police power and no intention or willingness to override national sovereignty.

In an article, "Human Rights at San Francisco," published in *American Jewish Archives,* April, 1964, Dr. Jerold S. Auerbach summarized the case against the "Declaration of Human Rights" in this fashion. He wrote that it had the following weaknesses: the successful amendments would not be able, despite their inherent idealism, to curb the power of the major nations upon whom, as with all the other governments, rested the responsibility for carrying out the provisions; there was no machinery for their enforcement; there was a built-in contradiction between the rights involved and other parts of the charter, such as no intervention in the domestic sovreignty or affairs of any nation and the freedom of each nation to determine its own system of government; the guaranty was a facade; and heightening and belligerent nationalism would never accept a system of international control in these areas. Auerbach pictured Proskauer as retreating from his stronger position of 1944, when he had stated his maximum demand— "International force to effectuate the decisions of international law"—to the lesser one where he was willing to accept the absence of a policing machinery. Judge Proskauer was also held at fault for espousing universal protection of these rights everywhere, rather than in specific, geographically defined areas covered by protective minorities provisions in the peace treaties (such as after World War I). Thus, international protection through sanctions was thereby sacrificed to domestic jurisdiction.

It is a little naive to assume that Proskauer and the other consultants were not aware of the political realities that stalked them. A concensus, certainly among the United States, the Soviet Union, Great Britain, and France, had to be reached. To any one of these powers the surrender of even a little of sovereignty, notably the imposition of sanctions and the creation of an international military force, was unthinkable. Proskauer, as did almost all of the others, well knew that, while charters endure and machinery can rust, without the machinery, on the international level and within each nation, charters remain mere scraps of paper.

Proskauer and his associates at San Francisco might also have been influenced by the example of Wilson at Versailles: if the principle is written into a document, then at least the basis for a possible later implementation is laid. The time to speak up and seek that implementation came swiftly enough on May 15, 1946. At a meeting of American church and civic organizations before the United Nations Commission on Human Rights, broad agreement was expressed that the United Nations declaration had to be made an integral part of international law and enforced by direct court action. Proskauer, representing the AJC, warned that the United Nations must not shy away from enforcement to escape the charge of interfering with the internal affairs of member nations. He pointed to Article II, Section 5 of the United Nations Charter which pledged the complete assistance of every member. He asked that the Declaration of Human Rights be made part of International law and that the International Court of Justice be empowered to deal with violations. In addition, he recommended, each member nation should pass laws providing for the strict enforcement of the document and of all the freedoms guaranteed by the charter.

Since 1948 the United Nations has adopted nine different human rights conventions. Only one of these, the Supplementary Convention on Slavery, was ratified by the United States Senate. (Four were not even submitted to that body for its "advice and consent.") In addition, two regional conventions, not binding as international law but having legal force, were later adopted. The declaration has been included in the Allied Treaty of Peace with Japan (1951) and in the General Convention between France and Tunisia (1955). It has influenced the constitutions of several new states, such as the Federal Republic of Germany, Haiti, Indonesia, Libya, and Eritrea. It has also found its way into a Paraguayan copyright statute, a Canadian fair employment practices act, a Bolivian education decree, and a Panamanian antidiscrimination law. Finally, the Declara-

tion of Human Rights or its individual articles have been cited in a growing
number of judicial decisions and opinions of national courts.

PROSKAUER AND PALESTINE 12

Joseph Proskauer stated in his *A Segment*...that he had no contact with or interest in the Zionist movement. "Instinctively" he wrote, "I was opposed to the creation of a state identified, however remotely with a religion." Of course, this was not strictly true. His profound faith in the efficacy of assimilation—that he was an American in his emotional and political attachment to the land of his birth—made him recoil at the idea that he could divide his loyalties. However, when he assumed the presidency of the American Jewish Committee and thus was plunged into a world of Jewish turmoil, he was forced to modify his thinking.

Two things turned Proskauer around. First, as World War II was drawing toward a close, Americans began to realize the enormity of the holocaust which had been visited upon European Jews. As tens of thousands of them, freed at last from Nazi concentration camps, began desperately to seek some place of asylum, the question of their resettlement became an all-absorbing one with Proskauer. The problem kept on gnawing at him between 1946 and 1948 and he spoke often of it with intense feeling. Secondly, as he became increasingly familiar with the members of the various British and American committees and commissions, he learned that far too many of the civil servants in the two countries having to do with the Near East were Arabists in their training, education, and sympathies. They were opposed to further settlement of the Jews in Palestine. And more fundamentally, they were opposed to the creation of a Jewish political state that Balfour and Lloyd George had envisaged. These men had great influence, both in the United States, particularly on Secretary of State George C. Marshall, and in England, particularly on Ernest Bevin, Secretary for Foreign Affairs in the Attlee Cabinet.

President Truman, in his *Memoirs,* completed almost ten years after the event, could still speak of the efforts of the American Arabists with cold hostility. "The Department of State's specialists on the Near East were almost without exception unfriendly to the idea of a Jewish state....Some thought the Arabs, on account of their number and because of the fact that they controlled such immense oil resources, should be appeased.... Some among them were also inclined to be anti-Semitic...I wanted to make plain that the President of the United States, and not the State Department, is responsible for making foreign policy."

Making foreign policy, in short, was a political decision. Truman knew that and Proskauer began to learn it from experiences and frustrations. When the crunch came, in the debate over the creation of an autonomous Jewish state, Proskauer, still anti-Zionist, was ready to make the decisions to support the partition of Palestine and to seek to influence the President in the making of his.

The year 1945 was one of mounting tension. The obduracy of the British as regards immigrant admissions; the unsuccessful direct appeal of Truman to Prime Minister Winston Churchill to accept 100,000 refugees and lift the restrictions "without delay"; the illegal resort of Palestine Jews to force open their doors to immigrants collecting in French, Italian, and Black Sea ports—all these involved not only Britain and the United States politically, but they also involved the non-Zionists of the AJC.

The illegality of the Palestine Jews took these forms. The Haganah, a defense organization, resorted to arms to fight off Arab attacks. At the same time, underground Jewish terrorists began to harass British forces and bring the fight directly into the Arab camp. The Haganah, assisted by funds pouring in from America, helped in the chartering and outfitting of ships secretly to carry immigrants to Palestine. The British, on their part, hunted down these vessels at sea, turned many of them back, captured others and sent off their human cargo to detention camps on the Islands of Cyprus.

In the spring of 1945 the British Churchill Government, defeated in a general election, was succeeded by Labour whose Cabinet was headed by Prime Minister Clement Atlee. For more than twenty years Labour had been pledged to support the Balfour Declaration but Atlee, now in office, became as unyielding as had Winston Churchill. The guerrilla war in Palestine, the mounting cost of maintaining the Mandate which was losing control of the situation, and unofficial and official pressures from America (Truman's among them) nevertheless forced Atlee's hand. In an effort to involve the United States directly, Atlee suggested to Truman the setting up of an Anglo-American Committee of Inquiry. Truman acceded and in January, 1946 it was formed, and was made up of six members from each side. It was instructed to investigate the condition of Jews in the displaced persons camps and to study the situation in Palestine. It was to hold hearings in Washington and London and issue a report, with recommendations. Before this committee, spokesmen for American Jewish organizations appeared—Proskauer following Rabbi Stephen Wise, one of the leaders of the Zionist Organization of America. Proskauer's carefully prepared statement had a profound effect on the membership of the committee. He urged them to act quickly in relieving the miseries of the thousands of European displaced persons and to encourage the governments of the countries which had admitted Jewish refugees to permit them to acquire citizenship. He called for the immediate creation, perhaps under the United Nations, of a trusteeship for Palestine and for improved relationships between Jews and Arabs. "I do believe," he concluded, paraphrasing Chaim Weizmann,

> . . . in a future co-operation of Jews and Arabs, and that a time will come when

both Jews and Arabs will understand that they can live and work together for a common end. There is one indispensable condition, and this applies equally to both sides—to Jews and Arabs—that neither should dominate and neither be dominated by the other, irrespective of their numbers.

Judge Ernest Hutcheson, the American co-chairman of the committee, opened the interrogation of Proskauer with this compliment: "I would like to say that your approach is familiar and pleasant to me because it is the approach and the attitude of what I call judicial. It is practical. It is definite."

Justice Sir John Singleton, the British co-chairman, questioned Proskauer closely, yet in friendly terms. The exchanges revealed the keenness and troubled concern of men who were groping for rational answers in a situation where terror already stalked. In his earlier remarks Proskauer had noted that the AJC was opposed to the partition of Palestine. No solution of the problem was possible without peace between the two sections of the population, he added, setting off a lengthy colloquy between himself and Justice Singleton in which Proskauer explained that he and the Zionists both believed that would need to "be a considerable period of years looking for conciliation [between Jews and Arabs] before a state is created."

Among the many auditors at Proskauer's appearance was Eliahu (Epstein) Elath, the Washington representative of the Palestine Jewish Agency (PJA), who twenty years later recalled Proskauer's impact on the committee. In 1967 he wrote Mark Hirsch a letter, stating that Proskauer had "demonstrated the fact that support in the Jewish community in the United States for Jewish rights in Palestine was not limited to official Zionist circles alone." He added that the fact that the AJC had come out "In favour of the abolition of all arbitrary restrictions imposed by the [British] Mandatory Government was of great public importance and had its share in further developments as far as the American Government's position in the matter was concerned."

The late Dr. Herbert Feis, in his *The Birth of Israel, The Tousled Diplomatic Bed* (1969), wrote one of the best accounts of these political discussions.

> All members [he stated] at the end of their examination of the problem verged toward several main conclusions. These were:
>
> That the idea of a National Home in Palestine was not a conception nurtured by wealthy foreign Jews but so deep a wish of many Jews of Western Europe, especially the refugees;
>
> That these Jews would not, no matter what the compulsion, return to their countries of origin where they had suffered so greatly and where their relatives and their communities had been wiped out;

That there was little or no chance that foreign countries, including the
United States, would accept any substantial number of them as immigrants;
That, therefore, Palestine should be opened to them.

The report of the committee, which was unanimous, recommended that
100,000 certificates of immigration be issued immediately. However, the
committee backed away from proposing partition, reasoning that the creation of two separate states might lead to civil war. But, as Proskauer had
recommended, it voted for a trusteeship under the United Nations. Until
that materialized the Mandatory should continue to facilitate Jewish immigration "to the extent that conditions permitted." Finally, the committee agreed that existing restrictions on the sale, lease, or use of land in Palestine to the Jews should be rescinded.

"These recommendations were welcomed in Washington and rebuffed
in London," Feis declared. Truman, always alert to the main chance,
scored a political triumph at home when he approved the recommendation that 100,000 refugees be admitted at once. But his silence on the other
proposals infuriated the British, Foreign Secretary Bevin, in particular.
The burden of maintaining peace in Palestine apparently was not going to
be shared by the United States. Besides, the report was bound to set the
whole Arab world on fire (where the British were trying desperately to
maintain their influence) but it could not satisfy the Zionists either in Palestine or the United States.

On May 1 the Prime Minister, addressing the House of Commons,
declared that Britain alone could not undertake the costs and responsibility
of carrying out the Anglo-American committee's recommendations. What
part of the military and financial obligations was the United States going to
assume? he asked. A few weeks later, Atlee, more and more the captive of
Bevin, rejected the recommendations of the committee.

Proskauer and Blaustein, for the AJC telegraphed Truman on June 14 as
follows:

> [Britain's decision] has caused great consternation among all Jewish groups
> and among all fair-minded Americans. This refusal to abide by the unani-
> mous recommendation of the Anglo-American Committee would result in the
> sacrifice of the lives of the displaced Jews in Europe. Bevin's statement and
> the reported arrival of the Mufti in the Near East tend to increase the danger
> of civil war in Palestine. We urge you to use your influence with the British
> Government for the purpose of taking immediate joint action to effect the
> prompt entry of displaced Jews into Palestine as recommended by you and the
> Anglo-American Committee. . . .

Proskauer did not know that Truman was under pressure from Under
Secretary of State Dean Acheson, from the Arabists in the Department of
State, and from his Joint Chiefs of Staff. According to Feis, the Joint
Chiefs of Staff warned Truman "against involving American armed forces

in carrying out the Committee's recommendations, against any step that would so inflame the situation in Palestine that the British troops might alone be incapable of controlling it. For the United States should not endanger Western oil interests in the Middle East, nor cause the Arabs to open their arms to Russia." At this point Truman yielded to Atlee and Acheson and consented to another study. Again, there were to be two groups, American and British. They were to work together and draw up recommendations. Called the Grady-Morrison Committee, after the two chairmen, they had no prior knowledge of Zionism and Palestine, according to Feis, and were not particularly concerned about the tragedy of the refugees. In fact, they were "rather indifferent officials."

Within a month the Grady-Morrison Committee made its report. It proposed a kind of cantonizing of the two Palestine peoples: two provinces, the larger one Arab and the smaller one Jewish, were to be created within a federal state. Immigration would be the charge of the central government whose executive would be named by Britain. The legislature was to have two houses, one elected by popular vote. Inasmuch as the Arabs were more numerous, it was obvious that they would control the processes of government. Now, Proskauer re-emerged. His papers and those of Truman reveal that Proskauer began seeking an appointment with the President as early as April, 1946. This effort failed, as did another, this time with James A. Farley as intermediary. Farley then wrote Truman that Proskauer had some interesting things to say (including Roosevelt's opinions about Zionism, for one):

> He is an extremely frank person [Farley went on], entirely reliable in every respect and any observations which he may pass on to you, you can accept with full assurance that you are getting from him a true picture that comes from experience and wisdom. I know that it is highly essential that you see him as soon as he returns east and when he communicates with The White House, I would appreciate it if you would make as prompt arrangements as possible so that he may have a visit with you.

Oddly enough, the letter was misplaced and did not turn up until late in August. By that time Truman was busy with the problems resulting from the Japanese surrender. Farley persevered and wrote Truman a second letter. It drew a polite reply from Truman's appointment secretary, stating, "We have not as yet worked out a time for Judge Proskauer to call on the President, but it is still on our pending calendar."

But events were moving fast and positions were changing with kaleidoscopic speed. As a result, this time it was President Truman who wanted to see Joseph Proskauer. Undoubtedly, Truman knew of the strong impression Proskauer had made upon the two chairmen of the Anglo-American Committee of Inquiry and, more important, he had learned, that even though all Jews were not Zionists, they all felt deeply about Palestine. In

August, 1946 Proskauer received a call from David K. Niles, the President's administrative assistant, who was his liaison with American minority groups. Proskauer went immediately to have his first long talk with the President. The result was, he was asked to take over two assignments. The first was to attempt to reconcile the conflict between the recommendations of the Hutchison-Singleton and Grady-Morrison committees. Proskauer conferred with representatives of both groups. Hutchison was indignant. He told Proskauer that his people had studied the situation in Palestine and Cairo and were deeply annoyed at seeing their work wasted. He was less than polite about Grady and his associates, calling them amateurs who did not know what they were talking about. Proskauer reported back to Truman and on August 12 the latter rejected the Grady-Morrison report.

Proskauer's second assignment was to meet with Nahum Goldmann, a spokesman for the PJA which had been recognized under the terms of the Mandate as a legal body to advise with the British administration in Palestine and to coordinate the activities of the Jews there. It also sought the economic and financial aid of non-Zionists in the development of the Jewish settlements, helped obtain the funds for the buying or leasing of the refugee ships, and was generally accepted as the political (and diplomatic) representative of the Palestine Jews. Although it had been originally designed to comprise an equal number of Zionists and non-Zionists, in practice it was run by the Zionists.

In Washington, Proskauer opened doors for Goldmann, doors on which he had been knocking futilely, for he was speaking for the PJA and the World Zionist organization. He had come to Washington to inform the proper officials that his people were willing to consider a partition of Palestine. He promised a Jewish state which would be Jewish only in the sense that Jews would constitute a majority of the population. American Jews would in no way be politically involved—even the name of the state would not include the word "Jews"—and the Agency would do everything possible to hold in check the activities of extremists who were opposed to partition. As Proskauer wrote in his *Reminiscences,* "My answer to that question [about Proskauer's help in pushing partition] depends on the attitude of the Government of the United States of America. I have an appointment this afternoon with Secretary [of War] Robert P. Patterson. I will discuss it with him."

Goldmann, who had been trying without success to see Patterson, was introduced to him by Proskauer. After their conference Goldmann left the room and Patterson said to Proskauer, as reported in his *Reminiscences:*

> Joe, it makes sense. This refugee problem is getting to be utterly insoluble. I don't know what to do with these poor people any more. I've got no place I can send them. This atrocious MacDonald White Paper keeps them out of Israel [*sic*]. I can't get them into America because of our terrible im-

migration laws. I'm for it, but you've got to clear it with the State Department.

Proskauer agreed and Patterson telephoned Dean Acheson to make an appointment for him. At that meeting, according to Proskauer in the *Reminiscences*, Acheson said:

> Joe, I'm going to save you a lot of time. I've been studying this thing all morning, and I'm ready to say to you that the partition of Palestine and the creation of a Jewish state is American policy not only because of your Jewish interests but for a number of other reasons, collateral, which I couldn't and can't go into. And if you will get the American Jewish Committee, which is a great non-Zionist organization, to back us up it will be a great help both to Palestine and to America.

In his *A Segment . . .* Proskauer had said this:

> Partition was now the project both of the Jewish Agency for Palestine and of the government of the United States, for it had become apparent that partition was the most promising, if not the only means of throwing open the gates of Palestine. From that time on, therefore, I gave my whole-hearted support to the accomplishment of the plan.

His first task was to persuade the AJC to come out openly for partition and also to become the partner of the PJA in the United States. The meeting of the Committee was a stormy one, but Proskauer succeeded in persuading a majority of the members to follow him, keeping all options open, but endorsing partition. The one overriding necessity was to get refugees into Palestine as soon as possible. Proskauer had learned an important lesson—to think politically, when confronted by a crisis. Said he, to justify his stand: "I have 'no position' on Palestine in the sense of a fixed idological plan. The one great overwhelming objective is to get immediate and substantial immigration into Palestine and within limits, of course, I don't care very much how I get it."

Actually, Proskauer had furnished President Truman with a highly influential non-Zionist Jewish constituency which was ready and eager to act politically about Palestine, whenever the President gave the word.

Proskauer's second task was to seek out Bevin, who was then in New York. On November 27, 1946 the two were to have met at the Waldorf Hotel. This is the story of their encounter the next day, as Proskauer told it in his *A Segment . . .* and in his *Reminiscences:*

Proskauer had asked Lord Iverchapel, the British Ambassador, who had accompanied the Foreign Secretary, how best to approach Bevin, to which Iverchapel had replied smilingly that he had noted Proskauer's proficiency with the "big damn" and, since Bevin was not inexpert in the same art, suggested he "might fairly employ that technique." When Proskauer came to their postponed appointment, protocol was set aside and

Proskauer commenced with this question: "Why the devil doesn't the Labour Government do something in Palestine to give its friends in America something to say for it?" Startled for a moment, Bevin asked Proskauer, "What the devil" did he mean by that? Proskauer continued:

Why does the British Government have to have such a good police force? Why do you have to 'catch' a negligibly few thousand poor Jews who are trying to get into Palestine to save their lives? What harm would be done to anybody by letting them go in? And more than that, after you 'catch' them, why in the world do you have to put them in a concentration camp in Cyprus instead of detaining them in Palestine and gradually letting them out?

Bevin retorted almost immediately: "Why, I never thought of that; it's a new idea to me." There then followed "a serious discussion of the perplexing problems created by the MacDonald White Paper."

The next day Proskauer sent Bevin an *aide memoire* of the conference:

My thesis is that your country as a matter of right and self-interest should find a way to permit substantial immigration into Palestine. You should follow this course no matter what your ultimate action may be, whether partition, federalization, status quo or anything else. You must concede that the MacDonald White Paper is wrong legally and morally . . .

After repeating some of the observations he had made to the Anglo-American Committee, Proskauer concluded: "I suggest time is of the essence, and my prayer is you may find some helpful suggestions in the views I express."

Proskauer had reason for some cautious hope. The meeting had lasted for two hours. And when he asked Iverchapel, who had been present throughout, whether he had gotten anywhere with Bevin, the other had replied that Bevin did not spend that much time with anyone who did not. The next day Proskauer received a note of thanks from Bevin for his memorandum. "Perhaps," observed the Foreign Minister, "I could take this opportunity of saying how interested I was in meeting you."

Proskauer's high hopes were soon dashed, however, for Bevin returned to England "and entirely discarded every suggestion which had been made to him."

Years afterwards, Proskauer believed he had found out the reason for Bevin's about-face. One day, in New York, he happened to be riding with Sir Hartley Shawcross, Attorney General in the British Labour Government, to a luncheon, given in Shawcross' honor by John W. Davis. During its course Proskauer related the Bevin episode. Shawcross, obviously upset, finally broke in to remind Proskauer that, as Bevin's secretary, he had been present and had heard the entire conversation. When Proskauer said he thought the "Arabia boys in the Foreign Office had got ahold of Bevin," Shawcross replied, "I can't answer your question directly, but I can say that you're a damned good guesser."

Two further major efforts by Proskauer, in behalf of Jewish immigration into Palestine and partition, were made in 1947. The British Government, under great pressure in Palestine because of the guerilla warfare, again sought an honorable way out of its dilemma. On April 2, 1947 it asked the United Nations to put the Palestine question on the agenda of the next meeting of its Assembly. In the debate that followed, much to Britain's surprise, not only did the American delegate, Warren Austin, favor partition, but so did the Russian delegate, Andrei Gromyko. For the next year Soviet Russia was to be a stalwart friend of Palestine Jews, first supporting partition, then (through Czechoslovakia) sending arms to the Jewish forces, and finally declaring for independence. Austin, now backed up by Gromyko, then proposed that the United Nations create a special commission to seek a solution. It was so decided, with the proviso that the commission exclude from its membership representatives of the great powers.

On May 31, 1947 the AJC submitted a statement, signed by Proskauer and Blaustein, which reviewed the various reaffirmations of the Balfour Declaration, the nature of the British Mandate in Palestine, and the situation confronting displaced Jews. Proskauer, who wrote it, attacked both the "illegal" White Paper and the British argument that large-scale immigration should wait upon a final clarification of the political status of Palestine. If Great Britain persisted in its stand and the United Nations was unable to reverse this, he offered two alternatives: first, partition; but, if that were not feasible, then the trusteeship arrangement. Partition was the "only possible solution": it had been urged the previous summer by the PJA and it was "the only one that does not turn over Palestine completely to undeserved Arab domination." If, for the time being the solution was a trusteeship, Proskauer stated, "The UN should assume an obligation, on the request of the administering authority, to furnish adequate means of policing the country, and should reserve the right, through its appropriate bodies, to do so without such request. . . ."

In September, after a thorough and painstaking investigation, the Special Commission on Palestine made its report to the Assembly. It was unanimously adopted. It recommended the end of the Mandate and the grant of some form of independence to Palestine under the auspices of the United Nations. Seven of the eleven members of the Commission favored partition into two states, untied economically. The British Government treaded water: it was ready to accept the majority report, partition, if both Arabs and Jews agreed to the proposals made by the Special Committee on Palestine.

Not so the United States Government. Under orders from President Truman the American delegate stated on October 11 that his government would accept the special report in principle and, more particularly, the majority recommendations on partition and immigration. (A few days earlier, on October 2, Proskauer had had an appointment with Secretary of State Marshall who was known to be unfriendly to the Palestine Jews and to the ideas of trusteeship and partition. Proskauer told him in no uncertain terms that partition was the only solution; that he had been constantly advised that that was the position of the United States Government; and that, if this was true, realities had to be faced. "General," he stated flatly, "you can't implement partition without a police force." His forthrightness evidently impressed Marshall who is believed to have convinced Truman and Acheson to redirect their thinking.) In any event, the United States now made the momentous decision not only to support the PJA openly, but also to abandon Great Britain.

On November 13 the British Government declared its relinquishment of the Mandate as of May 1, 1948 (later changed to May 15) and the evacuation of its military forces by August 1. It would maintain law and order until that time, but it would have no part in the partition plan. From this point on Truman openly directed American policy. As Feis reported the subsequent events, the United Nations Assembly set up an ad hoc committee to draw the maps of the two countries that were to emerge from the partition. The committee was inclined to recommend that the Negev (which the Special Committee had proposed be in the Jewish state) be given to the Arabs. Truman declared he believed the Negev should be Jewish. Former Secretary of State Welles in his book, *We Need Not Fail* (1948), stated: "By direct order of the White House every form of pressure, direct and indirect, was brought to bear by American officials on the countries outside the Moslem world who were known to be uncertain or opposed to partition." And David Niles, Truman's administrative assistant, who was bypassing the officials of the Department of State, gave orders to Hershel Johnson, the American appointee on the ad hoc committee, to use any devices or any sort of pressure needed to get favorable votes for the resolution.

The division was close: success in all likelihood depended on how the Communist countries were going to vote. When the Russian ambassador to the United Nations told the PJA people that Soviet Russia was going to vote for the resolution, the long, hard struggle for the creation of an autonomous Jewish state seemed assured of success. On November 29 the Assembly voted—thirty-three for the resolution and partition and thirteen against, with ten abstentions.

With the partition decided upon and a Jewish state now a virtual reality, Proskauer wrote a letter to the New York *Herald Tribune,* January 19, 1948. In it he threw to the winds his old fear (namely, that the fulfillment of the Zionist dream would mean a Jewish nation requiring the undivided loyalty of Jews everywhere): but he was, in effect, reassuring the American people in general and President Truman in particular of this fact:

We are told by the anti-Semite, through malice, and by some small sections of American Jewry, through confusion, that this partition has created a problem of possible inconsistency between our obligations as Americans and as Jews. There is no such problem. Five years ago our Committee stated: 'There can be no political identification of Jews outside of Palestine with whatever government may there be instituted.' These words state an axiom and remain true today. The Jews of America suffer from no political schizophrenia. Politically we are not split personalities, and in faith and in conduct we shall continue to demonstrate what the death rolls of our army on many a battlefield have attested that we are bone of the bone and flesh of the flesh of America.

If 1947 had its alarums and excursions, 1948 had nightmarish qualities. The announcement of the United Nation Assembly's vote led to the outbreak of large-scale hostilities in Palestine. Egypt and the other Arab states indignantly rejected the decision and their governments threatened intervention. British forces proved ineffectual in maintaining order and the PJA failed to contain the attacks of terrorists. Arab bands moved into Palestine from Syria, Iraq, and Trans-Jordan; illegal Jewish immigrants, bearing arms, seeped into Palestine in increasing numbers. Would the Arabs formally declare war? What would Russia do? Would there be an embargo on Arab oil going out to the West? The United States Government marked time.

Truman was exhorted, cajoled and attacked as a "traitor" by American Zionists. Would he not do something to save the hard-pressed Palestine Jews? Truman, who was a highly courageous man, resented such pressures. Even ten years later, in his *Memoirs,* he voiced his annoyance: "Individuals and groups asked me usually in rather quarrelsome and emotional ways to stop the Arabs, to keep the British from supporting the Arabs, to furnish American soldiers, to do this, that, the other."

Meantime, Proskauer maintained cordial relations with Truman and David Niles and, to some extent, with the Department of State. He wrote Under-Secretary Robert A. Lovett several letters, offering him suggestions, proposals, and advice. Lovett acknowledged them in friendly fashion. One such communication, dated February 13, 1948, pointed out that the United Nations Security Council already had the power to see that the partition of Palestine would be accomplished peaceably, without aggression, invasion, threat, or violence. Legal questions, if unnecessarily submitted to the International Court of Justice, would result in chaos in Palestine. Inasmuch as the Assembly resolution favored partition and the United States Government had supported it, the Security Council was bound by that decision to determine whether there was a threat to peace.

On March 1, 1948 Proskauer wrote Lovett a second letter, insisting that the United States follow a consistent policy on partition and actively display leadership in the Security Council. The United Nations in effect, he said,

had become trustee of Palestine since Britain had virtually surrendered it,
and that, therefore, the Assembly resolution was in order. Even if the
Security Council could not use force to implement partition, it could at least
counter the force of those who would block it.

On April 1, in his third note to Lovett, Proskauer suggested the lifting of
the American arms embargo and the early recognition by the United States
of a Jewish state:

> I feel I am a sort of sounding board for the [State] Department [he wrote].
> I say to you frankly that on all sides I hear what was brought to explicit expres-
> sion in the meeting held at the Waldorf last week, where sixty-three [Jewish]
> organizations expressed views similar to the one that I am here setting down.
> I was consulted about the form of the resolution that the meeting passed and,
> against opposition, I had excised from it bitter criticism of our government.

The Security Council of course did not act, for Britain, despite the fact
that it had bowed out, was still the Palestine trustee. But Proskauer
refused to stop trying. In *A Segment* . . . he reported that at the end of
April he held a conference with Dean Rusk then a high functionary of the
State Department, which Moshe Shertok (Sharett), the spokesman for the
PJA, also attended. The meeting was spent in an "interminable discussion of details." On April 28 Lovett acknowledged Proskauer's labors in a
telegram: "Rusk has told me of the very real help you have given him and
of the fine letter you have written. Our delegation has been instructed to
do its best to accelerate action on the entire problem of Jerusalem and Rusk
has just phoned to say they are complying gladly. Best regards."

A political decision could be made only by President Truman and for
weeks he was a prey to indecision. He was worried about war, Russia, and
the warnings of his Joint Chiefs of Staff. On March 19, presumably with
Truman's concurrence, at the United Nations Warren Austin called for a
suspension of partition for the time being and the assumption by that body
of a temporary trusteeship on May 15, when the British Mandate was to
end. This proposal failed.

> These efforts having come to naught, Truman thereafter let events take
> their course [according to Feis]. But he had apparently by then made up his
> mind, secretly and stubbornly, that if no interim arrangement for the govern-
> ment of Palestine was established when on May 15 (May 14 Washington
> time), the British forces left Palestine, and the Jews proclaimed a National
> State, the American Government would recognize it.

A few days earlier President Truman, harassed by the American Zionists, had declared that he was not going to talk to any Zionist spokesmen,
not even Chaim Weizmann, who had been trying to get an appointment.
At this juncture, Eddie Jacobson, Truman's Jewish partner in World War I
days in the haberdashery business, entered the picture. He persuaded

Truman to see Weizmann and Truman consented. In his *Memoirs* Weizmann wrote that they talked of many things, among them again the importance of the Negev to the Jewish state. Truman, in his own *Memoirs,* reported that he "felt that [Weizmann] had reached a full understanding of my policy, and that I knew what it was that he wanted." In any event, Jacobson recorded, Weizmann left the President's office pleased and reassured. Yet, on the very next day, American foot-dragging took place at the United Nations Assembly.

This and the subsequent events troubled Truman greatly. On March 20 he asked his general counsel, Samuel Roseman, to tell Weizmann "that there was not and would not be any changes in the long [*sic*] policy he and I had talked about." At this Weizmann once again took heart. Three days later, according to Jacobson, Weizmann called him and said:

> Don't be disappointed and do not feel badly. I do not believe that President Truman knew what was going to happen in the United Nations on Friday [the 19th] when he talked to me the day before.... Don't forget for a single moment that Harry S. Truman is the most powerful single man in the world. You have a job to do: so keep the White House doors open.

Jacobson did so and on April 12 told the President that he had talked with Weizmann. Feis reported this meeting in these words:

> Truman authorized him [Jacobson] to tell Weizmann that he stood by the promise he had made; and he agreed with Jacobson that the American Government should recognize the new Jewish state if and when it came into existence. Whether this affirmation was relayed to Weizmann, and by him relayed to Palestine, and whether it may have influenced the course of the Palestine Zionists before and during the mid-May climax, is still not known.

Weizmann now had the ear of the President. He felt that he could personally inform him of the plans of the PJA and the Palestine Jews. On May 13, therefore, he told the President that the Zionists were going to proclaim the existence of a Jewish state on midnight May 14. Truman called in Marshall, Lovett, Clark Clifford (his legal counsel), David Niles, and others for a conference. Marshall was for delay: why not talk it over with the British and French governments? Truman was not: the moment of truth, the time for a political decision, had come and he, Truman, was going to make it.

Truman instructed Clifford to reach Eliahu Epstein (Elath), the political spokesman for the PJA in Washington, and arrange to coordinate their actions. Elath submitted a formal request for the recognition of a Jewish state which would be called Israel, as the United Nations Assembly resolution of November 29, 1947 had contemplated. Eleven minutes after the establishment of the State of Israel was proclaimed in Tel Aviv, May 14, 1948, the announcement went out that the United States

Government had granted it *de facto* recognition.

Why did President Truman hurry? One may speculate that he wanted to get there before the Russians. He had made a promise to a distinguished man, Chaim Weizmann, whom he respected and Weizmann, although old and ailing, was probably going to become the first president of the new republic. Truman also sought the good will of the American Jews. He knew that virtually every Jew in the United States, non-Zionist as well as Zionist, favored the creation of the Jewish state. Thus, he could truthfully say that what he was doing was in the interest of all Jews everywhere, and not just the Zionists. Feis concluded that Truman's *Memoirs* suggested he was paying off the Arabists, the permanent civil servants of the Department of State and the British Foreign Office, all of whom had tried to do his thinking for him. Or was Truman thinking of the forthcoming presidential election, when he would need the electoral votes of the states in which Jewish voters played important roles—particularly, California, Illinois, Massachusetts, New York, Ohio, Pennsylvania?

The establishment of the independence of the state of Israel was one thing, but winning it and holding it another. A full-scale war now broke out in Palestine (there were large numbers of Egyptian troops augmenting the earlier Arab irregulars) and it was touch and go for several months before the Arabs cried quits. At last, Jews had gained their independence in the field and their security was now based on their own armies.

> For many weeks thereafter [following May 14, 1948, Proskauer wrote in *A Segment*...] it was my lot to sit in conference after conference with our State Department and with the representatives of the new State of Israel, together and separately, in the endeavor to reach proper conclusions for the treatment of the Israeli situation. My function was to be a kind of catalyst.... At the very inception of these conferences I discovered that it was the fundamental objective of the President, with whom I had the honor of conferring, and of the State Department, to end hostilities by a general truce. While I personally agreed to do all in my power to aid in the accomplishment of this objective, I strongly urged at all times that what the situation required in the first instance was a policeman, not a mediator.

Grateful for Joseph Proskauer's labors, Israel's Prime Minister David Ben Gurion, wrote the AJC April 19, 1949: "We in Israel will never forget the noble efforts of Judge Proskauer in helping to secure the political conditions which facilitated the emergence of the Jewish State."

Proskauer, on his part, mindful of the earlier Zionist efforts to embriol all Jews in their activities and quarrels, wanted a *quid pro quo*: that Israel would not seek to undermine the independence and integrity of American Jews in their own country. He got two pledges: Israel and the Palestine Jewish Agency would not proclaim publicly that the Jews outside of Israel were "living in exile"; and that they would not seek to encourage mass emigration of American Jews into Israel.

In August, 1950 Ben Gurion entered into an "entente" with American Jews. In a letter to Jacob Blaustein, Proskauer's successor as president of the AJC, he declared:

> The Jews of the United States . . . owe no political allegiance to Israel. . . . We, the people of Israel, have no desire and no intention to interfere in any way with the internal affairs of Jewish communities abroad. The Government and the people of Israel fully respect the right and integrity of the Jewish communities in other countries to develop their indigenous social, economic, and cultural institutions in accord with their own needs and aspirations. . . .
>
> Our success or failure depends in a large measure on our cooperation with and on the strength of the great Jewish community of the United States, and we, therefore, are anxious that nothing should be said or done which could in the slightest degree undermine the sense of security and stability of American Jewry.

THE LAST TWO
GREAT TRIALS

13

By 1947 Joseph Proskauer had turned seventy, but he was in the center of a maelstrom which required every physical, mental, and emotional resource he possessed. In order to play his unique role in the creation of the State of Israel, he was in and out of Washington constantly, consulting with the representatives of the Palestine Jewish Agency who had come to depend upon him increasingly.

And it was when he was in his seventies that he was the outstanding man, among many, in two of the most complex cases in his long career. Thanks to his skill at presentation and cross-examination, and his command over the subtleties of the law, both were legal triumphs which were reported in the law journals and entered into legal textbooks.

Early in January, 1947 Proskauer was "briefed" by Aramco (the Arabian American Oil Company, which was a subsidiary of the California-Texas Oil Company, wholly owned by the Texas Company and Standard Oil of New Jersey), to defend it in a heavy damage suit involving Arabian oil and American companies. This came at the very time when Proskauer was seeking to persuade the United States Government to forget about its interests in Arabia and come out squarely for the Palestine Jews. After two years of preparation, the jury trial (known as *Moffett* v. *Arabian American Oil Company*) came before the United States District Court on February 1, 1949.

The plaintiff was James A. Moffett, one-time chairman of the Board of Directors of the Bahrein Petroleum Company and the California Texas Company and former head of the Federal Housing Administration. He claimed the defendant owed him $6 million dollars for services rendered in keeping petroleum moving out of Arabia to Britain during the early years of the World War II. According to his plea, in 1936 Aramco had acquired important oil concessions from King Ibn Saud of Saudi Arabia. Annual royalties were to be paid, as were the expenditures of devout Moslems making their pilgrimages to Mecca (and their gifts to the King). Together these were the chief sources of the King's revenues. In 1941, when the outbreak of the war put an end to the pilgrimages, leaving Saudi Arabia in financial straits, King Ibn Saud asked Aramco for an annual advance of $6 million against royalties on pain of termination of the oil concession—a loss which would have seriously damaged the war effort of the hard-pressed British who were then standing alone against Nazi Germany.

The company hired Moffett, or so he alleged, to keep the Arabian oil flowing. He was to use his good offices and friendship with President Roosevelt to persuade the United States Government either to make the funds over to Great Britain to satisfy Ibn Saud's demands, or to pay off Ibn Saud directly. Moffett contended that he went to see Roosevelt and at his suggestion had obtained a conference with Jesse Jones who, as Federal Loan Administrator, was in process of arranging a loan to the British government under the Lend Lease Act. Moffett heard from Jones that the American government itself could do nothing, of course, since the country was still neutral, but at the instance of the President and the Secretary of State, he, Jones, had "suggested to the British Ambassador that Britain continue providing King Ibn Saud with such funds as in its opinion were necessary to meet his requirements."

And so it turned out. Britain got its loan of about a half billion dollars from the United States and from 1941 to 1943 paid Ibn Saud $33 million in advances. Satisfied, King Ibn Saud stopped putting the heat on Aramco. Moffett claimed that he had not been compensated by the company and was now suing it for $6 million.

When the case came to trial, it held out all the promises of a first-rate scandal, involving people in high places, including President Roosevelt— at least, Moffett's counsel, William Power Maloney, a highly skilled trial lawyer, made this charge in his opening statement. In 1941, when Moffett was chairman of the board of the Bahrein company, he had been hired by Aramco to rescue it, presumably by getting the United States Government to pay King Ibn Saud.

Proskauer's opening statement for Aramco was simplicity itself, yet he did not reveal the crushing argument that was destined to leave the Moffett case defenseless.

Proskauer began by saying, "I expect to prove to you that the outline of facts made by my friend, Mr. Maloney, is one of the most fantastic interweavings of admitted truths with utter fabrication that ever came to the attention of a jury." Moffett, in contending that because of him Roosevelt spoke to Harry Hopkins and Hopkins to Jones and Jones to the British Ambassador, was not stating the facts. Quite the reverse was true, he argued. Roosevelt was not influenced by Moffett, Jones received no instructions from Roosevelt, and he did not twist the British Ambassador's arm. Simply put, the British had moved solely in their own interest. They were helpless and thus compelled to give in to King Ibn Saud's blackmail.

The direct examination of Moffett by his counsel attempted to show the following. On April 9, 1941 Moffett had an appointment with the President who told him that he had no legislative sanction for what Moffett sought. He suggested that perhaps a government agency might buy oil from one of the Arabian refineries. But Moffett, in a memorandum to Hopkins, persisted in harping on his original notion:

> If the United States government will advance to the King of Saudi Arabia
> six million dollars annually for the next five years, we feel confident that we

can work out with the King an arrangement whereby he will deliver [the oil] through us. . . . Unless this is done, and soon, this independent Kingdom, and perhaps with it the entire Arab world, will be thrown into chaos.

In June, Hopkins relayed the memorandum to Jesse Jones, along with this covering note:

The President is anxious to find a way to do something about this matter. . . . I am not sure what techniques they ought to use. It occurred to me that some of it might be done in a shipment of food direct under the Lend Lease Bill, although just how we could call that outfit [Saudi Arabia] a 'democracy' I don't know. Perhaps instead of his using his royalties on oil as collateral, we could use his royalties on the tips he will get in the future from the pilgrims to Mecca.

In July Roosevelt wrote Jones: "Will you tell the British I hope they can take care of the King of Saudi Arabia. This is a little far afield for us." A few days later Jones wrote Hopkins that there was no legal way the United States could help out. "With approval of the President, I suggested to Lord Halifax [the British Ambassador in Washington] and Sir Frederick Phillips, also Mr. Neville Butler, that they arrange to continue taking care of the King."

Proskauer, in taking over the cross-examination of Moffett, once again displayed his great abilities as a trial lawyer. Moffett admitted that he had no written contract with Aramco for what he had set out to do and that his efforts were not "the producing cause of the British advances to the King of Saudi Arabia." The agreement making a United States Government loan to Britain under Lend Lease had been signed the day before Moffett began working to get a stipulation. Neither Hopkins's letter to Jones nor Jones's memorandum, written in October, made mention of a stipulation. In fact, when Moffett later requested such a letter from Jones, Jones "did not give Mr. Moffett such a letter, because it would not have been true."

In every particular Jones, who had given testimony in a pre-trial examination, supported Proskauer's defense. He had told Moffett, "When they spoke to me about helping the King of Saudi Arabia, that there was no way we could do it. Furthermore that Saudi Arabia was in the British sphere and that if the British thought the King needed assistance, it was up to them to furnish it." When asked whether the President had ordered him to get an agreement out of the British loan delegation, he replied that he had not. To the question, "Did you ever state . . . that it was a term or condition of the collateral loan that the British should furnish aid, whether in money or supplies, to Saudi Arabia?" Jones answered in the negative. And he added that he had never told Moffett that he had obtained such a stipulation.

Proskauer, who was building his case very carefully, argued that it was consistent with British policy and in the British interest to keep on friendly terms with the Arabs. To support his position he introduced the testimony of James M. Landis, former dean of the Harvard Law School and director of United States economic operations in the Middle East during 1942-1945. Said Landis: "In my opinion, the danger is that these events [of 1941] will be treated as an isolated episode and not as part of a long continued policy going far back. The 'inevitability' of the British action in 1941 rose from its consonance with everything that had occurred in the past. The purpose and even the technique is similar and some of the personnel carryover from one period into the next."

The case was closely argued by both sides. Moffett's counsel, Maloney, yielded not an inch, and Proskauer, for his part, was pressing at every point. In the second week tempers flared and the two lawyers grew angry and sarcastic with each other. At one such exchange, the Court chided Proskauer, suggesting that he "count ten" before next speaking.

Proskauer, who knew how to handle a jury, guided and informed rather than admonishing and exhorting. Said he, "Don't get the idea for a moment please, that when Moffett collapsed on points on the witness stand that there was anything of legerdemain on my part, or that when nothing was done to my witnesses on cross-examination that it emanated from any lack of skill on the part of [Maloney]. If he fell down it was not because he is not as good a fighter as I am; it is because he just did not have the shots in the locker." Carefully reviewing the evidence, he ended simply: "Never in God's world would any man or woman on this jury in any affair which affected his or her own life or conduct say that Moffett had sustained the burden of proof of convincing you of this fantastic and outrageous claim."

Maloney, when his turn came, was the reverse. His client had been ill-treated and imposed upon by a giant corporation. He stated, "You have witnessed one man pit his honesty and raw courage against the unlimited resources and corporate might of this defendant.... [and] the combined efforts of a battery of legal, eminent legal talents, so numerous that there was not even room for them to sit at the counsel table...." And then his appeal to class prejudice, "[You have seen] one corporate hireling after another up on the witness stand.... They are fat, sleek, and, oh, so well paid."

After five hours the jury returned with a verdict finding for the plaintiff and awarding him damages of $1,150,000. It was not unexpected to Proskauer; in fact, earlier in the proceedings he had touched upon the grounds on which he would make his appeal. After Maloney had completed his case, and before beginning his, Proskauer had made the usual motion to dismiss the complaint because it was contrary to the weight of the evidence, adding that "the claim asserted and testified to is void as against public policy.... It is against public policy to permit the plaintiff to predicate any recovery on the amounts which he claims were lent by the British government.'' This motion of course had been denied.

To the talismanic phrase, "against public policy," Proskauer returned after the jury had handed up its verdict. He called upon the Judge to set aside the verdict as "against public policy" because the "personal solicitation of the President, the Governor, or heads of departments for favors or for clemency is not the lawful subject of a contract." He cited precedents, and ended: "And there is no use of my piling Pelion on Ossa. I have got ten cases on my brief which hold that up as an absolute norm." This would turn out to be a brilliant *coup*.

The jury had rendered its verdict February 15, 1949. Two months later, on April 25, the Judge made public his opinion. He went at length into the evidence and he examined the law. And then, he stated,

> All we have left is a hope by the President that the British 'can take care of the King'; a *suggestion* by Jesse Jones 'that Britain *consider* providing King Ibn Saud . . . with funds'; or the showing of the President's note by Jesse Jones to the British representative, . . . with the *request* that the British government furnish [Ibn Saud] with whatever funds it felt were desirable and necessary. Whether it be a hope, a request, or a suggestion, it in no way approximates the claim of the plaintiff.

Of course, all this had been clearly set out by Proskauer. Said the Court: "The services contemplated under this contract are the kind the law says may not be compensated for. They are against public policy. . . . In all conscience I felt I should set this verdict aside and direct a verdict for the defendant."

The case went before the Second Circuit Court of Appeals in its October 1950 term. Proskauer wrote the brief and made the oral argument for the defense. An opinion by Judge Jerome N. Frank, for the three-judge panel, affirmed the lower court, not on the grounds of public policy Proskauer had stressed, but more narrowly: "There was no proof," said Frank, "that plaintiff had performed the services for which he claimed compensation." The public policy argument probably was too touchy and opened up too many wide vistas.

Proskauer, the wise old professional, was overjoyed. All along he had played it both ways. In a letter to a friend he wrote,

> [It] furnishes one of the few examples of getting what you have gunned for. When I left the courtroom after the argument, some of my assistants were critical . . . because they thought I spent too much time in the discussion of evidence rather than of public policy. I had stayed awake the night before . . . and I decided that public policy was pretty well going to take care of itself on the brief, and that my job on argument was to get the Court to realize the complete hollowness of the case. By the grace of Providence it came out that way.

In February, 1951 Moffett petitioned the United States Supreme Court for a writ of certiorari. But again Proskauer had considered every contingency and plugged up every hole. On March 12 the case was irrevocably closed, when the Supreme Court denied certiorari and Moffett's plea for appeal.

For a man of seventy-four the Moffett case, in all its ramifications, was a virtuoso performance. But Joseph Proskauer was destined to surpass even that landmark. When he laid the ground work for his last case of note, he was almost eighty years old—yet he did it so well that it ended in the complete vindication of his client.

The case was officially known as *United States* v. *Standard Oil Company of California, et al.* It had its inception in August, 1952, when the Department of Justice brought suit against a number of oil companies for having overcharged the government $100 million in the sale of Saudi Arabian oil to European countries under the Marshall Plan. In this connection the Department of Justice had appointed Milo V. Olson, a highly regarded Los Angeles lawyer and a special assistant to the Attorney General, to work up its cases and bring them to trial.

Earlier, in 1948 the Marshall Plan had been broadened into the Foreign Aid Program. Under this, the so-called Economic Cooperation Administration (ECA) was to finance in U. S. dollars purchases of needed commodities (in this case, oil) by foreign nations which would put up the equivalent in their own currency. The price to be charged for the American commodities was determined by formulas contained in regulations of the ECA whose policy it was to finance at the "lowest competitive market price." The government suit revolved about the allegation that, for a long period of time, the prices for oil sold abroad had exceeded the lowest competitive limit and, therefore, the companies had been ineligible for government financing. As a result, the government was asking for the return of all or at least part of these funds.

Olson first had decided to sue Standard Oil of California, the Texas Company, Bahrein Petroleum Co. Ltd., Caltex, Ltd., Caltex Oceanic, Ltd., and Mid-East Crude Sales Co. As the trial opened in New York on April 15, 1957, before Judge Thomas F. Murphy, Bahrein, Caltex, and their sales subsidiaries were represented by the Proskauer firm. Standard Oil of California was being defended by Cahill, Gordon, Reindel and Ohl, and the Texas Company had as its counsel Webster, Sheffield & Chrystie. In all, there were fifteen attorneys appearing for the defense.

Certainly, Proskauer was a peer among peers in this impressive array, if not *primus inter pares*. Despite his age and the highly technical questions involved in the case, he plunged into its preparation with gusto, working out a strategy of defense that was simple and yet overwhelming. He conceded that the oil companies, in good faith, had complied with every applicable price regulation throughout the period of the sales. But, more importantly, these prices were the lowest "competitive market prices" as practical businessmen would determine them in competition with each other and in the higgling between sellers and buyers in the market place. This was the central argument he developed in his opening presentation, and when the prosecution offered a key witness, Paul G. Hoffman, the first head of the ECA (1948-1950), he seized the opportunity to isolate and dramatize the issues in Hoffman's cross-examination.

When Olson opened for the government, he agreed that crude oil was among the important commodities the hard-pressed European countries needed. In fact, during the first year of the administration's operations, almost half a billion dollars worth was paid for to be delivered at the "market price." Olson submitted, and he had facts and figures to prove it, that during the first four years of such sales the oil companies had over-charged the United States almost one hundred million dollars.

Proskauer opened for the defense, addressing the Court for more than two hours. He was completely at ease, his speech colloquial, his manner friendly and disarming. He was not seeking to obfuscate but to inform, he said, and in the first few minutes of his presentation he drove home the simple issues on which he was going to rest his case:

> There are certain postulates in this case that nobody can deny [he declared]. The first is that we never sold any oil in America or to America, and when I say 'we' I mean Caltex and its group. . . .
>
> Second, as my friend Olson . . . substantially concedes, nobody in Europe, with his sole reservation about that UK transaction . . . , could buy oil for a penny less than we were selling it for, and I interject that we were not selling it to the ECA. The ECA . . . was a kind of investment banker here, and we sold oil for $1.75 as a willing seller to a willing buyer in a market which I shall show you was competitive in the extreme, and nobody could get it for less. . . .
>
> My last observation . . . is that you don't build up lawsuits by casual conversations, by heated debates, by experts, by inter-office communications, one of the most important of which I am going to show you was never even communicated to us. You fixed our obligations with respect to what was eligible for ECA financing by regulations duly adopted and printed in the official Register in accordance with the statute. And in that, your Honor, I am taking no technical position because I shall show you that every dictate of justice requires that the ECA be held to that obligation.

Proskauer's second opportunity came a few days later, when Olson put Hoffman on the stand. After he was cross-examined by other attorneys for the defense, Proskauer took his turn. Hoffman was no tyro, no government functionary suddenly invested with mysterious and extraordinary powers, trying to work his way out of a vast tangle of conflicting claims and interests, he stated, flatteringly. Quite the contrary. From humble beginnings Hoffman had climbed up to become the knowledgeable and highly-respected president of the Studebaker Corporation. In every respect he knew his way about the intricacies of tricky business-management matters. Such a witness, he continued, was to be treated with the respect due his abilities, accomplishments, and troubling problems. In a few questions Proskauer skillfully established this rapport with Hoffman, in effect, making him his own witness. After an exchange of pleasantries, Proskauer asked Hoffman whether he had difficulty in reaching any conclusion about prices on the crude oil sales. "Speaking personally, that is true," Hoffman replied, adding that he realized that any advice his consultants had given him "became effective only if [he] translated it into a regulation." Proskauer then suggested that Hoffman's consultants themselves "had a difficult time coming to an agreement" and Hoffman again agreed. Next, Proskauer asked his witness whether he knew of a certain clause in the regulations which required the ECA "to impose additional limitations," in the event the rule of competitive prices "was not met." When Hoffman replied "yes," Proskauer added, "And it was not your idea, was it, that a seller...had to go through the *Congressional Record* to find out what your regulations were?" Hoffman replied, "No."

Proskauer expressed the opinion that, when one oil company reduces its price, competitors usually meet it—and that in this case the ECA approved and financed a lower figure "for a long time." After Hoffman had answered affirmatively, the exchange continued as follows:

> *Proskauer:* But that was a very important factor, about the most important factor that you can think of, the enormous volume of sales in Europe which were being made both ECA-financed and not ECA-financed, both to affiliates and non-affiliates, all during this period of controversy?
>
> *Hoffman:* Well, Judge, in all honesty I would say it was that question that I brought the consultants in to answer because I wasn't sure I could answer it.
>
> *Proskauer:* I know you were not sure you could answer it, but you are a very practical businessman. I am going to ask you sitting there with the responsibility of decision which was on you, and not on the consultants, wouldn't you now man to man talking to me and looking me in the eye say if you were trying to ask yourself the question, what is the lowest competitive market price as far as practicable, that enormous sales all during this period on the continent of Europe was at least a very important factor in answering that?
>
> *Hoffman:* That I will answer yes.

Upon receipt of these satisfactory replies, Proskauer had actually won his case against the government. Hoffman, guided by Proskauer, had agreed that the oil companies had all along been acting in good faith—and the colloquy continued:

> *Proskauer:* Now, when these people were reducing the prices all the time, as I have indicated, you knew that they were trying to live in peace and harmony with you, didn't you?
>
> *Hoffman:* Yes, I think that might have been a factor.
>
> *Proskauer:* I beg your pardon?

Hoffman: I think that was a factor.

Proskauer: You know it has been conceded in this case that there was no fraud or over-reaching in any respect in all our dealings?

Hoffman: I never felt there was any fraud or deceit at all.

Proskauer: And you never thought there was any fraud in connection with anything we did, the selling of oil, the supplier's certificates, or anything else?

Hoffman: No, that is quite true; I did not.

Proskauer: So we can assume there is no suggestion of fraud or over-reaching in any aspect of this case as you saw it develop?

Hoffman: That is correct.

The remainder of the case was anticlimax. A little later Proskauer asked Hoffman about the government's business with Korea and, by so doing, was not only moving outside the areas covered in direct examination, but was making the witness his own and therefore was bound by his replies. Olson objected—Proskauer was cocky now. He had bested the younger man. When Olson again objected, Proskauer actually humiliated him. Said he, "I am not going to have many opportunities to talk to Mr. Hoffman again, and if [Olson] wants me to I will make him my witness on any excerpt here. I don't know of any witness I would rather have. I am surprised at you, Mr. Olson."

It was no wonder that Proskauer could say, after he had released Hoffman: "Oh! It's not been a bad day." Three months later, when the trial was over, he received this salute from the vanquished but admiring Olson: "I thought that your cross-examination of Paul Hoffman was one of the finest bits of cross-examination I have ever had the pleasure of listening to. . . . The job you then performed was a masterpiece."

Proskauer's appearance did not end the suit. It went on before Judge Murphy who, on July 17, 1957, in a long opinion found on every point for the defendants. Said he, following the Proskauer argument:

> We cannot conclude . . . without saying and finding as a fact that the defendants' proof showed beyond contradiction that the prices financed by ECA were in fact the lowest competitive prices. Throughout the entire period the ECA continued to finance at such prices, which perhaps more than anything else indicates ECA's acknowledgment that the prices charged were in fact the lowest competitive market prices.

Two years later the Circuit Court of Appeals affirmed the Murphy decision. In time, when the case appeared on the Supreme Court docket, certiorari was denied. But Proskauer had bowed out in 1957—this had been his last great case. When it came to the preparation of the brief on appeal, in July, 1958 Proskauer, with his usual sixth sense in these matters, jotted this note to his youngest partner, George M. Shapiro, who was working it up, "Don't hide the forest with trees. This case will be won by my opening and Hoffman cross-exam." And so it turned out.

THE NEW YORK STATE CRIME COMMISSION

14

A democratic society has to go through a house cleaning periodically. Unless there is constant vigilance in all its branches, the agencies of government—public bodies and officials, elective office holders, party functionaries—either become flabby or succumb to the temptations of corrupters. Various devices have been created to expose the weaknesses that creep in: investigations of legislative committees, broad grand jury inquiries, executive commissions. Legal codes have been drawn up to give such ad hoc instrumentalities effective tools with which to work—the rights to subpoena witnesses for questioning and records and documents for examination, in limited degree to offer for cooperation immunity against prosecution, to use the power of contempt to compel the recalcitrant to testify.

Sometimes the results have been the removal of errant office holders. Sometimes new legislation. Among the significant consequences of such free-wheeling inquiries is exposure: of want of diligence on the part of police and prosecutors, the links between organized vice or crime and public officials, the sale of public offices, the growth of overweening power in government itself. Most important is the exposure to the electorate of its own indifference to open or uncovered wrongdoing in its own institutions. These may be political parties, trade unions, public offices, privately- or publicly-owned corporations. (Devices used to this end are self-appointed "citizens' committees" and "reform" movements within political parties.) The only cure here is not more legislation but internal reform through the organization and action of the people. The argument in support of a democratic society is that such popular intervention does sporadically take place. And the defense of the public investigation—despite its hue and cry, the daily sensationalisms fed to the press, the occasional hurt to the reputations of decent men and women—is that it does have such an effect.

When the economy is flourishing, with full employment and new investments creating increases in wealth and income, the slackness in the management and responsibility of public bodies and the indifference of the electorate are most likely to occur. And contrariwise, when employment and business have ceased expanding, when the electorate has become critical of the ways of its servants, investigations by public bodies flourish like the green bay tree.

The end of the 1940s and the opening of the 1950s was such a time. A pattern of self-examination was set in 1950 and 1951 by the activities of the Senate Crime Investigating Committee, headed by Senator Estes Kefauver. Inquiries were launched in California, Florida, New Jersey, and

Texas. In every case ad hoc legislative committees were looking into the pervasiveness of criminality and its relations to public agencies, business, and trade unions. And one of the greatest such public inquiries was that of the New York State Crime Commission, of which Joseph Proskauer was chairman during 1951-1953, in his seventy-fourth to seventy-sixth years.

New York's Governor Thomas E. Dewey had won fame and political success for his "crime-busting" in the 1930s, first as a special prosecutor in New York County and then as its elected district attorney. From that office he had moved into the executive mansion in Albany in 1940. Twice, in 1944 and 1948, he had been the Republican Party's unsuccessful candidate for the presidency. By 1950 he had become alarmed by disclosures of crime and racketeering on the New York port waterfront, made by a citizens' organization called the Anti-Crime Committee. It was becoming apparent that one of the city's great industries was being endangered. And Governor Dewey decided to act.

Meanwhile, Kefauver and Dewey had become less than friendly. The former had accused the latter of failing to give assistance to the Senate committee's staff; the latter suspected that Kefauver was aiming to make New York the centerpiece of his political tale of horrors. As for Kefauver, he was actively seeking to get the life of his committee extended in the Senate, with additional funds, because he planned to move into New York, Dewey or no Dewey, and Dewey, in consequence, had decided that New York should best wash its own dirty linen.

Using as warrant a 1917 statute, on March 29, 1951 Dewey created the New York State Crime Commission with sweeping quasi-judicial and investigative powers. It was given all the rights and responsibilities possessed by Governor Dewey and his Attorney General and, therefore, could inquire into anything concerning the public peace, public safety, and public justice. The commission was given the responsibility of looking into the relationship between organized crime and any unit of state government. It was to examine the relationship between the government of the state and local criminal law enforcement, with reference to but not limited to the following: the role of the state police; the power of removal by the governor of local public officers; the possible enlargement of the power of the state over local units; the desirability of creating a new state agency of investigation to keep a continuous check on criminal enforcement; the desirability of establishing a uniform jury system for both grand juries and trial juries; and the examination of problems raised by criminal activity as it spilled over county or state boundaries. It could also conduct public or private hearings, administer oaths, examine witnesses, subpoena persons, books, papers, records, cite witnesses for contempt or request the courts to issue warrants of attachment, and call upon any state department and agency for assistance. The mayors, district attorneys, and the commissioners of police were required to assist the commission in its work.

As commissioners Governor Dewey named these highly regarded citizens: Joseph M. Proskauer, chairman; Samuel S. Capen, chancellor emeritus of the University of Buffalo; Edward P. Mulrooney, former New York City police commissioner; Lithgow Osborne, former ambassador to Norway and a trustee of the Osborne Association for Penal Reform; and Ignatius M. Wilkinson, dean of the Fordham University Law School. Commentators noted the commission was well-balanced, containing a judge, an educator, a police administrator, a diplomat and penal reformer, and a lawyer-educator. One was a Jew, two were Protestants, and two Roman Catholics. However, it was also noted that Dewey named neither a woman nor a labor leader.

In an interview with Mark Hirsch, October 4, 1963, Dewey told why he had chosen Proskauer as chairman. He had been an excellent judge, ranking high in his profession, and he was one of the leading trial lawyers in the country. Said Dewey, "I knew he would throw his great energies into it. His integrity was complete. He could be trusted to do a strong, impartial first-rate piece of work." Moreover, in 1934, when Dewey was only thirty-two and in private practice, Proskauer had invited him to assist in a law case involving two of New York's great banks. At that time Proskauer, said Dewey, had made "a beautiful and brilliant summation to the jury." As "old friends," Dewey was now repaying Proskauer.

Governor Dewey took immediate steps to organize the new commission and provide it with an appropriation of $250,000 for a year's study of organized crime. Each member was immediately apprised of progress (Proskauer, who was traveling abroad at the time, was kept in touch by radio-telephone). And the first decision was the choice of John Marshall Harlan as chief (and later general) counsel to head the legal staff of the new body. In his *Reminiscences* Proskauer observed that Dewey was responsible for the selection of Harlan—but the fact is that Proskauer, himself, by radio-telephone at sea, had made the offer so appealing that Harlan found it impossible to refuse. (The two men had known each other as far back as 1927, when Proskauer had been close to Al Smith.) In addition to Harlan, actually as chief of staff, was named Ben A. Matthews, a very good lawyer who was made assistant chief, but who later, toward the end of the work in 1954, was promoted to chief counsel.

When Joseph Proskauer returned to New York on April 4, he and his associates called on Governor Dewey at once. Proskauer was particularly delighted to begin work with Harlan. Together they visited Senator Kefauver—Proskauer did not want to prejudge the situation. While he had been off the bench for twenty-one years, he did "still have a little judicial temperament" and he hoped he could "be educated within the next week." These facts suggest that Proskauer had every intention of keeping a tight rein on himself. Harlan, who accompanied him to Albany and to Washington, observed his colleague with detachment and amusement.

Later, recalling the relationship, Harlan characterized Proskauer's deportment as "restless" and "impatient" and described him as "essentially a
partisan [who] had to identify himself with causes. His is not a judicial
temperament. He finds it irksome to have to be impartial." Of himself
Proskauer said: "I am a little in awe of this new job." Harlan disagreed:
"Proskauer got right into the cage without waiting for developments. He
pitched in with all the enthusiasm and imagination into the amorphous
assignment to investigate crime and the politics of people in public life."

In beginning its work, the commission held a series of private hearings
(which were at first closed to permit attorneys to line up their raw materials, assemble witnesses, and examine records and documents). These
were followed by public hearings in four widely separated parts of the state
and a fifth which dealt exclusively with the Port of New York waterfront.
These hearings were actually showpieces. Testimony of witnesses who
were regarded as pertinent or newsworthy was reported fully in the newspapers of the state. Although Dean Wilkinson was vice-president of the
commission, Proskauer usually presided. Harlan as a rule examined, but
Matthews occasionally substituted for him and took over entirely when
Harlan withdrew. In the important waterfront investigation, the arrangements were virtually the same, except that Theodore Kiendl, a partner of
the John W. Davis law firm, acted as special counsel.

Together Proskauer and Harlan made an impressive team. They
received a wide press, some of it dealing with the sensational, as one might
expect, but almost all of it presented carefully and soberly. As a means of
creating public awareness, the hearings succeeded admirably. Harlan was
a skilled, insistent, keen examiner, and Proskauer was more than a mere
spectator. His attitude was "quasi-judicial" and he was careful to preserve "the division between prosecution and defense." According to Harlan, he maintained "his objectivity and a sense of fairness, and also the
dignity and impartiality of the proceedings." In this particular, Proskauer
was an excellent chairman. He made clear and succinct opening remarks.
He was quick to protect the blameless, and he replied in formal statements
to those who questioned the good faith of the inquiry. However, he did not
hesitate to rebuke, to order, to warn, or to advise. He listened closely and
from time to time commented wryly and often wittily. There is no doubt
that he enlivened the proceedings. His dialogue with witnesses, such as
the one with a New York City Democratic district leader who was testifying
on behalf of Frank Costello, a well-known gambler with apparently great
political influence, made a good show—and excellent copy for the state's
newspapers.

One part of the investigation, which may be called "Crime and the
Public Servant," was made in three communities where this relationship
was stressed, Ogdensburg, Hudson, and Staten Island. It centered about
dice games, slot machines, the maintenance of horserooms, and the

operating of the numbers racket, in one group, and prostitution in another. They were considered crimes against society, those that might be called "victimless crimes." The commission also set about to expose their wide prevalence in the state and the culpability of the law enforcement authorities in either winking at them or accepting regular bribes from them. A characteristic incident occurred in Hudson. The witness was the former police commissioner who at the same time was the chairman of the City Democratic Committee. Under oath he admitted that he "knew that at least by widespread heresay the numbers racket was flourishing, that there were horserooms, that there were crap games and that 'The Block' had operated with house of prostitution for many, many years."

The commission, in total, issued five reports, the first four of which were findings and recommendations and the last a summary of accomplishments. The first, dated January 23, 1953, set out to demonstrate that there were basic shortcomings in the criminal law enforcement in the state machinery which demanded immediate remedial action. Evidence was adduced that there were payoffs for "protection" to police officers and other public officials or as contributions to political organizations. At the public hearing in Staten Island one witness, a former state senator and county attorney, reported this conversation with one Mr. Ruppell, then Republican county chairman:

> Well, I can't exactly place the date, but I had some conversation with him in which he indicated to me that he wanted a very normal administration of the district attorney's office. That's the way he put it. He said he didn't want the toes of people stepped on, and he didn't want a reform administration in the district attorney's office. He said there were certain contributors to the Republican party who would be adversely affected if we had a reform administration.

The upshot was that Governor Dewey was advised to supercede the district attorneys of St. Lawrence, Columbia, and Richmond counties. He did so at once and their successors proceeded to prosecute matters arising out of the investigation. Many such trials and convictions followed, as well as the removal or resignation of public officials for refusing to waive immunity and testify. In this first report the commission also made some general observations, including these:

> Whether the reason for failure of the law enforcement machinery has been bribery, political deals, inefficiency or loyalty to old friends, the evidence conclusively established . . . a serious breakdown in law enforcement. It further showed that the local law enforcement officers failed to realize the serious degradation of the public service that arose from either their complacence or their malfeasance, or, realizing it, did not fear discovery or retribution.

However, the commission had no desire to impair the viability of local home rule, believing that law enforcement should remain in local hands. And it declared that "the best way to preserve local autonomy in the administration of the criminal law is to save it from itself and its inherent weaknesses. If local law enforcement machinery ceases to function, local autonomy in this respect must ultimately wither and die." The commission offered as "a more basic step towards a permanent solution" the creation under Governor Dewey of a permanent Commission of Investigation with the continuing function of doing what itself had been doing. Dewey and the legislature accepted the recommendation, except that the new agency consisted of but one commissioner who was given wider powers. The law was passed in 1953. Subsequently, it was amended to expand the agency to three members.

The second phase of the commission's investigation, unique in public annals, led to fascinating disclosures which, in turn, led to significant changes in the New York election laws. It took place wholly in New York County (which was deemed representative) and the witnesses were largely party district leaders, members of party committees, and office holders. To play bass to their treble were known figures of the gambling and racketeering world, with whom the politicians were friendly. On the first day of the hearings, November 13, 1952, the New York *Times* headlined its story, "Tammany Leaders Admit Racket Ties." In its report of March 9, 1953 the commission put the problem of the relation of the regular party machinery to the democratic processes of government in this way:

> The investigations of the Commission have made it apparent that political committees and their leaders, selected, organized and functioning pursuant to the Election law, occupy a position of the greatest importance in the operation of democratic government. . . . Therefore, it is a matter of grave importance that steps be taken further to encourage men of high character and ability to become leaders of political committees. It is equally important that steps be taken looking to the elimination of unfit persons, and to the prevention of the choice of undesirable persons for political leadership.

Proskauer's key role in this investigation and his clear understanding of how government was affected by the integrity or want of it, of the party leaders, exemplified the position he had taken very early in the commission's work. When the hearing in Hudson was meeting with recalcitrance from the Republican county leader, for example, Proskauer made these illuminating remarks:

> A political committee in New York is not a voluntary body. It is created by statute. It is elected at the primaries held at public expense and the chairman of a county committee has a very grave responsibility, if he discharges his duty properly. . . . And to have the chairman of a county committee . . . come here and refuse to answer these questions on the grounds that they might tend to incriminate him, is a shocking blow at democratic government

in the State of New York. I'm calling that to the witness's attention in the hope that if he can see his way clear to steer clear of a criminal charge, he will answer these questions.

Matthews and Proskauer opened the New York County proceedings with declarations of their intentions. Matthews said there were to be four phases, to wit: to show the unsavory caliber of some of the party leaders in New York County; to indicate the method by which political leaders perpetuate themselves in power; to point out the important powers exercised by these leaders, particularly in the selection of party nominees; and to illustrate some of the results of entrusting party leadership to persons unfit to assume honestly their manifold responsibilities. As for his part, Proskauer reminded his listeners that the purpose of the inquiry was not simply exposure. It was established to make "recommendations to the Governor and to the Legislature for the adoption of curative measures," he said.

In his opening remarks at the second phase of the inquiry, that having to do with political power and its misuses, Proskauer outlined the four matters the commission was charged to explore: (1) evidence of the existence of improper political tie-ups; (2) the methods by which those responsible for the tie-ups are chosen and remain in power; (3) the possible defects in the election machinery that enables them to remain in power, and (4) the extent to which the exercise of that power has given influence to underworld characters and resulted in a serious deterioration of public service. The party county committees were very powerful, he said, in great part because their existence had been confirmed by law, they were "creatures of statute. . . . They are public bodies, and they exercise a dominating influence in the formulation of public policies and in the designation and choice of public officials."

The commission's counsel had no difficulty in showing that some of New York County's political leaders were unfit to hold their positions. There was evidence presented that divulged incomes for which the recipients could not account; admissions to association with known criminals; and the acknowledgment that Frank Costello was known as "The Boss." It was also evident that underworld figures made contributions to party funds in violation of the election laws. Again and again, the enormous and virtually unchallengeable power wielded by political leaders was demonstrated. The hearings read like a sophisticated and cynical commentary on the seizure and retention of political power. An outstanding case in point was the testimony of a Bronx County Republican leader who had been an assembly district leader for nearly forty years. Under cross-examination he testified that a "suggestion" made by a county leader was tantamount to election, adding that it was all "cut and dried" and that the results were known "before the convention meets." It was also revealed that the county leaders controlled the appointment of personnel to exempt positions in the courts. In fact, the leaders themselves sought and obtained the jobs of secretaries and clerks to judges where they received regular salaries and did little or no work. As of January 1, 1952, in the five New York City counties under investigation, 57, or 29 percent, of the 199 leaders of both parties were then employed in the courts. Furthermore, it was ascertained that the great majority of them were non-lawyers who held positions where legal experience was considered necessary.

These revelations prompted newspapers to declare that the commission was also investigating the judiciary. At this point Proskauer stepped out of his formal role of chairman to make a statement which had widespreading effects:

> We are investigating the relationship between political committeemen and undesirable characters, and one aftermath of that is the kind of thing that touches on the judiciary. . . . We believe that after all our evidence is in, there should be basis for a thorough investigation into the whole judicial system, not so much chiefly, or mainly, with respect to any wrongdoing . . . but with respect to a study of the organization of the courts in this State, with the ultimate objective of getting some kind of reorganization, both as to the organization of the courts, and the methods of selection, which has been successfully accomplished in the State of New Jersey.

Governor Dewey incorporated this idea in his annual message to the legislature in January, 1953, calling for the creation of a Temporary Commission on the Courts which was to have "as its goal the complete re-evaluation of the court system." During that session the legislature passed an act, setting up a commission consisting of eleven members who were charged to look into the following problems: problems relating to the administration, structure, procedures and personnel of the courts; alleviation of calendar congestion; revision and simplification of practice statutes and enlargement of rule-making powers; reduction in costs of litigation; improvements in methods of selection of the judiciary; changes in substantive law to empower the administration of justice; and the evaluation of the present jury system.

The commission's examination of party machinery and the voluminous testimony it took indicated that the election law was being persistently circumvented. All sorts of difficulties stood in the way of independent candidates for district leadership who wished to be on primary ballots. In short, the work of the Board of Elections, a creature of one or the other major party organization, creaked under numerous and unnecessary technicalities.

In its second report the commission sought to eradicate the evils that had crept into the party and electoral processes. "Political leaders should have the dignity and be given some of the attributes of public officers" it stated, adding:

... leaders and officers of political committees on the assembly district, city, county and state levels should be given a status similar to that of public officers, and along with that status some of the duties and responsibilities of such officers. Legislation ... should require ... that each 'party officer' take an oath of office and be subject to forfeiture [of it] if, when duty called upon to testify concerning the performance of his official duties, he fails to waive immunity. Legislation ... should so clarify and give recognition to the fundamental importance of party leadership as to attract more people of ability and integrity to ... party service.

Inasmuch as the election law had got into a tangle, the commission decided that the legislature should create an appropriate body to overhaul the whole system and make needed corrections:

... to give to the enrolled members of the political parties the opportunity to express an intelligent and effective choice as to party leadership. A thorough revision of the Election Law ... would provide the means for, and encouragement of, a more active and effective participation by the electorate in the selection of political leaders and, thereby, in party affairs and the formulation of party policies.

The report concluded with these wise observations concerning the weaknesses and strengths of a democracy. The hand of Joseph Proskauer is evident in the phraseology:

Democracy is not self-executing. To make it function successfully, the great body of honest voters must exercise its power. ... If the Election Law is amended ..., a great forward step will be taken in the achievement of righteous and effective government. That step, however, must be followed by continuous and intelligent participation in party government by the voters themselves. ...

The stream of government rises no higher than its source. With us, all power stems from the people. One function of our disclosures has been to arouse the public to the need for it to exercise its power. ... Full enrollment, full primary voting, active service in committees—these are the elements of that eternal vigilance which we must have to safeguard and prosper the process of democratic government in our State.

Once more Governor Dewey took note. In a special message to the legislature, March 14, 1953, he called for legislation that would guarantee certain party officers a status similar to that of public officers; and for a thorough review of the provisions and procedures under the election law and party rules. In both the legislature complied. It amended the 1953 election law and it established a bipartisan joint legislative committee composed of three senators and three assemblymen. The committee began work at once and in 1954 proposed a series of meaningful amendments, including a provision in party rules for the direct election of district leaders in New York City, elimination of the requirement that signers of independent nominating petitions register for current elections, simplification of the mode of acceptable signatures on independent nominating petitions, and the permanent use of voting machines at primaries. The legislature approved and Dewey signed such a bill into law. Thus were many of the conditions criticized by the commission immediately corrected.

The New York waterfront investigation, which was begun in November, 1951, was long and herculean. For it a separate staff was set up, headed by Assistant Chief Counsel Leslie H. Arps with, as special counsel, Theodore Kiendl. On its roster were attorneys, investigators, and accountants, who established close cooperation with the New Jersey authorities and the police of both the city and state. All together, behind closed doors, the staff examined hundreds of witnesses, held about a thousand hearings, conducted more than four thousand interviews, and amassed about thirty thousand pages of testimony. Accountants examined the records of nearly one hundred steamship, stevedore, and trucking companies, local unions, and miscellaneous individuals and corporations. Public hearings ran from December, 1952 to March, 1953, and on May 20 the report was filed. After a brief holiday Proskauer served as chairman of the final public hearings; and on July 22, 1953 he appeared before the subcommittee of the United States House of Representatives Committee on the Judiciary which had begun hearings on a bill whose purpose was to permit the states of New Jersey and New York to enter into a compace to create a Waterfront Commission. As a key witness, his testimony was looked forward to eagerly.

The voluminous evidence the commission had collected indicated that, not only was the Port of New York in danger of losing the supremacy in the country of its maritime commerce, both coastwise and foreign it had so long maintained; but also that the accompanying evils were bound to damage the entire New York business community. There had been both public neglect and indifference behind the Port's decline. One factor was the deterioration of the piers. Another was a structure of discriminatory freight rates about which the Interstate Commerce Commission had done nothing to rectify, despite numerous appeals. But the most important factor threatening the welfare of the Port, said the commission's report, was "the entrenched existence of deplorable conditions involving unscrupulous practices and undisciplined procedures, many of which are criminal and quasi-criminal in nature." These had remified into many organizations and operations, including prolonged delays of berthed ships which, of course, resulted in excessive costs and even open invitations to blackmail. The report went on: corruption had penetrated the activities and methods of work of both the steamship and the stevedoring companies. Union officials, in the International Longshoremen's Association (ILA), including its president Joseph P. Ryan, and in the locals serving the Port, had flagrantly disregarded the welfare of their members and the public. Thus, the commission found that there was collusion between steamship and stevedoring companies on the one hand and with union officials on the other; that it was not unusual for certain stevedoring companies to make payments to officials of the steamship companies to gain or continue stevedoring contracts; and that most of the stevedoring companies expended large amounts of cash for which they could not account, paying off in this way shipping people and union officials.

In such secret and illegal transactions there was always a *quid pro quo*. Testimony revealed that cash payments were made to union officials by stevedoring companies for "services rendered" or for goodwill. The president of Daniels & Kennedy, a large trucking and stevedoring company, declared under oath that for five successive years he had made such cash payments of $1,500 to Joseph P. Ryan. (When questioned, Ryan stated that the money had been used to "oppose Communists.") The vice-president of the Jarka Corporation, the largest stevedoring company, admitted that between 1947 and 1951 his company had paid out $58,000 "for services rendered" outside regular work hours to men who were organizers or agents of local unions. The commission was also appalled at the cynical ways by which trade union officials had betrayed their trust to the rank and file membership. It declared flatly that Ryan and his organizers, whom he appointed personally, were demonstrably unfit for their posts and that his international union had failed in its supervision of the local affiliates. In addition, the commission proved that Ryan had withdrawn large sums from his union which he used personally and for which he made no effort to account. The report also cited many examples of appointees to union positions for which they were obviously unfit. One such case was that of Edward J. McGrath, an organizer, who had "a criminal record showing 12 arrests for crimes ranging from petty larceny to murder and including two convictions for burglary." Six Brooklyn locals, known as the "Camarda Locals," were for at least ten years, stated the report, "under the control of a group of notorious criminals." One of them was Anthony (Tony Spring) Romeo, who, according to the testimony of the financial secretary of one of the locals, demanded money that "came in from dues. . . . Maybe . . . $20,000, something like that."

Small wonder, that the waterfront locals fell into general disrepute and failed to carry out the functions for which they were ordinarily designed. According to the commission report, which was buttressed by a wealth of evidence, known criminals ran many important ones, at the same time using the presence of the unions on the docks as covers for their own illegal activities. Evidence indicated that they shook down the companies, and were guilty of pilfering, loan-sharking, extortion, and gambling. Their system of recruiting laborers, known popularly as "the shape-up," was found to be "vicious and antiquated." Usually, the period of employment of a man was for only four hours. However, at the more active piers, a gang was hired as a unit, and the team which made it up was chosen by the gang boss.

> The hiring foreman has complete control over what method shall be used at the shape-up and who shall be employed [the report stated]. There is no seniority; an individual or gang may have worked for years at a particular pier and yet can be refused employment at any time, with casuals getting the work. . . . During the year 1951-52 there were 44,000 men employed as dock workers on the waterfront. More than half of these men earned under $1,400 a year.

Because 44,000 men were far in excess of the number actually needed, a good deal of friction had developed in the fight for control of workers, including strikes, work stoppages, and in corrupt hiring practices involving kickbacks. Presumably, and under the contract written between the ILA and the New York Shipping Association, the employers (that is, the steamship and stevedoring companies) selected their own foremen, but in reality they were chosen by the union officials. Thus was the corruption doubly compounded. The testimony showed that many of the foremen exacted tribute from workers, dispensed patronage to relatives, friends, and criminal associates, and kept the piers in a constant state of turmoil as a result of work stoppages and wildcat strikes.

The report characterized another dock procedure, so-called "public loading," that is, the moving of cargo from a pier and stacking it in trucks, and the reverse operation, as a racket. Formerly, the truck drivers had loaded and unloaded their own trucks, but in 1949 Ryan had issued a charter to a local union legalizing the practice of "public loading." Despite this, public loaders operated as individuals, partnerships, or corporations. Some were members of locals unions, and all of them used the labor weapons of picketing and strikes, as well as coercion and extortion, to obtain loading concessions. The commission cited, as an example, the case of George Sellenthin, Inc., a company which did all the public loading on Staten Island. It employed men at a "shape-up," had gross receipts of close to two million dollars for 1947-1952, and its thirty-one stockholders were all members of the ILA locals.

Finally, commissioners attacked the watchman system on the piers as ineffective, costly, and hurtful. The watchmen's union, despite the law which required it to be an independent organization, was in fact closely associated with Ryan's longshoremen. Thefts and pilferage ran to millions of dollars a year and watchmen were discouraged and even reprimanded for reporting them. When several steamship companies tried to improve their security service, they were forced to abandon their efforts because of pressure from officials of the ILA.

The recommendations of the commission were wide-sweeping. The first called for the creation of the Division of Port Administration, under the authority and supervision of the state, which was to be given the power to abolish the "shape-up" system by setting up Employment Information Centers; to license and supervise all stevedoring companies and individuals whose responsibility it was to hire dock workers; to license and supervise persons engaged in the loading and unloading of trucks; and to license port watchmen. The body, was also to have the authority to investigate waterfront conditions and to issue subpoenas, administer oaths, and conduct hearings. The second proposed piece of legislation was designed to assure dock workers that their unions were bona fide and would honestly and constantly represent their proper interests. Labor organizations were to keep complete financial records, maintain bank accounts, and make payments only by check. All officers were to be elected by secret ballot, at least every four years, and these elections were to be supervised by state authorities. Similar safeguards were to be set up as regards voting by union members on the ratification of collective bargaining agreements.

Governor Dewey and the New York legislature moved at once. He held public hearings on the commission's recommendations on June 8-9, 1953 and, following these, summoned the legislature into extraordinary session on June 25. The bill that issued from the Governor's office was bolder than the commission's proposal of the creation of a State Port Commission. It called for a compact between the states of New Jersey and New York (which would require Congressional consent), under both of which a "Waterfront Authority" would operate. The legislature unanimously passed the Waterfront Commission Act and Compact, a counterpart of which was subsequently passed by the New Jersey legislature. Dewey signed this bill on June 30 and Congress following suit, gave its consent and President Dwight D. Eisenhower signed it into law on August 12, 1953.

The new compact provided for two commissioners, one to be named by each governor. The essential provisions of the document (which followed closely the recommendations of the Proskauer commission) were these:

Licenses were to be required for stevedoring firms, pier superintendents, hiring agents, and port watchmen operating in the New York Port. Proof of good character was to be a requisite to the issuance of a license.

Longshoremen were to register with the Commission. The Commission would withhold registration if the applicant had a significant criminal record or otherwise constituted a danger to the public peace and safety to the waterfront.

Like powers existed with respect to the revocation of licenses and registrations.

'Public loading' was banned.

Collection of dues on behalf of a union representing persons licensed or registered pursuant to the Compact was misdemeanor if the union had an official who had been convicted of a felony.

The rights of licensees and registrants were safeguarded constitutionally where threatened with revocation, by providing for public hearings, notice of charges, right of counsel, and court review.

The Commission was given full power to investigate racketeering on the waterfront, including the power to subpoena in both States.

The second recommendation of the New York State Crime Commission (a statute providing that labor organizations be required to meet certain minimum standards) was made, as the commission had suggested, to give unions time to put their own houses in order by voluntary action. Governor Dewey had decided on this course as a result of the public appearance and testimony of George Meany, president of the American Federation of Labor. Meany, referring to the report of the New York State Crime Commission, had declared: "I do not hesitate to say that I cannot find anything resembling legitimate trade-union activity on the part of [ILA]." And in reply to a question from Mr. Kiendl, Meany added, "I do not think there is any question that you have an intolerable situation, that any New Yorker, that is a real New Yorker, as I am, would be ashamed of. As a trade unionist I am ashamed of the situation down there."

Proskauer signed the report on the New York waterfront on May 20, 1953 and promptly announced that he planned to retire at the end of the year. On July 22, in Washington, he testified before the House of Representative's subcommittee of the Committee on the Judiciary on the New Jersey-New York Waterfront Commission Compact, speaking extemporaneously and with great eloquence. When certain members of the subcommittee asked for more time for study, he replied at length, cautioning them that delay or inactivity would "hearten every crook on the waterfront."

> I have dedicated more than two years of my life to the work of this Crime Commission [he concluded], and if I speak with some feeling in my prayers to you not to thwart what I regard as the crowning achievement of my life, you will understand that I speak from a full heart, from an abiding conviction that this thing is right, and that no cavilling and no petty faultfinding shall operate to stop the wheels of decency and of progress.

On December 17 Proskauer formally notified Governor Dewey of his desire to resign from the New York State Crime Commission, "now that its work is completed." Dewey replied promptly, with the friendliness and warmth that had long characterized their relationship:

> In undertaking this great public responsibility in the Spring of 1951 and carrying it through to notable success in every branch of the work, you have once again demonstrated your unselfish devotion to the welfare of the people of the State and the Nation. Certainly, the State of New York has no right to call upon you for further service. In accepting this immense responsibility, lavishing upon it your great talents, all without compensation, you have, I do believe, climaxed a life of extraordinary effective contribution to the public welfare.
>
> I am deeply grateful to you personally and I know I speak for all of the people of the State in expressing deep gratitude and admiration.

PROSKAUER GOES TO ROME 15

Proskauer had taken his first step towards recognizing his Jewishness in 1947-48, when he was 70 years old; that was his emotional identification with the Jews of Palestine and his acceptance of the State of Israel as a very important fact in his life. It was the beginning of his retreat from assimilationism; his assumption that his Jewish birth and his formal adherence to Judaism would raise no barriers to full social and economic equality, to access to all its opportunities for growth and development in the country of his nativity. He was a loyal American; that was enough to assure him equal rights under the laws and mores of his country.

The second step was necessary: and that was to understand the basis of anti-Semitism: it was anti-Semitism that stood in the way of giving him that security and peace of mind that he, as an assimilationist, sought; it was the bar sinister under which all Jews in the Christian world lived. He was a member of the Jewish people who had killed the Son of God. And in 1965, when Proskauer was 88 years old, he took the second step: he raised his voice against this ancient calumny and called upon the Catholic Church, in its Second Vatican Council, to repudiate the charge of "deicide"—and begin the long and difficult journey in the fight against anti-Semitism not only in its liturgy, educational work, and sermonizing but also in its relations with the Jews. By taking this second step, Proskauer's renunciation of assimilation was total and whole and his identity as a Jew, his rounding out of his Jewishness, was now complete.

Other Jews among his contemporaries had embarked on a similar quest. These three notably: the late Sir Lewis Namier, distinguished English historian; Georges Friedmann, equally distinguished French sociologist; and the late Jules Isaac, French historian and educationist. Each of these, like Proskauer had considered himself a citizen of his country of birth or adoption. Each had found in it intellectual and professional fulfillment. Not until the agonies of the 1940s and 1950s had they come to the decision that they were Jews as well as English or French.

Namier, Russian-born (from Galicia, a part of which was in then Russian Poland) who had espoused Roman Catholicism in his youth, had come to realize during the terrifying decade of Nazi domination in Europe that Jews could never become masters of their own destiny until they were able to establish themselves, geographically, as a nation. From his fruitful pen had poured essays, occasional pieces and notes that harped on a double theme: the belief of assimilation in any country had betrayed the Jews; the "one real hope and escape" for all was the creation of a Jewish state with which they could identify psychologically and emotionally. Jews, he declared, must face up to their history and their fate.

> There must be a country [he said] where Jews can live, work, and amuse
> themselves as they please; but, like all nations, among themselves, not under
> the eyes of strangers. . . . If having concluded the Great Journey we shall
> become humdrum and mediocre, that, too, will be our affair: but our children
> will have a better life—and this suffices. No nation need justify itself in its
> own home, and it matters little what nations think of each other.

Namier frankly admitted this was the first, the all-important step; and he
had lived to hail the birth of the State of Israel—but he remained and died a
Roman Catholic, in 1960.

Georges Friedmann, professor of the University of Paris, a Frenchman
by birth, education, sympathies, and loyalties, but a sceptic in religion,
took the next, and a much longer one, twenty years later. He had been
entirely disinterested in Zionism until the events of the 1940s and 1950s
created in him the same unease that had affected Namier. He had seen the
establishment and early struggles of the State of Israel and had gone there
as a casual visitor. Before writing his book, *The End of the Jewish People?*
(1965), he had steeped himself in the works of numerous French Jewish
scholars. His work, therefore, was more than an intelligent traveler's
journals; it was, really, the record of a pilgrimage in quest of a man's
identity. Friedmann wanted to know why he had become a Jew and by
what means Jews could continue to maintain their collective destiny in the
face of world-wide harassment. For he, a native-born Frenchman, had
come to accept his Jewishness "as a fact of my life, without pride or provo-
cation but also without embarrassment or shame." He had come to the
conclusion, as he wrote in *The End of Jewish People?*:

> Christianity worked indefatigably over the centuries to make the Jews
> odious by attributing to them collective responsibility for the death of Christ.
> . . . [By inflicting] on them the rigid and degrading rules of the ghetto . . . [it
> produced] a pathological human condition deprived of the most elementary
> rights, primarily the right most essential for normal development of the per-
> sonality, freedom of choice of work; and it made 'education in contempt' and
> hatred systematic, official, and consistent.

Thus, a sense of interdependence because of the sharing of a common experience, both as people of the Book and the Law and as victims through
more than a millennium of Christian scorn and hatred, was inevitable. This
is what Friedmann meant by his Jewishness as a fact of his life.

It was no accident of history that brought together the three men who put
the Roman Catholic Church on the right road, after more than one thousand years of "education in contempt," in its relations with the Jews.
These were all the products of their time. Jules Isaac, Augustin Cardinal
Bea, and Pope John XXIII. Isaac, a Jew, French-born, an outstanding
French historian, climbed the ladder in his country's public service to become an inspector general of public schools—until he was dismissed in
1940. Bea was a German theologian and a Jesuit and the only German

Jesuit in the College of Cardinals. And John XXIII, born Angelo Giuseppe Roncalli, named cardinal and patriarch of Venice in 1953, at the age of seventy-seven five years later was elected the Church's sovereign pontiff.

During the German occupation of France, Jules Isaac saw his wife and daughter and many of his friends and associates carried off by the Gestapo to die in Nazi prisons or in gas chambers. From that moment all his thinking centered on the scourge of anti-Semitism and more particularly its origins. For him it was too simple to assume that Nazism was solely or chiefly responsible for the wide dissemination of anti-Semitism. It was too deeply embedded in Christian teaching and, in fact, in all the Christian churches, and it was this education that had become part of the consciousness of all Christians. It was, according to Isaac, "the primary and permanent source of anti-Semitism, like a permanent, powerful stock root on which all the varieties of anti-Semitism grafted themselves." Three of his books, all written late in his life, had a profound influence in France and were widely read in more than theological circles: *Jesus and Israel* (1948), *Genesis of Anti-Semitism* (1956), and *Education in Contempt* (1962), which was written one year before his death. The burden of his closely documented argument was that, in his own time, Jesus had a popular following among the Jewish masses and his opposition had come from the leaders of Judaism, among them "the high priesthood, the orthodox, the notables, a number of Pharisee doctors." It was the fathers of the Catholic Church, beginning in the sixth century, however, who had singled out all Jews as responsible for Jesus' passion. Although the intention was theological and designed to unite the warring factions in the early Church, the method was through popular education; that is, the use of the Church's catechisms, and the liturgy of the Mass to "educate in contempt" all Christians against all Jews. This was, according to Isaac, in the mainstream of Christian thought. It depicted the Jews as accursed, debased, and doomed to perpetual servitude. With it were associated three themes: the dispersion of the Jews was a providential punishment for the crucifixion of Jesus; Judaism was already a degenerate religion at the time of Jesus; and all Jews, then and now, were guilty of the crime of deicide.

Isaac's thinking had a profound influence on Cardinal Bea, who reluctantly had come to the conclusion that the Nazi doctrine on the Jews was not enough to explain a universal phenomenon. Pope John XXIII also knew of the writings and the work of Isaac in a French interfaith organization and there is no question that Isaac's ideas prompted John to include the "Jewish question" on its agenda when he summoned the Vatican Council in 1962.*

In 1960, at the request of the French Embassy to the Vatican, an audience was arranged for Isaac at the Holy See. After passing from

---

* Note follows at the end of chapter.

cardinal to cardinal, Isaac finally came to Bea, who brought him and John XXIII together. The Pope listened to Isaac with great sympathy, finally instructing Bea to establish contacts and advance dialogues designed to improve relations with non-Catholics. The American Jewish Committee, of which Joseph Proskauer was now honorary president, responded immediately by sending Bea three memorandums, each of which followed closely the preparatory work for the summoning of Vatican Council II.

By early 1962 Bea's secretariat had drafted a statement reflecting the Roman Catholic attitude towards Jews and Judaism which, with Pope John's approval, was to be introduced at the first session of the Vatican Council, October 11 - December 8, 1962. Controversy between the "conservative" and "progressive" elements within the Church developed at once. The former listened to the Arabs in attendance that a Jewish declaration would involve the Church in the political struggle of Arabs. The "progressives" felt that the time had come for both significant institutional and doctrinal changes. They were restive under the "Roman" mentality of the Curia; they talked, notably the bishops, and particularly the American bishops among them, of "collegiality"—a wider sharing of responsibility and the decision-making powers within the Church; they spoke of the need for liturgical reforms, came out boldly for religious liberty, and took seriously what Bea had been saying about close intergroup relations to fight common dangers.

When Pope John died in the summer of 1963 (Isaac died a few months later), his successor, Pope Paul VI, announced that the Council would continue its work, but it was obvious that he meant to go slow. In September-December, 1963, at the second session, the Vatican itself issued a firm declaration which was introduced personally by Augustin Cardinal Bea. He deplored the "ancient anti-Semitic tradition" of the Roman Catholic Church, adding,

> Nazi propaganda has been effective, and has even insinuated itself among Christians. It has therefore been necessary to re-establish the truth. Let us not forget that the majority of the Jewish people did not agree to kill Jesus. . . . thus the Jewish people is not deicide, as certain Catholics claim.

Despite the fact that Bea implored his colleagues to follow the "example of burning charity of the Lord himself upon the Cross," the opposition was strong—the declaration never came to a vote and the second session adjourned.

Bea, refusing to lose heart, came to the United States a second time (his first visit had been in March, 1963) to urge American well-wishers to bring pressure upon their American prelates to take a firmer stand on religious liberties and upon the Jewish declaration. And when the Vatican Council met for its third session on September 16, 1964, Bea's commission presented a new schema entitled "On the Relation of the Church to Non-Christian Religions."

News of the new schema was leaked out to the New York *Herald-Tribune:* but the charge of deicide against the Jews was going to be dropped, the story stated further; instead, the Church was now going to renew its age-old attempt to convert Jews as the price for attacking anti-Semitism. This report blew up a storm both inside and outside the Vatican Council. The British primate condemned the textual changes. So did 170 out of the 240 American bishops in attendance. The American Catholic press' comments ran the gamut from concern to dismay. A Jewish declaration—not drawn up by the Bea commission—was introduced on September 25. Predictably, it was attacked by Arab prelates who wanted no declaration at all; and by the "progressives" who were now at last in full cry.

The result was a triumph for the "progressives" and the Bea commission resumed its work once more. Another new schema, stronger than the first and entitled "The Relationship of the Church to Non-Christian Religions," went before the Council November 19, 1964. It again included condemnation of the deicide accusation. The unsavory bargain of trading conversation of Jews for the fight against anti-Semitism had disappeared. Hatred and persecution of Jews were denounced and mutual respect and "dialogues" stressing brotherhood were endorsed.

On November 20 the vote on the Jewish declaration was cast and it was carried 1,770 ayes to 185 nays. But the omnibus schema into which the declaration was incorporated (there were 1,651 ayes for it and 99 nays) had 242 votes for with reservations. Obviously, the declaration was not yet in safe waters. The relevant passage of the declaration ran as follows:

> The Church . . . cannot forget that she received the revelation of the Old Testament from the people with whom God in His ineffable mercy concluded the former covenant. Nor can she forget that she feeds upon the root of that cultivated olive tree into which the wild shoots of the gentiles have been grafted. Indeed the Church believes that by His cross Christ Our Peace reconciled Jews and Gentiles, making them one. . . .
>
> Since the spiritual patrimony common to Christians and Jews is of such magnitude, this sacred synod wants to support and recommend their mutual knowledge and respect, a knowledge and respect that are the fruit, above all, of Biblical and theological studies as well as of fraternal dialogues. Moreover, this synod, in her rejection of injustice of whatever kind and wherever inflicted upon men, remains mindful of that common patrimony and so deplores, indeed condemns, hatred and persecution of Jews, whether they arose in former or in our own days.
>
> May, then, all see to it that in their catechetical work or in their preaching of the word of God they do not teach anything that could give rise to hatred or contempt of Jews in the hearts of Christians.

May they never present the Jewish people as one rejected, cursed or guilty of deicide.

All that happened to Christ in His passion cannot be attributed to the whole people then alive, much less to those of today. Besides, the Church held and holds that Christ underwent His passion and death freely, because of the sins of all men and out of infinite love.

In April 1965 Proskauer went to Rome, this time met on holiday-bent as he had done so many times previously. He went as a Jew and he went to the scene of one of the great events of his time, the meetings of Vatican Council II. In his early years his Jewishness had been only of a formal and occasional kind. In the Mobile synagogue and its Sunday school, as a boy, he had learned his prayers and the Hebraic responses of the Reform services; but in his manhood in New York his connection with the synagogue had attenuated. He was an irregular attendant and synagogue business, synagogue polemics and Jewish education (including that of his children) left him cold. To him his Jewishness meant simply that he had been born in a religious faith called Judaism through which he had become associated with Jewish philanthropies and the American Jewish Committee. He was of course aware of anti-Semitism. He had known about it since childhood, but he did not know what to do about it. He believed that educational campaigns, intergroup conferences, appeals to reason, the exposure of the restrictive practices of liberal-arts colleges and medical schools would slowly but in time succeed. Not until the end of World War II did the dream of a Jewish state as the focus of Jewish aspirations hold a strong attraction for him. He came around to Palestine as a ''homeland'' narrowly: here was a place of refuge for the more than one hundred thousand Jews in central Europe who had somehow survived the Nazi holocaust. A homeland for them had to be created even if it meant taking up arms against the British Mandatory and the Arabs, for a national homeland in Palestine had to become a reality.

Proskauer had always had an acute political sense. It had directed him into the camp of Al Smith, taken him to San Francisco in 1945 where the charter of the United Nations was being written, and to the White House to work with President Truman in 1947-48. He had had the courage to admit the error of his earlier life and he had turned around his assimilationist professions. Now they read that his loyalty to a Jewish nation did not weaken his American ties. It was this same political sense that was again at work so late in Proskauer's life in the 1960s. This time the question involved was even a more fateful one than the creation of a Jewish state, it was the necessity for exposing and tearing up the roots of anti-Semitism. Only the renunciation of the dreadful charge that all Jews were deicides could lead to those associations men of good will sought, the brotherhood of man, interfaith trust, and interfaith relations and cooperation.

Thanks to the pioneer work of Jules Isaac, Cardinal Bea, and Pope John, and to the activities of Father Felix Morlion who had founded the Pro Deo movement on an international scale, and to Proskauer's friendship with Rabbi Julius Mark of Temple Emanu-El (which he had joined) and with Cardinal Spellman of New York and Cardinal McIntyre of Los Angeles, Proskauer's education was now proceeding apace. Wittingly or not, he was preparing himself for a new role.

Its time came in the spring of 1965. Vatican Council II, as we have seen, had adopted a straightforward statement on Christian-Jewish relations, at the end of its third session, on November 20, 1964. It seemed to "progressives," to liberal-minded Catholics and to the outside world, that Isaac, Bea and Pope John had finally won—but a crack had been left open of which the untutored were unaware. The overwhelming vote in favor of the new schema had been on principle alone. Among those who had cast favorable ballots for it were 242 prelates who had said yes, but with reservations (*placat, justa medum*); and that implied further reconsideration on details and possible rewriting.

In the following months Rome became a large whispering gallery of rumors and innuendos accompanied by overt threats and overt and covert anti-Semitic attacks. The Arab bishops renewed their hostility to the schema, in which they were supported by Arab diplomats assigned to the Holy See. The declaration, they declared, was a political and not a doctrinal statement. It gave aid and comfort to Israel and by that token was both siding openly with the enemy of the Arab countries and exposing Catholics to persecution. Other "conservative" bishops—from Italy, Spain, South American countries—joined in the assault. Pope Paul seemed to be bending before the wind, for in a Lenten sermon on Passion Sunday in a small Roman Catholic church, he characterized Gospel lesson of the day to which he was preaching as a "grave and sad page narrating the clash between Jesus and the Jewish people—the people predestined to await the Messiah but who just at the right moment did not recognize him, fought him and slandered him, and finally killed him." And now the rumor-mongers were in full cry.

So much for the background for Proskauer's trip to Rome—but two other events gave it plausibility. One was the fact that Father Felix Morlion, the rector-president of the so-called Pro Deo University, had engineered an extraordinary *coup*: he had obtained official papal sanction for his institution, and a special Apostolic Brief, signed by Pope Paul, was in process of preparation. Morlion, a Belgian Dominican priest, had in 1932 begun a movement known as the "Council for the International Promotion of Democracy under God"—an organization whose philosophy was "to introduce the American spirit into European education, to fill a void which the European universities, most of them founded centuries ago, could not fulfill." Its keynote words were "democracy" and "brotherhood." Later, it became known as the "Pro Deo" movement to indicate its Roman Catholic inspiration and in 1944 Morlion had moved its headquarters from Brussels to Rome, and four years later had converted it into a "university," at the request of Pope Pius XII.

Father Morlion had long been associated in the new work of the American Jewish Committee and thus had met Proskauer. Indeed, the Committee had contributed funds to further the "Pro Deo" as an international union. Moreover, Proskauer had been president of the Henry Kaufmann Foundation when its directors voted to erect a building at Pro Deo University in memory of Kaufmann. With this in mind, Father Morlion suggested that Proskauer should personally go to Rome to inaugurate the new structure and this was the second event. The timing was perfect, for the Jewish declaration before the Vatican Council was in grave danger. Proskauer enthusiastically accepted the invitation, and the date was set for April 29, 1965.

Before he left for Rome Proskauer went to visit his old friend, Francis Cardinal Spellman, who had recently been hospitalized. Spellman, who was strongly in favor of the Vatican Council declaration, told Proskauer that he was unhappy because he could not be in Rome for the meeting, but that he was planning to go in the fall. In fact, he had already asked Pope Paul for a private audience, he said. There was no question about where Spellman stood: as far back as April, 1964 he had come out unequivocally in favor of the declaration in an address before the annual meeting of the American Jewish Committee:

> Anti-Semitism can never find a basis in the Catholic religion [he had said].
> Far from emphasizing the differences which divide Jews from Christians our
> Faith stresses our common origins and the ties which bind us together. . . . It
> is high time to stress the bonds of brotherhood which should characterize our
> relationship.

Meanwhile, the Vatican had followed the Pro Deo movement very closely. In 1948 its name was changed to the International University of Social Studies and by 1964-1965 a total of 1,929 priests and laymen were enrolled, one-third of whom were at the graduate level. Nearly three hundred students from fifty-one nations were pursuing their specialties under professors and lecturers (Roman Catholics, Protestants, Jews, Moslems, and Buddhists) from Belgium, Brazil, France, Germany, Great Britain, the Netherlands, Switzerland, Spain, and the United States.

On the afternoon of April 29, 1965, for the Kaufmann pavilion dedication, Father Morlion had succeeded in gathering together an impressive company. Eleven cardinals were present, including Amleto Cigognani, Secretary of State of the Vatican; Eugene Tisserant, Dean of the Sacred College; Gregory Peter Agaianian, prefect of the Sacred Congregation, top ranking dignitaries of the Dominican Order, prelates from the Holy Office and the Sacred Congregation of Seminaries and Universities, bishops attending the Vatican Council, and professors, students, and friends of the university. The speakers were to be the Master General of the Dominican Order, Cardinal Cicognani (who was to deliver the Apostolic Brief), Father Morlion, Josef Cardinal Beran, archbishop of Prague (in exile), and, of course, Joseph Proskauer.

Pope Paul VI opened the ceremonies by hailing the work of his predecessor, Pope Pius XII who he said, had "brought about the foundation of institutions which scattered fertile seeds in the culture of the spirit, in the political, economic and social thinking of peoples who desire to be brought together by links of brotherhood"—one of those was the "International Union" whose very name manifested its purpose.

> From the very outset ['Pro Deo'] has in fact dedicated its best energies to the aims that men of study and men of action from different nations who recognize in God the supreme source of authority in public and private life should join in a common work to establish unity among all these who inhabit the earth. . . . [he said].
>
> It therefore properly pertains to these kinds of studies and other activities designated by the name 'Pro Deo,' to work towards a harmonization of the principles of the anthropological and social sciences with the principles of theology and philosophy, in order that conclusions gathered therefrom might be useful for solving the spiritual problems of our time and others which concern matters.

Cardinal Cicognani was succeeded by Father Morlion who introduced Joseph Proskauer as the "eminent lay orator of the meeting. . . ., renowned throughout the world as a fighter for brotherhood."

Proskauer, deeply moved by this flattering introduction, kept his voice under perfect control, speaking clearly, slowly, simply, and briefly for about twenty-five minutes. He paid tribute to Henry Kaufmann and his foundation and to the ideals of "this great International University of Social Sciences." Both were of the same cut: "The combined achievements of Kaufmann and of this University have become a vital factor in the effort to realize our dream of a great brotherhood of mankind." To that theme Proskauer then addressed himself as follows:

> This twentieth century is marked as an era unsurpassed in the achievement of human brotherhood. Two of its years merit the title 'annus mirabilis.' The first was the year 1945. Then the nations of the world met in our city of San Francisco and adopted the Charter of the United Nations. Its preamble recites the objective 'to reaffirm faith in fundamental human rights, in the dignity and work of the human person and in the equal rights of men and women.' . . .
>
> Here for almost the first time the sanction of law was given to this ideal of brotherhood. . . . 'Where do we go from here?' The answer is that we go ever

upward and onward on the path to gain individual liberty against the forces of bigotry. . . .

The second wonderful year came almost two decades later in 1964. The Ecumenical Council voted approval of the declaration on the attitude of the Catholic Church toward non-Christian religions, and particularly toward the Jews. . . .

Proskauer described the large company which had gathered to honor Augustus Cardinal Bea, on his visit to New York. He recounted the story of the 1928 presidential election in the United States and the Smith-Marshall exchange of letters which were published in the *Atlantic Monthly.* He recalled the time when Governor Alfred Smith was defeated because of anti-Catholic propaganda.

However, [he added] Smith had closed his letter [to Marshall] with these words: 'I join with fellow Americans of all creeds in a fervent prayer that never again in this land will any public servant be challenged because of the faith in which he has tried to walk humble with his God.' Though he lost this election, his prayer was granted in the subsequent election of John Fitzgerald Kennedy, our martyred President.

Proskauer, now leading up to the chief purpose of his visit, again spoke of "brotherhood." But, boldly, he also spoke of justice:

The declaration of the Ecumenical Council, in its amplified version which was voted in November 1964, declares that the Church cannot forget that she received the Revelation of the Old Testament from the people with whom God in his ineffable mercy concluded the Abrahamic Covenant. . . .

The declaration asks of its communicants that they never present the Jewish people 'as despised, rejected, cursed or guilty of deicide.' We Jews welcomed that statement as an act not of favor, but of justice. Father Morlion has greeted me today as a fighter for human brotherhood. As such, in this gathering I voice a prayer. I pray that the God of all of us will bring to all of us the realization that the preservation and implementation of the words I have quoted from the declaration will be the greatest possible step forward for the cause of human brotherhood. The declaration continues: 'All men, therefore, but especially Christians, must refrain from discrimination against or harassment of others because of their race, color, creed, or walk of life.' It is noteworthy that important non-Catholic Christian Synods have endorsed these views.

Did Proskauer have a role in the final fate of the Jewish declaration? Did he help turn the tide? These facts are indisputable. The document was not taken out of Bea's hands. It remained on the agenda for the fourth session of the Vatican Council, and its secretary general made that pledge publicly. Cardinal Spellman was able to return to Rome, where he had a private audience with the Pope and from which he came reassured. The American junior prelates at the Vatican Council, the bishops, the great

majority of whom supported the original schema at last got around to saying "collegiality starts right now." They were openly restive of Vatican
authority. These were not discrete occurrences but straws in the wind.
One has every reason to assume that Joseph Proskauer had helped turn it
into a favoring one.

The final act of the drama was played out between September 30 and
October 15. On the earlier date the new text of the "Declaration on the
Relation of the Church to Non-Christian Religions" was placed before the
Vatican Council. It was immediately apparent that there were changes in
the statement affecting the Jews. As Judith Hershcopf, writing in the
American Jewish Yearbook (1966) put it, "To some, the differences in
language between this and the 1964 version seemed minimal, more nuance
than substance; to others the nuances added up to a significant difference
in content: a generous statement curtailed here, a grudging or legalistic
phrase inserted there, appeared to tip the scales of the entire document."
Neither Proskauer nor Cardinal Bea agreed with this judgment. The argument really swirled and eddied about three passages, the first and the final
versions are here presented in parallel columns (italics added):

1964 Text

Moreover, this synod, in her rejection of injustice of whatever kind and
wherever inflicted upon men, remains mindful of that common patrimony *and so deplores, indeed con-
demns*, hatred and persecution of
Jews. . . .

May they never present the Jewish
people as one rejected, cursed, or
guilty of deicide.

May, then, all see to it that in their
catechetical work or in their preaching of the word of God they do not
teach anything that could give rise to
hatred or contempt of Jews in the
hearts of Christians.

1965 Text

Furthermore, in every rejection a-
gainst any man, the Church, mindful of the patrimony she shares with
the Jews and moved not by political
reasons but the Gospel's spiritual
love, *decries* hatred, persecutions,
displays of anti-Semitism directed
against Jews at any time and by any
one.

. . . Although the Church is the new
people of God, the Jews should not
be presented as *rejected or accursed by God,* as if this followed
from the Holy Scriptures. . . .

All should see to it then, that in
catechetical work or in the preach-
ings of the word of God they do not
teach anything that does not conform to the truth of the Gospel and
the spirit of Christ.

Augustin Cardinal Bea made a strong plea for the new text. The first
version had not been weakened; the omission of the word "deicide" had

not represented a change of heart, for the schema still openly condemned anti-Semitism. The declaration was "clearer and more accurate in such a way that the substance of the text which was approved last year by a large majority would be faithfully retained." Bea, who had become worldly-wise in political maneuvering, knew that a head-on collision between the "conservatives" and the "progressives" threatened the Jewish declaration. Father Morlion took the same line. The new text was better. He said, "The one before had more regard for the sensitiveness of the Jewish people, but it did not produce the necessary clearness in the minds of Christians. In this sense, it was less effective even to the very cause of the Jewish people."

One acute American commentator, Joseph Roddy, in *Look,* January 25, 1966, noted that "Morlion knew just what the Jews did to get the declaration and why the Catholics had settled for its compromise. 'We could have beaten the dogmatics,' he insisted. They could, indeed, but the cost would have been a split in the Church." Apparently, so believed the Vatican Council Fathers, for on October 15, toward the end of the fourth and final session, the schema, including the changes, was approved as a whole by a vote of 1,763 to 250.

At a luncheon on December 5, 1965 Proskauer spoke of his visit to Rome and of the final passage of the Jewish declaration, warning,

> When some of our learned brethren indulge in semantics and want to split hairs and dot i's and cross t's, I suggest that the great movements of the world were never furthered by semantics and that those words [of the adopted schema] mean exactly what they say. Furthermore in her rejection of every persecution against any man, the Church, mindful of the patrimony she shares with the Jews, and moved not by political reasons but by the Gospel's spiritual love, decries hatred, persecutions, displays of anti-Semitism, directed against Jews at anytime and by anyone—this is what that final form of the declaration did.

And on September 22, 1966, when he was the toastmaster for a dinner given by the American council of the "Pro Deo" movement to welcome to New York Paolo Cardinal Marella, he spoke with his usual grace and wit. Turning to Mr. Augustus C. Long, who was the chairman of the evening, he said:

> At this moment, I am reminded of a speech made by your dear friend and mine, Governor Smith. He was addressing a Bar Association dinner and, looking down at the audience, he said: 'I have it all over you fellows. You had to study and pass examinations to get your law degree. All I had to do to become an LL.D. was to be elected Governor of New York four times. And so, all I had to do, Mr. Long to get this encomium from you was to live to 89 years of age and have my two co-chairmen of this organization—Mr. Luce and Mr. Grace—absent.'

Proskauer, still full of the things he had said and done in Rome, praised "this great 'Pro Deo' movement in its university in Rome." He said:

"We know that we shall achieve that unity of mankind; that common brotherhood of mankind under the common fatherhood of Almighty God," to which the Apostolic Brief, in chartering the university, and the Jewish declaration had dedicated themselves. Once again he hailed the two "wonderful years," 1945 and 1965 in which he had played a part. He quoted Pope Paul: "The actions must follow the ideals; the facts must follow the words" and he greeted affectionately their guest, Cardinal Marella, whom he had met in Rome and who had been named president of the Secretariat of the Holy See for relations with non-Christians. He has "the will, and soul, the spirit and the power to recreate this strife-torn world into a common brotherhood of all mankind under a common fatherhood of Almighty God," Proskauer concluded, evidencing his firm belief that interfaith cooperation would eventually achieve this goal.

---

* The Church's liturgy, particularly that for Easter, was full of anti-Jewish animosity. The Good Friday prayer *Oremus pro perfidis judaeis* appeared as early as the eighth century in the celebration of the Mass; and to highlight its serious and offensive nature, the genuflection following it was intentionally omitted. An American missal, widely used, and having an English and Latin text, was published in 1948 under the imprimatur of Francis Cardinal Spellman of New York. The prayer in English ran as follows:

"Let us pray for the unfaithful Jews, that our Lord and God may take away the veil from their hearts, so that they too may acknowledge Jesus Christ our Lord." (*Not* followed by "Let us kneel.")

To this was added the further prayer:

"Almighty, eternal God, Who repellest not even Jewish faithlessness from Thy mercy, harken to our prayers which we make in behalf of the blindness of that people, that, recognizing the light of Thy truth, which is Christ, they may be delivered from their darkness. Through the same." (*Not* followed by "Let us kneel.")

In 1959, on his own initiative, John XXIII ordered the elimination of the word *perfidis* (unfaithful) from the *Oremus pro judaeis* and the prayer was given the right of genuflection. This was a whole year before John and Isaac met personally. The Catholic missal referred to, with the prayer in its original form was still being used by the family, in whose home Hacker saw it, for the Good Friday services as late as 1969.

However the missal was revised in 1970 (in the Latin edition) and an English translation was published in 1973. It carried on its title page the following: "The Roman Missal. Revised by decree of the Second Ecumenical Council and published by authority of Pope Paul VI." The revised version of the Good Friday service referred to above now ran:

"Let us pray for the Jewish people, the first to hear the word of God, that they may continue to grow in the love of his name and in faithfulness to his covenant."

"Almighty and eternal God, long ago you gave your promise to Abraham and his posterity. Listen to your Church as we pray that the people you first made your own may arrive at the fullness of redemption. We ask this through Christ our Lord."

Apparently the English missal of 1973 was regarded as a stopgap. It was never publicly issued for it was felt that more work had to be done on the liturgy. New Vatican guidelines were issued in 1975 and these fell in with the thinking of the United States Conference of

Catholic Bishops. A storm blew up in 1976 in the United States over the so-called Missalette (a pamphlet or brochure) for Holy Week which, in addition to the regular service, contained the suggested songs and chants congregations might use as part of the liturgy celebrating Good Friday.

Inadvertently or not, this part of the liturgy contained the celebrated *Improperia* or "Reproaches," an ancient hymn which had its origin as far back as the fourth century. The "Reproaches" presumably were directed by God and Jesus against the Jews. The first verse, which was typical, ran as follows (God speaking):

> "My people, what have I done to you?
> How have I offended you?
> Answer me.
> I led you out of Egypt, from slavery to freedom,
> but you led your Savior to the cross.
> My people, what have I done to you?
> How have I offended you?
> Answer me."

When this was called to the attention of outstanding Catholic churchmen—as in violation of the 1975 Vatican directive—most of them deplored the inclusion of the "Reproaches" in the missalette. An excellent story, printed in the New York *Times* quoted Msgr. John Oesterreicher, director of the Institute of Judeo-Christian Studies at Seton Hall University as follows: The hymn had a low liturgical status and probably was infrequently used. "I would not object to any clarification or change or elimination, but I don't consider it of great importance."

How much work still had to be done by Catholic spokesmen themselves to eliminate anti-Semitism from the Church's liturgy—as it already had done in the formal services and the training of its clergy—was pointed out by Rabbi Henry Siegman of the Synagogue Council of America. The *Times* story quoted him as saying: "The hymn underlines a stark and unpleasant truth, that the liturgical and mythological life of the Church remains a significant source of anti-Semitism. Obviously still much work lies ahead." It is important to point out that the debate was being conducted without rancor on both sides.

PROSKAUER IN UNDRESS **16**

Proskauer was an elegant Edwardian in style. He dressed well, kept his hair, which he wore in a three-quarters part, and a small brush mustache trimmed carefully and, until the last years of his life, his weight and figure were neat and spare. Five feet and seven inches tall, he weighed about one hundred and sixty pounds. He was athletically inclined, often riding his horse in Central Park. To old and young alike, both men and women, he was an attractive man. Perhaps, his most striking feature was his face. It was longish and not fleshy, with a sharp straight nose and almost round sparkling brown eyes.

Proskauer was a gourmet. He set a very good table, and had first-class taste in food, wines, brandy, whiskeys, and cigars. He was a member of half a dozen clubs, the Harmonie, Lotos, Manhattan, Whist, Lawyers, and City, each of which he attended regularly, dining and playing cards, mostly bridge and gin rummy, with his many friends.

Proskauer was passionately fond of travel. Preferring ships to the air, he was well known on the great transatlantic liners and, when these began to disappear, on many of the cruise ships plying the Mediterranean and Caribbean seas. On land he put up at the best hotels, rented automobiles with chauffeurs, and hired guides for the length of his stay. Traveling thus in the grand manner, like an English milord, he was partial to cities, London, Paris, Amsterdam, Geneva, Madrid, Barcelona, Athens, Rome, Florence, Milan, and the Italian smaller hill towns. He frequented art museums, churches, and other famous places and often stopped at spas to take the waters and to gamble in the casinos. On his many visits abroad there were always companions, usually his wife and children, when they were younger. After her death in 1959, he was accompanied by a grand-child or by Helen and Phillip Haberman, his dear friends.

Although the Proskauers lived very well, their town and country dwellings were not ostentatious. In the early years of their marriage they lived in various apartments on New York's West Side near Central Park, when it was a fashionable residential district. There they remained, even after many of the wealthy and the bon ton had moved to the East Side. In 1923 they settled down in 205 West 57th Street, on the northwest corner of Seventh Avenue. When the house became the Osborne, a great ten-story cooperative made of red sandstone, they bought their flat and remained there. It was large and formidable, a proper setting for the Proskauer family.

Here they had ten rooms on the eighth floor, of which four were master bedrooms and three were servants' quarters. (They kept two live-in maids, one a cook, when Mrs. Proskauer was alive.) The entrance hall and living room were immense, with high ceilings. They were furnished in Spanish style, with heavy tables, chairs, hangings, and a large grand piano. These were never changed and took on a well-used, even musty air with time.

The dining table accommodated fourteen and it was often filled, for Proskauer liked very much to entertain. The company was usually his friends and card-playing cronies and their wives, and business partners. Proskauer picked the menus, including the wines, but he refused to serve cocktails. He always dominated the conversation.

Proskauer had no study in the Osborne and he brought no work home from his office. His love of music was his great passion. At one time he kept a player piano which he personally operated, playing roll after roll as his evening recreation. However, he never learned to play an instrument or master musical notation. Music, nevertheless, he knew well, his knowledge having been acquired entirely by ear. Except for Bach, he preferred Romantic composers, from Mozart and Beethoven through Tchaikovsky, whose symphonies and concertos (arranged for piano) he knew by heart, just as he did the works of his favorite poets (again the Romantics).

Located as he was at the Osborne, Proskauer was in easy reach of Carnegie Hall. Although he also went occasionally to the other, smaller ones, the Aeolian, the Steinway, and Town Hall, Carnegie was his favorite, not only because it was the home of the New York Symphony Society and the New York Philharmonic Orchestra, but also because there he could listen to many other distinguished orchestras, those of Boston, Philadelphia, Chicago, and Cleveland. Proskauer was a constant and devoted visitor at Carnegie Hall and in time became known to the outstanding orchestra leaders of the 1920s, 1930s, and 1940s, including Arturo Toscanini, George Szell, Bruno Walter, and Eugene Ormandy. In fact, Toscanini's conducting so moved Proskauer that he wrote a sonnet to him which was included in his *A Segment of My Time* and was once reprinted in the New York *Times*. Many of the piano and violin virtuosos of the day were acquaintances of Proskauer, among them, Horowitz, Rubinstein, Godowsky, Heifetz, Elman, Kreisler, and Zimbalist. He heard them regularly, when they came to New York to accompany the orchestras or to play in their own concerts.

Despite his love for music, Proskauer may have been an irritating patron of the many concerts he attended. As he listened to the music, he had the habit, perhaps it was unconscious, of acting the part of conductor, flinging his hands about to guide the various sections of the orchestra as well as the soloist. One may imagine how the real conductor or the soloist must have silently reacted to this idiosyncrasy.

Another of Proskauer's loves was the New York State north woods of his Lake Placid home and its immediate environs. He had become acquainted with the region when he was a young man and had made frequent excursions to it. When he was in funds, he acquired a summer property on Buck Island in Lake Placid in 1934, extending his holding until he owned twenty-six acres. This he named Camp Highwall and there he went every year, usually arriving at the end of May and staying until Labor Day. Originally, he traveled by overnight train on the New York Central, but later he went by automobile. He never flew, although the airport at nearby Lake Saranac was considered quite safe.

Lake Placid, lying in a heavily wooded and mountainous area, is almost fifteen miles long and eight miles wide. It is actually cut up by two large islands, one of which, Buck Island, is pear-shaped, two miles long and two miles wide. Access to it is from the small town of Lake Placid and the stretch of water is about a mile long. Here Proskauer and the family and their guests were met by the caretaker and ferried across to a landing, where Proskauer had put up a large boathouse.

Buck Island, like the rest of the region, is largely woods and rising hills. Its highest elevation is about two thousand feet, with the clearings and habitations on or near the shore, facing the town across the water. The original Proskauer property was a large house with a living room, a dining room, a kitchen and pantry on the ground floor and six master bedrooms on the second. His two daughters and his son and their spouses and their children were welcome; and all looked forward to coming. They all agreed that there was to be a general assemblage of the whole clan for Proskauer's birthday in August. For this a bungalow was built with additional bedrooms and a living room. The boathouse was improved, so much so that in time it served as well for Proskauer's study and music room. For, when hi-fi recording came in, Proskauer put his record player and its speakers into the boathouse and there he was to be found, when he was not at his meals or out fishing. There too he did his reading (the lives of the poets and painters of whom he was fond, history, public affairs) and worked on the puzzles of the *New York Times Magazine*.

The dining room of the main house had a large window facing east and from it on a clear day there was an excellent view, twenty miles away, of the whole of Whiteface Mountain, rising about five thousand feet, one of the noblest peaks of the Adirondacks. Alice Proskauer was a committed and highly imaginative gardener. Every spring she laid out a large series of flats of flowering plants and shrubs which she tended indefatigably and with great success. All who knew the garden praised it. Melville Cane said of it, "Each recurrent spring meant a fresh struggle against the odds of desperate Adirondack weather. Each summer proclaimed a fresh triumph. Alice flowered with her garden."

Proskauer, despite his deep attachment to the north woods, was no woodsman. Other than his horseback riding, he had no country skills; nor could he drive a car or motor boat. In fact, he never learned to swim. His pleasures at Highwall were visual rather than manual. He was the original conservationist, deriving his pleasure from gazing at Whiteface, taking a turn in Alice's garden, riding his horse, and tramping about the island. With one exception: he could fish all day. He fished for bass on the lake from a boat and he cast for trout around and about the neighborhood, sometimes as far away as forty miles. With his friends he would spend the day out-of-doors, preparing for them luncheons over an open fire. Then back to Highwall he would take them, tired and triumphant, to listen to classical recordings and play bridge.

For a good part of August the family, second, third and even fourth generations came, and when fully assembled they made a cheerful and noisy company. The elder daughter and the first-born, Frances, was the wife of Paul Cohen, a lawyer of Buffalo; the second was Ruth Smith, once married, but divorced, who lived in New York; and the third was Richard, a highly respected physicist, who lived in Old Westbury, Long Island. His six grandchildren and eight great-grandchildren came, too, staying for varying periods of time but never missing Joseph Proskauer's birthday.

Proskauer's relations with his immediate family, his wife and three children, were something of a puzzle. Towards them his conduct and attitudes may be traced back to his early manhood perhaps. He had trained himself to be an Edwardian gentleman; that is, he assumed his obligations toward his family, maintained a good home and educated his children, but companionship, as such, he sought and found outside the home. The whole family—until the children got out of their teens—traveled in Europe together and Highwall was their home as well as his. But of the warmth and affection considered normal in modern parent-child relations, there was apparently little in Proskauer's life. This left a void in the lives of his children, a void which perplexed them and about which they often spoke in their maturity.

There is no doubt that in his earlier and middle years Proskauer worked hard at his law practice, as he sought to climb up the ladder to success and security. This left him little time for an expansive home life. Perhaps it was because his mind worked so quickly that he was impatient with the fumblings, hesitancies and silences of children growing up. Perhaps there was too much of the German in him, from his own childhood upbringing: Kinder, Küche, and Kirche were women's duties. Or perhaps his wife and children stood too much in awe of the public man in him that they were afraid to try to break into the human person inside.

Proskauer's seventieth birthday was celebrated twice, the first time at a family party at Highwall on August 6, 1947, and the second at a dinner where his friends and New York's notables assembled at the Plaza Hotel the following December 4. At the first and more important, Ruth Smith and Paul Cohen were the chief actors in a little skit called "Life with Father," with Ruth as Alice and Paul as Dio, the family caretaker. The songs and the dialogue were a compound of the many emotions which revealed how the family regarded their master's many peccadillos and were able to poke fun at his high opinion of his self-importance. All this Proskauer accepted in good spirit, albeit with his usual stand-offish aloofness.

There is no question that Proskauer and his wife drifted apart as they grew older. They did not separate (there was never any thought of that) but, except for their summers together at Highwall, there were very few things they did together. Whether this was because Alice was not a demonstrative woman or because Proskauer was the reverse, or because both found their outlets in their work will never be known. The children were deeply attached to their mother and always spoke of her only with affection. She was a beautiful woman, considerate of everybody, they often said. "If she was immersed in her civic and philanthropic activities, this was only an expression of her concern for others." As Cane once wrote, "She was deeply serious without being solemn, always with a strong sense of responsibility, and loyalty not only to friends and family, but to those less fortunate in the world at large. . . ."

Alice Proskauer's civic interests were of the activist kind and this may have been the cause of her husband's impatience with her: he was the commanding officer, she the foot soldier. Alice was one of the founders and for many years a director of the Citizens Housing and Planning Council of New York. Starting with the early days of Roosevelt's "New Deal," she was on the housing committee of the Women's City Club and chairman of the housing section of the Welfare Council. She was one of the founders of Freedom House, an association to which the Willkie Memorial Building was dedicated. She was an active official of the American Association for the United Nations, the Urban League, the Euthanasia Society, the Joint Defense Appeal of the American Jewish Committee, and the Anti-Defamation League. During the last ten years of her life she was inflicted with a painful and irritating malady which she refused to let slow her down. She died March 18, 1959 in her seventy-seventh year. James Rosenberg, an old family friend, reported that Proskauer was broken up over her passing.

For many years Proskauer stopped seeking out the companionship of his wife, but this in no way is intended to suggest that there were other women in his life; on this there is general agreement. He attracted women, of course, and some even pursued him, but he assumed they were to be used to serve him and to be at his beck and call. He was vain; they were admiring; and Proskauer settled for that.

It was younger people—also attracted to Proskauer for his charm, wit, steady flow of fascinating talk—that gave him companionship when he grew older. He was deeply attached to his younger partner, Phillip Haberman, and his wife Helen, and when Phillip died suddenly in July, 1971, Proskauer mourned him like a son. George Shapiro, another partner, still younger, was very close to Proskauer and idolized him. Closest of all were his growing grandchildren. Gail and Anthony Smith, Steve Proskauer, and

"Ginger" Cohen. It was as though Proskauer was seeking a way to make up for the indifference he had shown to his own children. There was more than that to it, however. Proskauer saw that young people were handsome and bright, and because he showed his fondness for them, they in turn adored him. He sought them out but they sought him out, too. Between them there was mutual confidence and affection.

All of this makes for a complex personality. On his seventieth birthday Proskauer's senior associates, Alfred L. Rose, Norman S. Goetz, and Walter Mendelsohn, wrote him a joint letter, part of which ran as follows:

> It has been said that a friend is one who knows all about you and still loves you. We not only have been your partners—partners on a letterhead—for seventeen years, but we are your friends. . . .
>
> We love you for your comings and goings, for your bursting into conferences for no good reason, for your soft ways and your tantrums. We love you because you are at once the experienced man of affairs and the perennial small boy. We love you for your unshakable loyalties and because you are sensitive and sentimental. We love you for your unquenchable joie de vivre. In short, we love you for the things that make you YOU.

Phillip Haberman, almost fifteen years later, in 1961, when asked to talk about the contradictions in Proskauer's makeup, speculated aloud to Hirsch as follows:

> I would say that Judge Proskauer's rough exterior—I don't mean rough in sense of unpolished—but his frequently aggressive or even brutal manner, which I heard him employ many, many times, was a cover for the softness of the man underneath. I think he has lived his whole life terrified for fear that someone would really discover that he was exceedingly kind but doesn't want anyone to know that.

Was Proskauer a vain man? asked Hirsch. Hirsch had tried that gambit on Supreme Court Justices Frankfurter and Harlan. Frankfurter said Proskauer was one of the vainest men he had ever known. Harlan believed the trait was just a cover for a very sympathetic, understanding, and sensitive personality. Haberman's reply plumbed more deeply:

> Vanity yes; but vanity in the sense that he loves a compliment, that he needs compliments, he lives on them, he lives on admiration. He knows it. He needs admiration the way most people need food and drink. To me, that implies something quite the opposite of vanity. To me that implies a certain deep-seated form of insecurity on his part that requires to be fed constantly or he can't live with it. He never walked out of a courtroom after an argument, as far as I know, he never did with briefs without being impatient for the moment when he could be alone with his associate or assistant to put the invariable question, 'How did I do?' He always wanted to be praised.

Proskauer was a better public speaker than he was a writer. He mastered the craft of the first, but failed to understand that the second also required constant work and practice to achieve proficiency. In his long career as a public personage he spoke on countless occasions—to honor the dead, to celebrate anniversaries, to fund-raising drives, to pay tribute to honored citizens, and for many worthy causes and events. He early mastered the technique of radio speaking. This helped him perfect his style. His extraordinarily good memory stood him in good stead also, for much of his speaking was seemingly extemporaneous. He learned to be brief, to come to the point at once, starting with an anecdote and finishing quickly. In his long life Proskauer made hundreds of such appearances and what he had to say always pleased, often delighted his listeners. A few of his more formal addresses were printed, but the vast majority remain only as fond recollections in the memories of those who listened to him.

This kind of rigorous training and performance made Proskauer a first-class conversationalist. He knew how to listen in the company of his peers, but the younger or the untutored he instructed, telling them about the places he had been, the great people he had met, his court triumphs, and the mistakes of his opponents. His speech was colloquial—he was not above the use of profanity when annoyed—and always apposite and entertaining. Sometimes he lapsed into a monologue but he knew how to pull himself up short, for no man was more aware of the perils of boring than he.

In 1950, when Proskauer was seventy-three years old, he published a short book he called *A Segment of My Times*. It started out by being a memoir and its best writing was in its first twenty-five pages, for it has to do with the personal and highly subjective recollections of his origins, boyhood, and youth. The first three chapters of the work Proskauer evidently labored over, and then, suddenly, he seems to have lost patience. Probably, he discovered that writing was a craft whose rules one had to learn by working at them, and that was not his forte. On May 19, 1949 he wrote a friend that he was "dictating a narrative," but as the work continued it turned into recollections of public men and events with whom he had worked or in which he had participated, including reflections on the law, philanthropy, and what he called bigotry. After he had finished the manuscript, he asked two people to read it—Edmund Fuller, a well-known literary critic, and George W. Alger, lawyer and essayist.

As a reader for the publisher Fuller wrote:

> Judge Proskauer's book is not couched in a style that is going to carry the book, regardless of content, as an intrinsic appeal. It contains certain detailed discussions of ideas and principles . . . they are the book's principal merit, since Judge Proskauer has not succeeded in personalizing the chronicle to any marked degree.

He objected to the poems in the earlier chapters, thought Proskauer "leaned too heavily on speeches, of which there are much too many and at too great length" and that the chapter on Israel was "perhaps the poorest of all."

Alger wrote Proskauer that he liked his book, but added, "Give your readers something more of the 'Joe' we know. You've done the 'Proskauer' very well. Let them know that a 'bully' time 'Joe' has had through all your life's vicissitudes. And give some notion of what I call your *elan vital*." In consequence, Proskauer added a few pages in which he talked of his fondness for travel, fishing, horseback riding, music, painting, and church architecture. "Music and art have been ministers to my pleasure," he said.

> Above all [he continued], I have followed a vocation most dear to me. My associates in it have been my warmest friends—and lawyers are heart-warming company. I have known great men in the association of common high endeavors. I have known them 'off stage.' That has meant a camaraderie of infinite satisfaction.

Of his family he wrote only this: "[My life has been] serene and beautified by the love of wife, of children and grandchildren." But faced with the necessity of saying what he had really done, he explained himself in this fashion:

> [I am hoping that these chapters] by disclosing the thoughts, the fears, the failures and the achievements in a limited segment of my times [will] make the problems and spiritual heritage of my era somewhat more understandable....
> There are lives like mine that have touched closely upon great events, yet have fallen short of highest command. Often, from the experiences of such adjutants, one may gain a picture of the times more veracious, in many respects, than that which is drawn from the life story of the generals themselves. The adjutants, though participating in history, necessarily are more objective in their view than the prime movers.

When *A Segment*... appeared in 1950, the reviewers took Proskauer at his word and their notices were uniformly friendly, warm, and equally unpretentious. For instance, George W. Alger, in *Survey Magazine* had this to say:

> The space allotted to this review is inadequate to bear tribute to the statesmanship, sobriety, and fair-mindedness of Judge Proskauer's leadership of his divided and bewildered people in their years of recent trial and agony....
> It is a well-written and thought-provoking book.

Alvin Johnson in the *Saturday Review of Literature* found the author "one of the really significant men of the generation now closing its books." And he praised his work as judge and philosopher of law:

For a time Proskauer served on the bench and won a reputation as one of the most just and intelligent judges in America. . . . It is hard to find in his record as a lawyer compensation for the loss of a powerfully intelligent judge. Still we may be grateful that his experience as judge produced one of the ablest criticisms we have of the conventional treatment of the criminal and of the American jury fetish.

Karl Schriftgiesser wrote in the New York *Herald Tribune Book Review* that,

As lawyer, judge, politician, Zionist [*sic*] and public-spirited New Yorker, Joseph M. Proskauer has led a busy useful and profitable life. . . . He tells about it interestingly in a slim volume that may well become, as he suggests, a valuable footnote to the history of our times. . . . In many respects it is an inspiring study in Americanism.

And Judge Jerome Frank added in the New York *Times Book Review:* "Here is a stirring narrative most engagingly written well worth reading by anyone interested in the past half-century of American life. . . ."

The American Jewish Committee worked hard to promote *A Segment* . . . by mailing a "basic review" to 7,000 newspapers and journals. It also sent a flyer to its membership, the full-page covering letter stating that

Joseph M. Proskauer's achievements more than justify the reference made to him at our last annual meeting as a 'legendary' figure, but while most of us know what he has done, only those who have worked closely with him know the colorful personality of the man as it is revealed in his book: his wit and charm his high-minded devotion to the welfare of the American Jewish community, his undaunted courage as a fighter for what is right.

Sales of *A Segment* . . . indeed were very modest—in nine months only 2,358 of the 5,000 copies were sold. Under the circumstances, Farrar, Straus & Co., the publishers, and Proskauer agreed that, if the author wished to make a final settlement, the former would be glad to consider the total account as balanced without further payment by either party to the other. Realizing that there might be some small revenue in the remaining unsold copies, the publishers offered Proskauer 500 copies of the book, at no cost. Finally, against the $7,500 Proskauer had paid out to have his book printed, he received in return, after all costs, less than $1,000. Obviously, a professional writer could not have afforded this kind of transaction, but Proskauer, as he discovered in sorrow, was not a professional and he never repeated the experience.

On the other hand, Proskauer's public speaking was of the highest order. He commanded all its varieties, from the formal oration to the familiar discourse, and he knew all the wiles and stratagems of holding the attention of his listeners. In an early address, delivered May 10, 1928 at the unveiling of a bust of Rufus Choate in the New York University Hall of

Fame, Proskauer demonstrated his abilities. After an opening paragraph he stated that Choate was a man "born of the Puritan and the sea." Next, he quoted some verses of his dearly-beloved Columbia friend and mentor, George Edward Woodberry, and then added, "Choate kept the tang and savor of his boyhood to the end. From his death-bed in Halifax, he whispered to his son, 'If a schooner or a sloop goes by, don't disturb me, but if there is a square-rigged vessel, wake me up.'"

Stating that Choate had been a successful legislator, congressman, and senator, Proskauer continued:

> He put aside the lure of political and judicial careers to make himself a great advocate, even as the seafarer steers straight to his course. His eloquence had in it that persuasive mastery with which the mariner dominates the adversity of the elements. Unconsciously he used the imagery of the sea. And there was subtly blended with these qualities something of Puritan austerity, manifested in his devotion to things of the mind and soul.

On January 29, 1933 Proskauer was asked to deliver the principal address at a conference of Jewish charity workers in Chicago. Introduced by Leo Wormser, he replied, "This is the first time in my experience, that I have ever known a really true friend to anticipate the decease of his pal by delivering an obituary in his life time." He went on to say he had attended carefully to the business session of the conference earlier in the evening. There he had discovered that they were having budgetary problems in Chicago as he and his friends were having in the Federation of Jewish Philanthropies in New York. Then he told this story:

> The discussion became heated, and, as usual, quite unintelligible. There thereupon arose a physician from the East Side representing the Jewish Maternity Hospital. He said: 'Mr. President, if what I am about to say is wholly unintelligible to everybody in the room it is no different from the speeches which have preceded me. The budget question seems to me to be this. Should the Federation tell my hospital in June that it should die in August or is it better to wait until February and say we should have died last September? In the Jewish Maternity Hospital, the budget is like this. A woman comes to hospital. I examine her. I say "Madam you are going to have twins, but Madam, you cannot have twins. This hospital is not budgeted for twins."'

Proskauer often used a phrase (italicized below) which had fashioned early in his career. On Armistice Day, November 11, 1936, he addressed the Jewish War Veterans of New York. Among other things, he said this:

> I can never forget one night in the year 1928, when I was on a railroad train with Governor Smith who was then making his campaign throughout the country. We drew into a Western town [Oklahoma City] and, as I looked out of the car window, I saw in the surrounding hills the blazing crosses of the Ku Klux Klan. I saw hooded figures grouped about them. In that lurid light I sensed

all that was bitter and malevolent in that movement which denied the very essence of America itself, *a common brotherhood of man under common fatherhood of God.*

It was not unusual for Proskauer to begin an address by identifying the opening music—such as, "The moving strains of that sublime andante of Beethoven you have just heard. . . ." And he often ended with these lines from Shakespeare's *King Henry VIII:*

> Still in thy right hand carry gentle peace
> To silence envious tongues: be just and
> fear not:
> Let all the ends at which thou aim'st be thy
> country's,
> Thy God's and truth's. . . .

On September 12, 1938, on radio station WHN, Proskauer was chosen to memorialize Patrick Cardinal Hayes, the late archbishop of New York. He hailed Hayes's ecumenism, saying: "He numbered among his friends Protestant and Jew and Catholic. His prayers were uttered often for those not of his own faith. He had the magnanimity of soul which enabled him to help and to love those who in other paths than his sought to walk humbly with their God."

On January 24, 1939 Proskauer spoke at a dinner given by the Committee for the Relief of German Christian Refugees in honor of Dorothy Thompson. His remarks were gracefully done and he came quickly to the heart of the matter. Unlike many of her contemporaries, he suggested, Miss Thompson, the distinguished journalist, had tried to warn her fellow Americans that Nazism was the scourge of all mankind, not simply the Jews alone. She was, he added, "A perfect woman nobly planned/ To warm, to comfort, to command." He called her "Cassandra-like" and went to Pope's translation of *The Iliad* to point up her "prophetic" and unheeded warning: "Injustice, suffered and unconfined/Sweeps the wide world and tramples all mankind."

Proskauer often dwelt on the Nazi horror which was already sweeping over Europe. Among those who were being driven into flight were "hundreds of thousands of great intellectual and spiritual leaders of the German people whose only offense had been that they would not bow their heads in abject submission to the tyranny of the Nazi regime," he said on October 19, 1939. Two months later, on December 12, 1939, before a mixed audience of Jews and Christians, he described the emancipation of the Jews in England and then made his pleas for ecumenism: "Our creeds of conduct today must rest upon the essential unity of the ultimate Hebraic and Christian ideal."

On February 23, 1943, with World War II raging and the intention of the

Nazis fully revealed, Proskauer was one of the key speakers at a series of
conferences called "Brotherhood Week" under the auspices of Columbia
University. He spoke not more than ten minutes and was more solemn
than usual. He again referred to what was taking place in Germany, emphasizing the heroic resistance of European churchmen. In conclusion he
offered this plea for American unity:

> I will discriminate against no man because of his faith or creed or race.
>
> I will daily deal with every man in business, in social and political relations
> only on the basis of his true individual worth.
>
> I will never try to indict a whole people by reason of the delinquency of any
> member.
>
> I will spread no rumor and no slander against any sect.
>
> In my daily conduct I will consecrate myself hour by hour to the achieve-
> ment of the highest ideal of the dignity of man, human equality, human fel-
> lowship and human brotherhood.

Proskauer accepted several invitations to eulogize his dear friend and
companion, Al Smith, who died in 1944. On October 7, the day Smith was
buried, he spoke on Radio Station WQXR, beginning by saying, "I choose
to speak, not of the statesman, but of the man." He took as his theme
Wordsworth's "Character of the Happy Warrior," quoted extensively from
it, adding: "This man was faithful unto death to every obligation that was
ever placed upon him. He had a singleness of aim—and that was to do his
duty. . . ."

"He was born of the people and many a hard-fought battle he waged for
their rights [he continued], but he knew no distinction of high or low, rich
or poor, strong or weak; and as he was faithful to his trust, so men of every
station in life came to put their trust in him as a true leader and a true
servant. . . .

"His moral fiber was granite, but in his heart lay a great and abiding
love. But his love went out far even beyond [his family and friends]. He
loved humanity; he loved every human being. . . . He was the most devoutly
pious man I ever knew. He gave no mere mouth service to the great Catholic religion, which he professed, but utter, complete, and unswerving devotion. May we all wish to be what Alfred E. Smith was. May that be the
lesson for us as we say farewell to this good, this great husband, father,
friend, statesman, lover of his church, lover of all mankind."

Proskauer also spoke at the dedications of the Governor Alfred E. Smith
State Office Building in Albany on May 16, 1946, and the Governor Smith
Memorial Park in New York's East Side on June 1, 1950. His ability to turn
a graceful phrase was never better in evidence than on the latter ceremony:

> If Alfred E. Smith were with us today he would have slight concern with
> [his] statue, but would choose as a memorial dearest to his heart this lovely

park. Sprung from the sidewalks of New York, his heart was filled with solicitude for the growth of this crowded city. So he would gladly welcome the association of his name with this happy place of recreation and refreshment.

Proskauer was eagerly sought out for speaking at such public events, largely because of the gracious, thoughtful, and honest comments he was able to make about the individual being memorialized. When his old friend, Irving Lehman, chief judge of the New York Court of Appeals, died in 1945, Proskauer's brief address was simple and beautifully done:

> He was a lawyer's judge. . . . He had the special learning of the erudite scholar but he was also a human judge, . . . a great judge, . . . a very truly good man. [He] made no show of being the spectacular witty judge. But he demonstrated that he was the learned one. He had no mere pretense of plausibility and no arrogance of overconfidence. He was both more reverend and more advised. . . .

Proskauer received many awards and honors, among them testimonal scrolls from all kinds of organizations, medals, election to boards of trustees, and honorary degrees from colleges and universities. Columbia University awarded him an LL.D. in 1929; so did Dartmouth College (1953), Brandeis University (1955), Colgate University (1957), and Fordham University (1967). Hebrew Union College granted him the L.H.D. in 1946, as did the Jewish Theological Seminary in 1948. Frequently, at these happenings Proskauer spoke, always succinctly and felicitously, seeking and finding a peg on which to hang a tale or a moral.

Columbia University gave him a testimonial scroll June 3, 1952 in connection with its religious counseling. On this occasion he spoke frankly of bigotry and persecution:

> We Jews have, above all men, the heritage of centuries of persecution. We have had to teach ourselves to live in a world which has at times tortured us, at times banned us. Even today—even in this country of our love where we enjoy complete equality under the law—we are discriminated against in many of the essential ways of life. . . .

In acknowledging an award given him by his own Congregation Emanu-El on January 22, 1957, he addressed himself to the subject of Jewish unity, first rejecting the talk of creating "some functional worldwide organization 'to speak for Jewry.'" But there were three purposes which could always link Jews together, he added: the preservation of the Jewish creed as a religion and a way of life, the presentation of Jewish identity, and "respect for the dignity of the individual, springing fresh the concept that man was created in the image of Almighty God."

On January 25, 1966, when he was nearing ninety years of age, a dinner was held in New York in his honor to announce the endowment by Brandeis

University of a chair in legal institutions named after him. He was saluted by many dignitaries, including President Abram L. Sachar and Judge Kenneth B. Keating of the New York Court of Appeals. Proskauer replied extemporaneously, refusing to take himself and his friends and admirers too seriously. To one of the speakers, a woman, he said, "I associate myself completely with you. You and I are the only two people in this room, except your little brother, who are living in the age of innocence." To Keating he said, "Kenneth, I once did you a great disservice. I didn't mean it. But I went out and worked my fingernails off to have you elected to the Senate."

After quoting Sir Edward Coke, Oliver Wendell Holmes, Samuel Johnson, and Louis D. Brandeis, he concluded:

> It was the elder Pitt who said that where the law ends, tyranny begins. And it would be my hope and belief and prayer that this university acting through this new chair of jurisprudence, will brand that concept on this world. For only in a world dominated by law can we reach those pinnacles of human brotherhood which are the greatest objectives that man has urged on this world today. . . . And as we look forward to what this chair in my profound belief can accomplish, it is to bring that peace to this world, recreating this strife-torn world into a brotherhood of man and a common fatherhood of Almighty God.

Proskauer was elected a member of the Board of Trustees of Brandeis University in 1957. At that time the Department of Mathematics was nominating for an assistant professorship a bright young man whose father was well-known as former secretary-general of the American Communist Party. The nominee was apolitical, but the whiplash of McCarthyism was still very strong in the country and Brandeis was young and struggling to win a secure place in the academic world. A general and confused discussion took place, with some members of the board demurring. Then, Proskauer, the new member, took the floor:

> I would imagine that it's exactly because we are so young and because we have no tradition that we have no alternative but to bring this man in. This is the time that you are setting your pattern. We have nothing to say about this man's character that is detrimental. His father was a bastard, but so was the father of Cardozo, and Hoover didn't decline consideration of Cardozo for the Supreme Court. Smith College had the problem when young Viereck was recommended for the history department and his father George Sylvester Viereck was indicted as a seditionist during World War II. I think we have no alternative but to bring this man in, and I so move. [This motion carried unanimously.]

Another Proskauer story was told by President John Sloan Dickey of Dartmouth College. This time the place was the dinner in celebration of Proskauer's ninetieth birthday on October 25, 1967. (Fourteen years earlier, at Dartmouth's commencement exercises several notables had received honorary degrees, among them Lester Pearson, Minister for External Affairs of Canada, John J. McCloy, United States commissioner to Germany, Proskauer and President Dwight D. Eisenhower, both of whom were to speak that day. Dickey reminded his listeners that, in 1953, "America was passing through one of the bitterest periods of recrimination and self-doubt [McCarthyism], even as bitter as that which we are passing through today. . . . I will not purport to use [Proskauer's] exact words, [when he came to speak] but the essence of it was, it is a sad day that this country should have men in its employ taking books out of American libraries and American embassies abroad and burning them."

That afternoon President Eisenhower, picking up Proskauer's thoughts, told the American people:

> Don't join the book burners. Don't think you are going to conceal faults by concealing evidence that they ever existed. Don't be afraid to go in your library and read every book, as long as any document doesn't offend our own ideas of decency. That should be the only censorship.
>
> We have got to fight communism with something better, not try to conceal the thinking of our own people. They are a part of America, and even if they think ideas that are contrary to ours, their right to say them, their right to record them and their right to have them at places where they are accessible to others is unquestioned, or it is not America.

And Dickey added, "These historic remarks were the beginning of the end for something which was very, very unworthy to America." Then, turning to Joseph Proskauer, he concluded, "And we owe our thanks for that to this man, and this man alone."

After his wife's death, when Proskauer's visits to the office were infrequent, he increasingly turned to traveling for solace and relaxation, usually in the spring of the year so that he could be back at Highwall in the summer. Between 1962 and 1970 he journeyed to Italy four times, to the Caribbean and South America twice, and to Europe once. On the last-named trip he was accompanied by his nurse, Miss Sadie Holmes.

Proskauer died on September 10, 1971 in his ninety-fifth year. He had been going about his regular affairs after his summer at Highwall, calling at his office to "pontificate" to his partners, lunching at the Harmonie, playing bridge, attending concerts, and visiting at the homes of his friends. On the ninth he was dining with his partner, Walter Mendelsohn, at his apartment in the Hampshire House on Central Park South, when he complained of being ill. He was taken to Lenox Hill Hospital, put in the cardiac intensive care unit—and there his stout heart simply stopped. He was buried from Temple Emanu-El on Monday, September 13. More than five hundred mourners gathered to do him honor and hundreds of messages of

sympathy arrived from home and abroad and from the high and the low.
The President of the United States sent his personal representative. The
Prime Minister of Israel, saluting Proskauer as "my friend," cabled her
condolences. And the New York *Times* commented editorially on his many
contributions: "The world, nation and city were all the beneficiaries of his
greatness."

Eight years earlier, Proskauer had written his own obituary. He had
said: "My fishing rods are bent with age now, but they've seen good use.
I've hunted, ridden, traveled, and worked. I think I have paid my debt to
life. I know that life owes me nothing."

BIBLIOGRAPHY

PRIMARY SOURCES

A. Manuscripts

The American Jewish Archives: Joseph M. Proskauer Correspondence

Central Zionist Archives (Jerusalem, Israel)

Citizens Union Collection (Columbia University)

Columbiana Collection (Columbia University)

Felix Frankfurter Papers (Library of Congress)

Charles Evans Hughes Papers (Library of Congress)

Herbert H. Lehman Papers (Columbia University)

The Mayors' Papers (Municipal Reference Library, New York)

Adolph Proskauer Collection (American Jewish Archives)

Joseph M. Proskauer Papers (Including correspondence of Alice Naumburg Proskauer)

Richard Proskauer Papers

Franklin D. Roosevelt Papers

Unpublished manuscript history of the law firm Proskauer Rose Goetz & Mendelsohn, by Alfred L. Rose

Alfred E. Smith Papers (State Education Library, Albany, New York)

Socialist Assemblymen's ouster materials in Tamiment Institute Library, New York University (Boxes A26 and A27)

Tammaniana Collection of Edward Patrick Kilroe (Columbia University)

Harry S. Truman Papers

B. Charney Vladeck Papers (Tamiment Institute Library)

B. Official Publications

Authorizations For Crime Control Investigations In Several States (The Council of State Governments, Chicago, February 12, 1952)

Civil War Naval Chronology, 1861-1865: Part III - 1865 (Naval History Division, Office of the Chief of Naval Operations, Washington, D.C.)

Department of State, U.S.A., *Foreign Policy Briefs, July 1, 1968*

Fifteenth Annual Report of the New York State Probation Commission, 1921 (Legislative Document No. 15, 1922)

New York State Reconstruction Commission. Report to Governor Alfred E. Smith on Retrenchment and Reorganization in the State Government, October 10, 1919 (Albany, 1919)

Report of the Joint Legislative Committee of the State of New York Investigating Seditious Activities, April 24, 1920, Senate of State of New York. Revolutionary Radicalism: Its History, Purpose and Tactics, 4 vols. (Albany, 1920)

C. Oral History

The Following Columbia University Oral History Project memoirs were consulted:

"The Reminiscences of William Wilson Cumberland"

"The Reminiscences of Mrs. Genevieve B. Earle"

"The Reminiscences of Stanley Isaacs"
"The Reminiscences of Herbert C. Pell"
"The Reminiscences of Joseph M. Proskauer"
"The Riminiscences of Lindsay Rogers"
"The Reminiscences of Laurence A. Tanzer"
"The Reminiscences of Leonard M. Wallstein"

D. *Newspapers* (including scrapbooks, collections, and clippings)

The American Israelite	New York [*Daily/Sunday*] *News*
Bronx Home News	New York *Evening Journal*
Brooklyn Daily Eagle	New York *Herald-Tribune*
Brooklyn Times-Union	New York *Mirror*
Coney Island Times	New York *Post*
Flushing Avenue Journal	New York *Sun*
The Israelite	New York *Telegram*
Jamaica Press	New York *Times*
Jamaica Queens-News	New York *Tribune*
Jewish Daily Forward	New York [*Morning/Evening*] *World*
Jewish Examiner	New York *World-Telegram*
Jewish Morning Journal	*North Side News* (Bronx)
Jewish Telegraphic Agency dispatches	*People's Law Journal*
Mobile *Daily Register*	*San Francisco News*
New Leader (New York)	*Staten Island Advance*
New York American	

E. *Autobiographies and Reminiscences*

James A. Farley, *Jim Farley's Story: The Roosevelt Years* (New York, 1948)
Fiorello H. La Guardia, *The Making of an Insurgent: An Autobiography, 1882-1919*
(New York, 1961)
Joseph M. Proskauer, *A Segment of My Times* (New York, 1950)
James N. Rosenberg, *Painter's Self-Portrait* (New York, 1958)
Alfred E. Smith, *Up to Now: An Autobiography* (New York, 1929)
Harry S. Truman, *Years of Decision* (Garden City, N.Y., 1955), *Years of Trial and
Hope* (Garden City, N.Y., 1956)
Grover Whalen, *Mr. New York: The Autobiography of Grover Whalen* (New York,
1955)
Stephen S. Wise, *Challenging Years: The Autobiography of Stephen S. Wise*
(London, 1951)

SECONDARY SOURCES

A. *Biographies*

Joseph Barnes, *Willkie: The Events He Was Part Of - The Ideas He Fought For*
(New York, 1952)
Bernard Bellush, *Franklin D. Roosevelt as Governor of New York* (New York, 1955)
Walter Chambers, *Samuel Seabury: A Challenge* (New York, 1932)
Paula Eldot, *Alfred Emanuel Smith: Reforming Governor* (unpublished doctoral
dissertation, Yale University, 1961)

Harry Fleischman, *Norman Thomas: A Biography* (New York, 1964)

Frank Freidel, *Franklin D. Roosevelt,* 4 vols. (Boston, 1952-73)

Claude M. Fuess, *Carl Schurz: Reformer, 1829-1906* (New York, 1932)

Frank Graham, *Al Smith, American: An Informal Biography* (New York, 1945)

Oscar Handlin, *Al Smith and His America* (Boston, 1958)

Norman Hapgood and Henry Moskowitz, *Up from the City Streets* (New York, 1927)

George S. Hellman, *Benjamin N. Cardozo: American Judge* (New York, 1940)

Mark D. Hirsch, *William C. Whitney: Modern Warwick* (New York, 1948)

Matthew and Hannah Josephson, *Al Smith. Hero of the Cities* (Boston, 1969)

Ely Jacques Kahn, Jr., *The World of Swope* (New York, 1965)

Ambrose Kennedy, *American Orator: Bourke Cockran, His Life and Politics* (Boston, 1948)

James McCurrin, *Bourke Cockran: A Free Lance in American Politics* (New York, 1948)

Herbert Mitgang, *The Man Who Rode the Tiger: The Life and Times of Judge Samuel Seabury* (Philadelphia, 1963)

Robert Moses, *A Tribute to Governor Smith* (New York, 1962)

Henry Moskowitz, *Alfred E. Smith: An American Career* (New York, 1924)

Allan Nevins, *Grover Cleveland: A Study in Courage* (New York, 1932)

Richard O'Connor, *The First Hurrah. A Biography of Alfred E. Smith* (New York, 1970), *Herbert H. Lehman and His Era* (New York, 1963)

Henry F. Pringle, *Alfred E. Smith: A Critical Study* (New York, 1927)

Cleveland Rodgers, *Robert Moses: Builder for Democracy* (New York, 1952)

Franklin D. Roosevelt, *The Happy Warrior, Alfred E. Smith: A Study of a Public Servant* (Boston, 1928)

Morton Rosenstock, *Louis Marshall, Defender of Jewish Rights* (Detroit, 1965)

Robert E. Sherwood, *Roosevelt and Hopkins: An Intimate History* (New York, 1948)

John Tebbel, *The Life and Good Times of William Randolph Hearst* (New York, 1952)

Rexford G. Tugwell, *The Democratic Roosevelt: A Biography of Franklin D. Roosevelt* (Garden City, N.Y., 1957)

Emily Smith Warner, *The Happy Warrior: A Biography of my Father, Alfred E. Smith* (Garden City, N.Y., 1956)

John K. Winkler, *William Randolph Hearst: A New Appraisal* (New York, 1955)

B. The German Jews

Cyrus Adler, *Jacob H. Schiff. His Life and Letters.* 2 v. (Garden City, N.Y., 1929)

Stephen Birmingham, *Our Crowd. The Great Jewish Families of New York* (New York, 1967)

Eli N. Evans, *The Provincials: A Personal History of the Jews in the South* (New York, 1973).

Nathan Glazer, *American Judaism* (Chicago, 1957, 2nd ed. 1972)

Oscar Handlin, *Adventures in Freedom* (New York, 1954)

———, *The Uprooted* (Boston, 1951)

——— and M. F. Handlin, "Century of Jewish Immigration" in *American Jewish Yearbook* (New York, 1948)

Eric Hirschler, *Jews from Germany in the United States* (New York, 1955)

B. W. Korn, "Jews in the Old South, 1789-1865" in *Publications of the American Jewish Historical Society*, No. 3 (March 1961)

———, *American Jewry and the Civil War* (Cleveland, 1961)

A. E. Zucker, ed. *The Forty-Eighters, Political Refugees of the German Revolution of 1848* (New York, 1950)

C. *The East European Jews*

J. B. Berkson, *Theories of Americanization* (New York, 1920)

C. S. Bernheimer, ed., *The Russian Jew in the United States* (New York, 1905)

Miriam Blaustein, ed., *Memoirs of David Blaustein* (New York, 1913)

Julius Henry Cohen, *They Builded Better than They Knew* (New York, 1946)

Maruice Fishberg, *The Jews: A Study of Race and Environment* (London and Newark, 1911)

Nathan Glazer, *American Judaism* (Chicago, 1957, 2nd ed. 1972)

Irving Howe, with the assistance of Kenneth Libo, *World of Our Fathers* (New York, 1976) Consult for complete bibliography

Oscar Janowsky, ed., *The American Jew* (Philadelphia, 1964)

Isaac Metzker, ed. and translator, *A Bintle Brief. Sixty Years of Letters from the Lower East Side to the Jewish Daily Forward* (New York, 1971)

Moses Rischlin, *The Promised City. New York Jews, 1870-1914* (Cambridge, Mass., 1962)

D. *General: The Southern Scene with*
special attention to Mobile, Alabama

Christopher C. Andrews, *History of the Campaign of Mobile* (New York, 1867)

Howard K. Beale, *The Critical Year: A Study of Andrew Johnson and Reconstruction* (New York, 1958)

Nash K. Burger and John K. Bettersworth, *South of Appomatox* (New York, 1959)

Vic Calver, *Romances of Mobile* (Chicago, c. 1921)

Hodding Carter, *The Angry Scar: The Story of Reconstruction* (Garden City, N.Y., 1959)

W. J. Cash, *Mind of the South* (New York, 1941)

Arthur Charles Cole, *The Irrepressible Conflict, 1850-1865* (New York, 1934)

Collections of the Minnesota Historical Society, XII (St. Paul, 1908)

Erwin Craighead, *Mobile: Fact and Tradition, Noteworthy People and Events* (Mobile, 1930)

Caldwell Delaney, *Remember Mobile* (Mobile, 1948)

———, *The Story of Mobile* (Mobile, 1953)

First National Bank of Mobile, Alabama, *Highlights of Seventy-Five Years* (Mobile, c. 1940)

W. Norman Fitzgerald, Jr., *President Lincoln's Blockade and the Defense of Mobile* (Madison, 1954)

Charles H. Fonde, *An Account of the Great Explosion of the United States Ordnance Stores, Which Occurred in Mobile, on the 25th day of May, 1865* (Mobile, 1869)

John Hope Franklin, *From Slavery to Freedom: A History of American Negroes* (New York, 1956)

Frank B. Freidel, *The Militant South, 1800-1861* (Cambridge, Mass., 1956)

———, *F. D. R. and the South* (Baton Rouge, La., 1965)

Peter J. Hamilton, *Mobile of the Five Flags: the story of the river basin and coast about Mobile from the earliest times to the present* (Mobile, 1913)

Ralph Selph Henry, *The Story of the Confederacy* (Garden City, N.Y., 1931)

William B. Hesseltine, *The South in American History* (New York, 1951)

Edward King, *The Great South: A Record of Journeys* (Hartford, Conn., 1875)

John E. Land, *Mobile, Her Trade, Commerce and Industries* (Mobile, 1884)

Stanley Blake McNeely, *Bits of Charm in Old Mobile* (Mobile, 1946)

Mobile Board of Trade, *Mobile Harbor* (circular, Mobile, 1883)

Albert B. Moore, *History of Alabama* (University, Ala., 1934)

A. G. Moses, "Jews of Mobile" in *American Jewish Historical Society Publications,* vi-xii (1904)

Polk's Mobile City Directory for Year Ending February 1, 1905 (Mobile, 1904)

Lyman P. Powell (ed.), *Historic Towns of the Southern States* (New York, 1900)

Publication of the American Jewish Historical Society, XII, 1904. See article by Rev. Alfred G. Moses, "A History of the Jews of Mobile."

———, *L. No. 3, March 1961.* See article by Bertram W. Korn, "Jews and Negro Slavery in the Old South, 1789-1865"

Whitelaw Reid, *After the War: A Southern Tour, May 1, 1865 to May 1, 1866* (Cincinnati, 1866)

Bernard Reynolds, *Sketches of Mobile from 1814 to the Present Time* (Mobile, 1868)

Lester B. Shippee (ed.), *Bishop Whipple's Southern Diary, 1843-1844* (Minneapolis, 1937)

F. B. Simkins, *Pitchfork Ben Tillman* (New York, 1944)

Charles Grayson Summersell, *Mobile: History of a Seaport Town* (University, Ala., 1949)

Holland Thompson, *The New South* (New Haven, 1919)

J. T. Trowbridge, *The South: A Tour of its Battle-Fields and Ruined Cities* (Hartford, Conn., 1867)

Edward L. Ullman, *Mobile: Industrial Seaport and Trade Center* (Chicago, 1943)

War Papers of the Military Order of the Loyal Legion of the United States (Washington, D.C., 1894)

C. Vann Woodward, *Origins of the New South* (University, La., 1951)

———, *Reunion and Reaction: The Compromise of 1877 and the End of Reconstruction* (Boston, 1951)

———, *Tom Watson, Agrarian Rebel* (New York, 1938)

E. The Proskauer Family

Barnard College, Alumna Record No. A27, Alice Naumburg

Barnard College, Columbia University, Academic Record No. 813, Alice Naumburg

Ella Lonn, *Foreigners in the Confederacy* (Chapel Hill, 1940)

Robert Emory Park, *Sketch of the Twelfth Alabama Infantry of Battle's Brigade, Rode's Division, Early's Corps...* (Richmond, 1906)

Simon Wolf, *The American Jew as Patriot, Soldier, and Citizen* (Philadelphia, 1895)

F. The Columbia Years

Harry Elmer Barnes, *A History of Historical Writing* (New York, 1962)

John W. Burgess, *Reminiscences of an American Scholar: the Beginnings of*

Columbia University (New York, 1934)

Nicholas Murray Butler, *Across the Busy Years* (Vol. 1, New York, 1939)

Class Book of the Class of '95, School of Arts, Columbia College (New York, 1899)

Columbia College Handbook of Information, 1892-93 and Register of Students, 1891-92; and also, *1893-94* (New York, 1892, 1893)

The [Columbia] Jester

Columbia Law School. Academic Record of Joseph M. Proskauer, Matriculation No. 1089

Columbia Spectator

The Columbian, 1896

Horace Coon, *Columbia, Colossus on the Hudson* (New York, 1947)

Joseph Doyle, *George Edward Woodberry* (unpublished doctoral dissertation, Columbia University, 1952)

———, "George E. Woodberry," in *Yearbook of Comparative and General Literature*, I, 1952

John Erskine, *The Memory of Certain Persons* (Philadelphia, 1947)

Julius Goebel (ed.), *A History of the School of Law* (New York, 1955)

Michael Kraus, *A History of American History* (New York, 1937)

Louis V. Ledoux, *George Edward Woodberry: A Study of His Poetry* (Cambridge, Mass., 1917)

Dwight C. Miner (ed.), *A History of Columbia College on Morningside* (New York, 1954)

Lloyd Morris, *A Threshold in the Sun* (New York, 1943)

Saturday Review of Literature, XXVII, Nos. 32 and 44

G. The Law

American Labor Year Book, 1921-22, IV (New York, 1922?)

Appeal Cases, J. M. P. (privately bound briefs, applications, papers, opinions, and decisions in library of the law offices of Proskauer Rose Goetz & Mendelsohn)

The Association of the Bar of the City of New York. *Yearbooks, 1920, 1921, 1932*

Joel Prentiss Bishop, *Bishop on Criminal Law* (Chicago, 1923)

Bulletin of the Association of the Bar of the City of New York, No. 12, March 1923. Report of the Committee on International Law.

———, No. 6, March 1921. Report of the Special Committee on the Permanent Improvement of the Real Property of the Association.

George E. G. Catlin, *Liquor Control* (New York, 1931)

Julius Henry Cohen, *They Builded Better Than They Knew* (New York, 1946)

Audrey M. Davies (comp.), *Moreland Investigations in New York State* (Institute of Public Administration, New York, 1936)

Walter K. Earle, *Mr. Shearman and Mr. Sterling and How They Grew* (New Haven, 1963)

Karl N. Llewellyn, *The Common Law Tradition: Deciding Appeals* (Boston, 1960)

John E. Missall, *The Moreland Act: Executive Inquiry in the State of New York* (New York, 1946)

New York State Crime Commission, Public Hearings.

New York State University. Abram I. Elkus, Regent of the University of the State of New York, 1911-19 (Albany, 1919)

Dexter Perkins, *Charles Evans Hughes and American Democratic Statesmanship* (Boston, 1956)

Reports of Cases Decided in the Court of Appeals of the State of New York, May 22,
   1947 - May 21, 1948, CCXCVII
Charles Reznikoff (ed.), *Louis Marshall: Champion of Liberty; Selected Papers and*
   Addresses, II (Philadelphia, 1957)
Charles Solomon, *The Albany "Trial"* (New York, 1920)
Various Reports and Supplements:
   Appellate Division
   Appellate Division Reports, New York
   F Supplements
   Hun
   Miscellaneous Reports, New York
   Miscellaneous Reports, New York. Supreme Court, New York Special Term,
      October, 1923
   Miscellaneous, New York
   New Jersey Equity Reports
   New York
   New York Court of Appeals
   New York Reports
   New York Supplements
   United States Reports

H. *In Service of Jewry*
A Dreamer's Journey: The Autobiography of Morris Raphael Cohen (Boston, 1946)
American Jewish Committee: numerous brochures and pamphlets dealing with the
   history, functions and purposes of the Committee. See, for example, "Questions
   and Answers about the American Jewish Committee" (brochure, 1964?); "Meet
   the American Jewish Committee" (pamphlet, 1966); and, "Milestones of the
   American Jewish Committee" (pamphlet, 1967)
American Jewish Committee. Records Division materials.
———, *Reports on the Foreign Scene, the United Nations and Human Rights*
   (November, 1963)
American Jewish Year Book, 5704 (1943-1944), XLIV, XLV
Annual Reports of the Educational Alliance
Jerold S. Auerbach, "Human Rights at San Francisco," art. in *American Jewish*
   Archives, XVI, April, 1964
Morris Isaiah Berger, *The Settlement, The Immigrant and the Public School* (un-
   published doctoral dissertation, Teachers College, Columbia University, 1956)
Jacob Blaustein, *Human Rights: A Challenge to the United Nations and to our*
   Generation (Dag Hammarskjold Memorial Lecture, Columbia University,
   December 4, 1963, privately published pamphlet, n.d.)
Miriam Blaustein (arr.), *Memoirs of David Blaustein: Educator and Communal*
   Worker (New York, 1913)
Borris D. Bogen, *Jewish Philanthropy: An Exposition of Principles and Methods*
   of Jewish Social Service in the United States (New York, 1917)
Business Men's Council, Federation for the Support of Jewish Philanthropic So-
   cieties, *Everybody's Federation,* (April, 1929)
Clarke A. Chambers, *Seedtime of Reform: American Social Service and Social*
   Action, 1918-1933 (Minneapolis, 1965)
Naomi W. Cohen, *A Dual Heritage* (Philadelphia, 1969)

Congress Weekly (American Jewish Congress)

Merle Curti, *American Philanthropy Abroad: A History* (New Brunswick, N.J., 1963)

East Side News

Abba Eban, *My People: The Story of the Jews* (New York, 1968)

Educational Alliance. Art School Alumni Exhibition, 1940

Maurice N. Eisendrath, *Can Faith Survive?* (New York, 1964)

Federation of Jewish Philanthropies of New York. "Summary of Philanthropic Activities of the Hon. Joseph M. Proskauer" (compiled by Sam Elkin)

———, *Handbook for Trustees* (1963)

Nathan Glazer, *American Judaism* (Chicago, 1957)

Philip R. Goldstein, *Centers in My Life: A Personal Profile of the Jewish Center Movement* (New York, 1964)

Samuel Halperin, *The Political World of American Zionism* (Detroit, 1961)

Ben Halpern, "The Impact of Israel on American Jewish Ideologies," paper in *Jewish Social Studies*, XXI, January 1959

Harmonie Club of the City of New York, 1967-1968

Harry N. Howard, "The United States in the Middle East Today," art. in *Current History*, July 1969

Oscar I. Janowsky, *Foundations of Israel: Emergence of a Welfare State* (Princeton, 1959)

———, (ed.), *The American Jew: A Composite Portrait* (New York, 1942)

———, (ed.), *The American Jew: A Reappraisal* (Philadelphia, 1964)

George Lenczowski, *The Middle East in World Affairs* (Ithaca, 1952)

Jacob R. Marcus, "Mass Migrations of Jews and Their Effects on Jewish Life," in Central Conference of American Rabbis, *Yearbook*, L, 1940

———, "Zionism and the American Jew," in *The American Scholar*, II, No. 3, May 1933

Arthur D. Morse, *While Six Million Died* (London, 1968)

92nd Street Y.M.-Y.W.H.A. Archives. "The Joseph M. Proskauer File"

Official Souvenir Book of the Fair in Aid of the Educational Alliance and the Hebrew Technical Institute, 1895 (New York, 1895)

Opinion, October, 1943

Max Raisin, *Great Jews I have known: A Gallery of Portraits* (New York, 1952)

Moses Rischin, "The American Jewish Committee, 1906-1956" (ms. in Library of A.J.C.)

Harry H. Rosenfelt, *This Thing of Giving* (New York, 1924)

Leonora Cohen Rosenfield, *Portrait of a Philosopher: Morris R. Cohen in Life and Letters* (New York, 1962)

Nadav Safran, *The United States and Israel* (Cambridge, Mass., 1963)

Statement of the American Jewish Committee on withdrawal from the American Jewish Conference ... [(pamphlet, New York, n.d.)

Georgiana C. Stevens (ed.), *The United States and the Middle East* (Englewood Cliffs, N.J., 1964)

This is Your Federation: A Handbook of the Histories, Services and Facilities of the Federation of Jewish Philantropies of New York and Its Member Agencies, 1966

Morris D. Waldman, *Nor By Power* (New York, 1953)

The Young Men's Hebrew Association Bulletin on the Occasion of the Laying of the Cornerstone of the New Association Building, November 17, 1929. [also, the Association's *Dedication Journal . . ., October 26, 1930*]

Young Men's and Young Women's Hebrew Association, New York City, *Building Character for 75 Years* (1949)

I. The Political Arena

William H. Allen, *A. E. Smith's Tammany Hall* (New York, 1928)

Book of Horrors (a looseleaf volume collection of anti-Catholic, anti-Alfred E. Smith material in the Special Collections Division, Columbia University Library)

Bruce Calvert, *Al Smith and the Presidency* (pamphlet, Mountain View, N.J., 1928)

John T. Casey and James Bowles, *Farley and Tomorrow* (Chicago, 1937)

The Citizens Union of New York: Citizens Union Archives, Folder C3.362: Committee on Judicial Nominations; Citizens Union Archives, "Joseph M. Proskauer File"; *Report of the Committee on Legislation of the Citizens Union for Session of 1909;* and, for sessions of 1910-1919; *The Searchlight,* 1914-1935; *The Searchlight: Voters' Directory,* V-XXII

David Ellis, editor, *A Short History of New York State* (Ithaca, 1957)

Federal Writers Project, *New York City Guide* (New York, 1939)

Charles Garrett, *The La Guardia Years: Machine and Reform Politics in New York City* (New Brunswick, N.J., 1961)

Ralph M. Goldman, *The Democratic Party in American Politics* (New York, 1966)

Andrew Hacker, *The New Yorkers,* (New York, 1975)

Institute of American Business, *Governor Alfred E. Smith on State Regulation versus Municipal Control* (pamphlet, New York, 1923)

———, *Symposium of Opinion Upon the Proposals of Governor Smith for Municipal Regulation of Public Utilities* (pamphlet, New York, 1923)

Donald Bruce Johnson, *The Republican Party and Wendell Willkie* (Urbana, Ill., 1960)

William E. Leuchtenburg, *Franklin D. Roosevelt and the New Deal, 1932-1940* (New York, 1963)

Charles C. Marshall, *Governor Smith's Catholicism* (New York, 1928)

Charles Michelson, *The Ghost Talks* (New York, 1944)

Henry Minor, *The Story of the Democratic Party* (New York, 1928)

Herbert Mitgang, *The Man Who Rode The Tiger, The Life and Times of Judge Samuel Seabury* (New York, 1963)

Edmund A. Moore, *A Catholic Runs for President: The Campaign of 1928* (New York, 1956)

Warren Moscow, *Roosevelt and Willkie* (Englewood Cliffs, N.J., 1968)

Gustavus Myers, *History of Tammany Hall* (New York, 1917)

William B. and John B. Northrop, *The Insolence of Office: The Story of the Seabury Investigations* (New York, 1932)

Roy V. Peel, *The Political Clubs of New York City* (New York, 1935)

Roy V. Peel and Thomas C. Donnelly, *The 1928 Campaign: An Analysis* (New York, 1931)

William A. Prendergast, *Public Utilities and the People* (New York, 1933)

Progressive Democracy: Addresses and State Papers of Alfred E. Smith (New York, 1928)

[Hilmar] Stephen Raushenbush, *The Power Fight* (New York, 1932)

Hilmar Stephen Raushenbush and Harry W. Laidler, *Power Control* (New York, 1928)

Cleveland Rodgers and Rebecca B. Rankin, *New York: the World's Capital City* (New York, 1948)

Eugene H. Roseboom, *A History of Presidential Elections* (New York, 1957)

Samuel I. Rosenman, *Working With Roosevelt* (New York, 1952)

Arthur M. Schlesinger, Jr., *The Age of Roosevelt: The Crisis of the Old Order, 1919-1933* (Cambridge, Mass., 1957)

————, *The Age of Roosevelt: The Politics of Upheaval* (Cambridge, 1960)

Theodore Schroeder, *Al. Smith, the Pope and the Presidency* (New York, 1928)

Frederick Shaw, *The History of the New York City Legislature* (New York, 1954)

H. C. Syrett (ed.), *The Gentleman and the Tiger: The Autobiography of George B. McClellan, Jr.* (New York, 1956)

Ruth C. Silva, *Rum, Religion and Votes: 1928 Re-examined* (University Park, Pa., 1962)

Robert P. Shuler, *"Al" Smith* (pamphlet, Los Angeles, 1928?)

M. R. Werner, *Tammany Hall* (New York, 1928)

J. Miscellaneous

Atlantic Monthly, CXXXIX, April, May, 1927

Current History, XXVII, March, 1928

David M. Ellis, James A. Frost, Harold C. Syrett, and Harry J. Carman, *A Short History of New York State* (Ithaca, 1957)

Mark D. Hirsch, "Royal S. Copeland," and "Morgan Joseph O'Brian," arts. in *Dictionary of American Biography*, XXII.

William J. Keating with Richard Carter, *The Man Who Rocked the Boat* (New York, 1956)

Estes Kefauver, *Crime in America* (Garden City, N.Y., 1951)

Library of Congress Information Bulletin, XVI, No. 31, August 5, 1957

New York City Advertising Club News

Joseph M. Proskauer Seventieth Birthday Celebration Testimonial (New York, 1947. Privately bound)

Saturday Review of Literature, July 29, 1950

Dore Schary, *Sunrise at Campobello* (New York, 1958)

Fred A. Shannon, *America's Economic Growth* (New York, 1940)

Time [Magazine], LXXV, April 18, 1960

Gus Tyler, *Organized Crime in America* (Ann Arbor, 1962)

Dixon Wecter, *The Age of the Great Depression, 1929-1941* (New York, 1948)

INDEX

PROSKAUER: HIS LIFE AND TIMES

was composed in Compugraphic Garamond

by Compsetters, Toney, Alabama,

printed by Thomson-Shore, Inc.,

Dexter, Michigan, and

bound by John H. Dekker and Sons,

Grand Rapids, Michigan.